Peter De Vries

Twayne's United States Authors Series

Warren French, Editor
Indiana University, Indianapolis

TUSAS 448

PETER DE VRIES
Photograph courtesy of Thomas Victor

Peter De Vries

By J. H. Bowden

Indiana University Southeast

Twayne Publishers • *Boston*

Peter De Vries

J. H. Bowden

Copyright © 1983 by G. K. Hall & Company
All Rights Reserved
Published by Twayne Publishers
A Division of G. K. Hall & Company
70 Lincoln Street
Boston, Massachusetts 02111

Book Production by Marne B. Sultz

Book Design by Barbara Anderson

Printed on permanent/durable acid-free
paper and bound in the United States of
America.

Library of Congress Cataloging in Publication Data

Bowden, J. H. (James Henry)
    Peter De Vries.

    (Twayne's United States authors series; TUSAS 448)
    Bibliography: p. 174
    Includes index.
    De Vries, Peter—Criticism and
    interpretation.
2. De Vries, Peter—Religion and ethics.
I. Title.
II. Series.
PS3507.E8673Z57 1983   813'.52   82-23421
ISBN 0-8057-7388-6

*for my grandmother, a very fine
woman, whose Calvinist-bred indomitable
iron-clad Will enabled her to overcome
every obstacle raised by her Calvinist-bred
indomitable iron-clad Will.*

Contents

About the Author

James Henry Bowden received the M.A. in English from the University of Louisville and the Ph.D. in American Studies from the University of Minnesota. He also studied at Seabury-Western Theological Seminary on a Rockefeller Scholarship, and later attended the Louisville Presbyterian Theological Seminary.

He has published verse, fiction, and essays in a variety of journals. Since 1966 he has taught at Indiana University Southeast, where he is Chairman of the Humanities Division. He is married and has three sons.

Preface

Most who read over the works of Peter De Vries would conclude that here is the quintessential *New Yorker* sort of writer: urbane, witty, concerned with savoir faire and with contacts and conflicts between those few who have it and the many who have it not. That judgment would be only partially correct, and even so would require an inquiry as to how he so became; hence a biographical chapter should come first.

In this first and in succeeding chapters attention will be given also to that undercurrent of theological inquiry that threads through the submerged chambers of all of De Vries's books. For it happens that this boulevardier is a product of a Dutch Reformed upbringing, and Calvinism is the most bourgeois version of Christianity. Out of conflicts such as these—sophistication versus pedestrianism—comes Art; in this case, Comic Art.

Like the work of most Comic authors, De Vries's world is comparatively static. That is, his outlook doesn't change. The central intelligence who progresses through these works, or, rather, who meanders through these successive novels, is somewhat like De Vries himself. So in a sense this study will all be a form of biography. (In this century, most good writing is.) De Vries's external world changes here, although the internal one does not, presenting a variation on P. G. Wodehouse's (non)sense of time: in Wodehouse it is always 1905 or so. And Bertie Wooster is around twenty-five. In De Vries, the clock ticks on, the scenery shifts, but the narrator is almost always early middle-age—about where the author was at the time of his marriage, say, or in the first years thereafter.

Indeed, practically all of his books (after the out-of-print first three) begin with people who are married or marrying, which would seem to disqualify De Vries from serious consideration as a writer: no major American novelist has written much that is favorable about that institution, unless William Dean Howells be major. A few have written things that *end* in marriage—Hawthorne in *The House of the Seven Gables*, say—but De Vries's usually start that way. Thus he is on at least one salient point un-American.

He is un-American on another point as well: not only is the typical American protagonist an "orphan hero" who has no personal history and who lives as much as possible outside social institutions, he also is traditionally a metaphysician. De Vries's people, on the contrary, are more likely to be theologians. There is a very big difference, namely in that the former is speculative, and any free-born son can engage in it; even Natty Bumppo theorizes about what is Beyond Nature. Not so with God-Talk, for theology implies intellectual rigor that depends in large part on an historical tradition and some degree of learning.

These two debits would not possibly be forgiven De Vries as a serious writer were it not that he is a serious *comic* writer. Flannery O'Connor somewhat similarly manages to write about theocentric people in a secular age, manages to bring it off by her Southern Gothic style; thus her positivist readers are willing to accept her view. De Vries writes about people who kick against the traces but who find the traces ultimately do them more good than harm, a view not at all congenial to Romantic (a redundancy) Americans; without any major recourse to surrealistic techniques, De Vries manages nonetheless to have a devoted readership. (Small but indiscriminating, he says.)

In Art, style and content are not separable; and in this case style and method determine each other. Because of the unpopularity of his subject matter—roughly, the limitations of being human, and the necessity of something like a bourgeois pattern of existence—De Vries's method is the devious one of comedy.

A very serious business, too. Most critics choose to study and explicate authors whose work they find has deciphered and then recodified the world in such a way as they, the critics, would have done it if they could have done it. Even so is this the case here. Thus, although it has been a serious work, it has also been a delight to undertake it.

My thanks to those who have made this study possible for me, including Donald Fiene, at present of the Slavic Department at the University of Tennessee, and his wife, Judy, a social worker in the same clime, who introduced me to the man (via *The Mackerel Plaza*) not so many years ago. Then there is the excellent bibliographical work done by Edwin Bowden—we're not related—of the University of Texas: with his *Peter De Vries, A Bibliography, 1934–1977*, the harder part of the needed research was done for me. Of most help of all was the man himself, Peter De Vries, who was never anything but generous with his time and commentary. Next would be Warren French, my editor, who must surely be among the gentlest and wisest of that breed. And, finally, spouse Colleen Carter, always willing to inform me when I am "exactly 360° off course."

J. H. Bowden

Indiana University Southeast

Chronology

1910   27 February, Chicago, birth of Peter, second child and first son of Joost and Henrietta Eldersveld de Vries, both immigrants from the Netherlands. Lives in Englewood district on S. Halsted.

1912   Birth of Anna, sister.

1916   Till 1923, attends Englewood Christian School. Stutters.

1923   Death of Engeline, older sister, at nineteen. Father becomes progressively more religious, mother less so. Attends Chicago Christian High School, 1923–1927, first team in basketball for two years, 1925–1927.

1927   Enrolled at Calvin College, Grand Rapids, Michigan. On the debating team four years, winning prizes. Edits *Chimes*, monthly student newspaper, during his senior year. Plays varsity basketball.

1931   B.A., English, Calvin College. Begins editing community paper in Chicago.

1932   Several months a patient at a church-run TB sanatorium in Denver.

1933   Involved in Democratic reform politics for two years.

1934   Begins running candy-vending machines and a taffy-apple route, free-lance writing.

1936   Father begins having breakdowns: melancholia, hypochondria; from 1937 onward spends time in church-run sanatorium in Grand Rapids, where he dies.

1938   Works on father's van lines, lectures to women's clubs, until 1941 is a radio actor. Associate Editor of *Poetry*.

1940   *But Who Wakes the Bugler?*

1941   Until 1944, editor of *Poetry*.

1943   16 October, marries Katinka Loeser. *The Handsome Heart*.

1944 At James Thurber's invitation, moves East to work on the *New Yorker*. Lives in the Village till 1946. *Angels Can't Do Better*.

1945 9 January, Jan De Vries born.

1946 $1,000 National Institute of Arts and Letters award in literature.

1947 26 March, Peter Jon De Vries born.

1948 Moves to Westport.

1949 26 October, Emily De Vries born.

1950 Mother dies.

1952 19 November, Derek De Vries born. *No But I Saw the Movie*.

1954 *The Tunnel of Love*.

1956 *Comfort Me with Apples*.

1957 Stage version of *The Tunnel of Love* on Broadway.

1958 *The Mackerel Plaza*.

1959 *The Tents of Wickedness*. Joost De Vries dies, at eighty-five.

1960 19 September, Emily dies.

1961 *Through the Fields of Clover*.

1962 Emily Clark Balch lecture at the University of Virginia. *The Blood of the Lamb*.

1964 *Reuben, Reuben*.

1965 *Let Me Count the Ways*.

1966 Lectures at Villanova University.

1967 *The Vale of Laughter*. Play, *Spofford*, on Broadway.

1968 Avery Hopwood lecture at the University of Michigan. Awarded D.H.L. by University of Bridgeport. *The Cat's Pajamas & Witch's Milk*.

1969 Elected to National Institute of Arts and Letters.

1970 *Mrs. Wallop*; death of sister, Anna De Vries Schoonveld, 1 March.

1971 *Into Your Tent I'll Creep*.

1972 *Without a Stitch in Time.*

1973 *Forever Panting.*

1974 *The Glory of the Hummingbird.*

1976 *I Hear America Swinging.*

1977 *Madder Music.*

1980 *Consenting Adults.*

1981 *Sauce for the Goose.*

1983 Elected to Chair No. 17 (formerly held by John Cheever) of American Academy of Arts and Letters. *Slouching Toward Kalamazoo.*

Chapter One
Chicago and Connecticut
Celestial City

Certain facts in the life of Peter De Vries are not subject to dispute—where he grew up, went to school, and so on—but when it becomes a matter of discerning the relation of these facts to his fiction the prospect becomes as slippery as telling Truth from Make Believe in a Pirandello play. And of course it is this relationship of fact to fiction that most matters in the biographical portion of literary criticism, where the task is not so much to distinguish the dancer from the dance as it is to study the dance by studying the dancer.

For one thing, the interviews De Vries has granted tend often to overlap, with similar questions and answers reappearing; furthermore, in some of his interviews his books are quoted, and in his books his interviews are quoted. The result often is an eerie sort of déjà-vu experience. One is left with a heightened sense of unreality or art or insanity, which in De Vries's work may amount to saying the same thing three times, anyway. Interestingly, he has expressed admiration for Proust, especially for *Swann's Way*, in particular for the last fifteen pages or so, where what he liked, he said, was that possibility "for the thing not to exist at all, the relativity of it."[1]

Roy Newquist gives this personal account of "the man who came to have this rarefied taste in literature":

[I] was born in Chicago in 1910 into a Dutch immigrant community which still preserved its old-world ways. My origins would have been little different had my parents never come to America at all, but remained in Holland. I still feel somewhat like a foreigner, and not only for ethnic reasons. Our insularity was two-fold, being a matter of religion as well as nationality. In addition to being immigrant, and not able to mix well with the Chicago Americans around us, we were Dutch Reformed Calvinists who weren't supposed to mix—who, in fact, had considerable trouble mixing with one another. We were the elect, and the elect are barred from everything, you know, except heaven.

I wasn't allowed to go to the movies, to dance, to play cards, go to the regular public schools or do anything much that was secular, even on weekdays. On Sundays we went to church (usually three times) and in between services we sat around and engaged in doctrinal disputation, in which we became adept at a very early age. It was said about us, "One Dutchman, a Christian; two Dutchmen, a congregation; three Dutchmen, heresy." We accepted and even repeated this without an apology or any suggestion that there was anything wrong with this religious pugnacity. We were the product of schism, and we produced schism.[2]

Writing of his parents, De Vries noted that after they immigrated in early youth both became bilingual, but added that while his mother soon lost her Dutch accent, his father never did. This he found curious and apparently a little embarrassing, although one notes that Dr. Henry Kissinger—a learned enough man—is a similar case. De Vries called his father an extremely complex mixture of opposites: nervous, temperamental, religiously austere and repressive, inflexible; but he was also emotional, kind, sensitive, outgoing, generous. He saw his son become increasingly alienated from the fold as a result, in part, of the schooling he sacrificed to afford. "One of the injustices of life," he said. His father had fierce pride in his children's successes, but had to endure seeing Peter's made outside the same fold. Joost (pronounced Yost) De Vries was a self-made man who worked in the ice (summers) and coal (winters) business, then became a furniture mover—from horse-drawn vans into trucks—and finally headed a warehouse business, owning three warehouses.

His father voted for Roosevelt the first time, but became a Roosevelt and New Deal-hater even while paying his own men higher wages than the minimum required by the NRA. The son thinks Henry Wallace's killing of pigs did it: "Imagine what that economic measure did to people who emigrated because of hunger and poverty, from European farm and fishing villages." As Joost grew older he became extremely melancholic for some years until his death at eighty-five in a church sanatorium, where the son recalls they ironically tagged his father, "Happy."

His mother, he says, had "the same disappointments, anxieties and tensions, but was less articulate. Pour soul." She was "a submerged and mute member of this highly provincial, narrow, insulated Dutch-American, Calvinist community in the heart of 'worldly' Chicago, in which she lived till 69." Family tensions arithmetically multiplied among members who were themselves individually tense, so much so that "Talk of a Generation Gap today makes me laugh." He calls today's situation "Child's play . . . a mere chink in the fencepost compared with the Grand Canyon that divided us." He added that perhaps his could be compared with the religious familial tensions and conflicts of present Jewish-American writers, which could be read as the "Same thing in another vein: to wit, the all-or-nothing point of view postulated from the parental side of the household, religiously based."[3]

Thus it would appear that George Bernard Shaw was wrong when he said it only bothered Catholics to lose their faith, that with Protestants it made no difference. Probably he was thinking of the tepid sort of Anglicanism he had grown up with in Ireland. Clearly his sentiments don't apply to sincere evangelicals, especially when linked to an immigrant culture that doubles—at least—in intensity the isolation that such a religious outlook necessarily brings anyway. Said De Vries:

. . . I suppose biographical or psychological analysts could make the case that my fascination with the sophisticated and "worldly" world is a vicarious escape from this (in many ways) painful immigrant childhood, with its sense of exclusion and inferiority, and that my satirizing of the upper crust is, well, a simultaneous appeasement of the household gods being flouted, etc. Who knows? Who cares? I don't. One just sits in the corner and secretes the stuff. Don't ask a cow to analyze milk.[4]

Cows aren't asked, but dairymen are—an appropriate analogy for the roles of the artist and of the critic—and the split between the saved and the sophisticated is present in his work. Out of such tension grows art, to the profit, very much at least, of De Vries's readers. But there was another, internal, split as well, one within his own home. In 1923, when she was nineteen and Peter thirteen, his older sister Engeline died. The reaction of the parents was markedly different: the father became more intensely religious, while the mother never again sang in church. This division also recurs from time to time in the literary work of their son. One parent believes, one does not.[5]

Such tension was doubtless salubrious so far as the writing De Vries later did is concerned: and it almost seemed that if he were to be a writer at all it would be a requisite that he detach himself from the church of his upbringing. Of all the religious traditions of Christendom, none is so deadly toward art as Calvinism. The John Miltons are rare, although quite a few artists who were at one time quite committed to a Calvinist reading of life—for example, Van Gogh—have come out of it. Calvinism is Augustinian and Pauline and Platonist, which ought to be enough, but it is also a particularly bourgeois expression of that mind-slant, and *that* is deadly. For art. (The Calvinist art form is Work.) Fortunately for De Vries, "One sees in [him] emotional attachment to religious attitudes intellectually discarded. The dogma has gone; the sympathy, the taste, the point of view remain."[6]

College and After

His parents had expected an ecclesiastical career for their son, but at Calvin College (1927–31), where he was "about as inconspicuous as a flamingo,"[7] he chose to be an English major instead. Known as "Dewpoint" in high school, he was high scorer on the 1927 basketball team that achieved a 10 and 3 season, and he played some in college: he recalls that he was varsity there, although the yearbooks do not bear that out. For four years he was on the debating team, representing his school during his junior and senior years in the Michigan Oratorical League: he placed both times, and in his senior year won the intercollegiate extemporaneous competition. In 1930, the year previous, he won the Broodman Contest, eliciting a later college yearbook statement that ". . . his Alma Mater feels honored to have had him as her outstanding forensic representative of the past two years" (1931, 80). Indeed, his prize-winning speech is reprinted in its entirety in the journal: entitled "Bolshevism or Vaccinate," it shows a rarely revealed political side of De Vries, a side that suggests Liberal accommodation to changing times. It is better, he argues, to get a small dose of the disease and be inoculated thereby, than to succumb to the real thing: a little socialism will enable us to muddle along.

Henry Stob, a classmate of De Vries and later a professor of religion at Calvin, said, "Everyone liked him, he was not arrogant, not standoffish, but was friendly, gracious, would quip a lot."[8] Others, concurring, embellish upon this. (There is a considerable amount of De Vries folklore at Calvin College recalled by those who studied there with him, who taught him, who dated or dated with him.) On dates he was quiet and gentlemanly, but in a crowd might become zany—help direct traffic, say—and at least once he was thrown out of class. Another time he mounted the counter of the De Luxe Café and gave a spontaneous oration on Buffalo Bill.

In 1931 De Vries edited the *Calvin College Chimes*, the student paper, then a monthly. He worked great changes in it, but also parodied the faculty and trustees, said Dr. Stob, and failed to last out the year. Of two loose associations of undergraduates about then, Conblow and Friggers, De Vries belonged to the former, a collection known mainly for monkey-shining and drinking; the other was more academic. His digs were next to a theater—not a proper Dutch Reformed environment—and he lived there in some disarray, throwing dirty socks, banana peels, and the like into one corner. Of that place, Dr. John Timmerman, emeritus of the Calvin College faculty, writes:

I once visited his apartment on Wealthy Street next to the old Wealthy Theater. In the course of the conversation he engaged in a heated diatribe against a print he had hanging on the wall. He then opened the refrigerator, took out an egg, and hurled it on the middle of the print. We all watched the egg dribble to the floor. Later it struck me as a prophetically symbolic act. (Dialogue, 21)

Then, for a year or so when just out of college, De Vries got $12 a week for editing a Chicago community newspaper, he said, "until in one of my 'Personality of the Week' sketches I described a local businessman as being a member of both the Masons and the Knights of Columbus."[9] There followed a term in a church-run TB sanatorium in Denver. Several of his college-era friends said in retrospect that they saw the illness building during his undergraduate years.

On returning to Chicago he operated a candy-vending-machine route—his ill father sometimes accompanying him on his runs—and then after a few years he "sold" some poems and became a part-time associate editor of the prestigious *Poetry* magazine. Still he worked two days on the candy-machine route and one day on a wholesale taffy-apple route, free-lanced as a radio actor (whatever his father's dialect, the son learned Standard General American), lectured to women's clubs, and was a furniture-mover on one of his father's trucks. On one occasion he also turned out a rhymed table of contents for an advertising magazine.[10] In sum, the way of the would-be writer is not easy. As T. S. Eliot said, such an aspirant must be prepared to earn his living some other way.

By 1938 he was an associate editor of *Poetry* and was giving it three days a week through 1941, as well as radio-acting, furniture-moving, and lecturing, for about $25 a week. His political activities by then were decreasing, although for a couple of years he had been active in reform politics; he worked for Paul Douglas, later a United States Senator; but in 1933 and 1934 the Kelly-Nash (mayor-boss) machine mopped them up. In 1936 the Reform party asked him to run for alderman, but he declined. This tension between politics and literature shows in his earliest novel, *But Who Wakes The Bugler?* (1940), although he seems to have made his choice after that. At Calvin, De Vries majored in English, but John Timmerman has written that "If someone had asked me in our senior year at Calvin, 'Is Peter De Vries going to be somebody?' I would have said, 'Most certainly.' If he had asked me 'What?', I would have said, 'Mayor of Chicago'" (Dialogue, 21).

In 1942 he became coeditor of *Poetry*, by which time the magazine was already thirty years old. However well established it was in literary circles, the journal still needed money; and it was decided that prominent figures would be invited to give benefit lectures on behalf of the coffers. Robert Penn Warren and Frank Lloyd Wright were both asked during De Vries's tenure, and so was James Thurber; this last choice occasioned a turning point in the editor's life. He sent an advanced copy of the December issue to Thurber, in which issue was an article called "James Thurber: The Comic Prufrock":

Thurber was instantly taken with the piece, in which De Vries held that Thurber had more in common with modern poets than with modern humorists (especially in such word-manipulating casuals as "The Black Magic of Barney Haller") and that the middle-aged man on the flying trapeze was really J. Alfred Prufrock in comic clothing. Thurber was struck not only by the editor's flattering analysis but by a critic taking him seriously, the bugbear of his middle age.[11]

That was in November. The month previous, De Vries had married Katinka Loeser, a sometime contributor to the magazine, later known mainly for her short stories. De Vries, warmed by Thurber's appreciative letter of response, invited him to speak in behalf of *Poetry* at the Chicago Arts Club and he did, on 4 April 1944. Since Thurber was nervous before crowds, he and De Vries schemed at Thurber's Ambassador East hotel room the night before the speech. De Vries would ask bogus questions the next night based on the relaxed conversation they'd already had:

In his hotel room . . . I was Mr. Interlocutor to Thurber's Mr. Monologuist. I realized his offhand lines were great, full of warmth and anecdotes about every subject under the sun. Our little stratagem seemed to make the event less painful for him, and cooking it up, we had a pleasant evening together with our wives.[12]

It went very well: De Vries's introduction was clever and flattering, and only one phony question was needed before Thurber was off and running. After that, he decided De Vries must come to work for the *New Yorker*. He showed some pieces of his to Harold Ross, who didn't expect much, but who changed his mind quickly on reading them. Over lunch at the Algonquin they were introduced, Thurber advising De Vries that he ought to take only a part-time job rather than a full-time one so that he could spend the extra hours on his own writing. By then he had three novels out and was still working on his verse. His military duty was behind him; he served briefly and was medically discharged. On Labor Day 1944 he and his wife moved to New York and a Village apartment.

The first three novels, out of print now and not listed by De Vries in his credits, were all composed in Chicago, and it was to be a decade before his first exurbanite book appeared. In the interim he worked for the *New Yorker* two days as a poetry editor and two days on the "rough basket," where newly submitted cartoons were screened; after 1947 he quit poetry and from then on did art only. His own verse he has never collected into a volume, he says, because he thinks it not good enough. He may be right; but it seems more likely that his standards are exceedingly high, or else that he has simply decided his true métier is not poetry but fiction.

Before he took that fork in the woods, it looked as though he could go either way rather than choose the one more traveled: in the biographical notes section of the January 1938 issue of *Poetry* it says that Peter De Vries is "a young Chicagoan, has contributed verse and fiction to *Esquire, Story*, etc., while solving the economic riddle with a candy and taffy-apple business."[13] They had published his "Late Song." By April he was listed with the magazine as an associate editor and by October as *the* associate editor; in that issue he had three poems, all of them good and seriously about himself but lacking the honed edge of wit that his later verse has.

A few of these may be read—anthologized, as it were—in *The Tents of Wickedness*, where he attributes them to his character Beth Appleyard. The best of these, "Sacred and Profane Love, or There's Nothing New Under the Moon Either," appeared originally in *Harper's Magazine* and was chosen by the editors for inclusion in a collection of theirs, *Gentlemen, Scholars and Scoundrels*, a book made up of the best verse that appeared in *Harper's* over a hundred-year period. That seems compliment enough. Two others, "Bacchanal" and "Christmas Family Reunion," were chosen by Kingsley Amis for *The New Oxford Book of English Light Verse*, and the former of these appears also in the third edition of *The Norton Introduction to Literature*. One poem also appears in *The Poetry Anthology: 1912–1977*—that is, an anthology of the best in *Poetry*—which isn't bad when one considers that Allen Tate has only two in it and Eliot has four.

By April 1944 Katinka Loeser was an associate editor of the journal, and from April 1947 through October 1947 she and her husband are listed as contributing editors. Although his formal connection with *Poetry* ended then, De Vries says he still sends them a yearly check. During this Chicago period three novels—*But Who Wakes The Bugler?*, *The Handsome Heart*, and *Angels Can't Do Better*—were published. Then came the hiatus insofar as long fiction was concerned, although in 1946 he received a $1,000 National Institute of Arts and Letters Award in literature. In 1948, after they already had the first two of their four children, the De Vrieses moved to Westport, where they have remained, although living in three different houses.

In 1952 came the first of two collections of the best of his short fiction and essays, *No, But I Saw the Movie*, most of which appeared first in the *New Yorker*, although other first-class magazines also are represented. Some of the pieces from the first volume are repeated in the second, *Without a Stitch in Time* (1972), and many of them appear in modified form in his novels. Since De Vries's novels are basically episodic and/or picaresque, there's not much difference between his shorter and longer pieces except that the former contain only *one* episode.

During the early exurbanite years—after assimilation had taken place—there came in rapid succession books that ridiculed the Westport way of life and love. *The Tunnel of Love* (1954), *Comfort Me with Apples* (1956), *The Mackerel Plaza* (1958), *The Tents of Wickedness* (1959), and *Through the Fields of Clover* (1961) all question whether Vanity Fair is quite what it's cracked up to be. At the same time he took care to defend the exurbs over the way of the city, and his family life went well. He argued in the local papers over a censorship attempt (of a play) by a local Roman Catholic cleric, during which quarrel he generalized a bit on such proclivities in the church the priest represented. Given that anti-Catholicism is the Liberal's anti-Semitism, some of this would be expected from De Vries; his novels, however, indicate a tolerant attitude, at least of those who will tolerate him.

Then, in 1960, the family lost their ten-year-old, Emily, after a long battle with leukemia. As would be expected, this disaster needed to be organized and exorcised fictionally by De Vries (Katinka Loeser De Vries wrote of it, too, in stories). This he did in *The Blood of the Lamb* (1960), and again in the paired novellas, *The Cat's Pajamas & Witch's Milk* (1968). Although De Vries has denied it, there was a noticeable blackening of the humor in the works that appeared between these two, also, in *Reuben, Reuben* (1964), in *Let Me Count the Ways* (1965), and in *The Vale of Laughter* (1967). The while, he ventured into academe—although only briefly, since he docsn't carc much for the milieu to give the Emily Clark Balch lectures at the University of Virginia (1962), to lecture at Villanova (1966), and to give the Avery Hopwood lecture at the University of Michigan (1968); the same year as the Hopwood, he was awarded the Doctor of Humane Letters degree by the University of Bridgeport.

In 1967, *Spofford*, a play based on the first section of *Reuben, Reuben*, was produced on Broadway; although it was not as great a success as the earlier adaptation of *The Tunnel of Love*, it did well. Two years later De Vries was elected to membership in the National Institute of Arts and Letters. About the same time he turned down a goodly sum from Princeton "to speak in any way he chose" on the general subject of religion and literature. He dismissed the offer as doubtless a "clerical error."[14] In 1970, the year his sister died, he published *Mrs. Wallop*, and, in 1971, *Into Your Tent I'll Creep*.

By 1973 and the publication of *Forever Panting*, the three surviving children were gone from home (he has no grandchildren; indeed, none of his adult three offspring is married); and he seems to have experienced settling down. The social analysis continues, generally between Chicago and Connecticut, but there is a mellowing. At the same time the decline and fall seem to be total; there comes some bit of hope that a new and equally silly synthesis will emerge. Thus *The Glory of the Hummingbird* (1974) deals with the love of easy money in Chicago and thereabouts, and *I Hear America Swinging* (1976) with the New Sophistication come to—gasp!—Iowa (whence comes his wife). The North Shore and Fairfield County generally make do for Vanity Fair since De Vries knows them best; and a portion of Chicago for the Celestial City, for the same reason. And if a part of Chicago can so serve, then surely so can any place.

Madder Music (1977), *Consenting Adults* (1980), and *Sauce for the Goose* (1981) all continue that arc across mid-America from Chicago or Michigan or Indiana to New York and Connecticut. That takes in most of us; and, as has been noted, the silliness there is likely to continue. De Vries's observation of the comedy is likely to last a while longer, too.

Chapter Two
The Trying-Out Books

First Things

Presumably the title of De Vries's first published novel, *But Who Wakes the Bugler?*, raises the basic cosmological question of the Prime Mover—whether there is one, that is—one of the more basic questions yet formulated. The issue never arises per se in the book, but the general madness that pervades it suggests that our succeeding confusions have as their birthplace that particular marc's nest. De Vries's line seems to be that since no one knows where we stand, no one can put his weight down. Eliot's Prufrock says he is not Prince Hamlet, nor was he meant to be; this makes Prufrock a comic Hamlet. Thurber's suffering men are, says De Vries, comic Prufrocks. If that be so, then Mr. Thwing is a comic Thurberman. The reviewers for both the *Chicago Daily News* (9 October 1940) and the *San Francisco Chronicle* (30 August 1940) were laudatory, saw the resemblance. The *New York Times Book Review* (8 September 1940) simply called it "first class fun" that "wabbles over on the far side of the [sanity-madness] line."

That's a lot of tin cans tied on the tail of one indecisive dog, and *But Who Wakes the Bugler?*, the story of a schlemiel getting up courage to marry, is probably one can too many. Indeed, De Vries thinks so, and believes that his out-of-print books are just where they ought to be. In this case he may be right, although it has a certain charm as a product of its time. And it *is* dated: not only is there a stage Negro, Jubal, who speaks in a thick dialect, but it's the man—Mr. Thwing—not his fiancée Hermina, who can't face up to matrimony. Now it's women who fear stifling. The illustrations, which by chance were done by Charles Addams, reinforce this period-piece flavor: first, just by being there, since illustrated novels are now passé; and, second, by their style.

The novel is essentially formless, but there is some pattern supplied by Mr. Thwing's attempt to solve an apparent murder in the Chicago rooming house he owns: a Dutch sea captain, Jehoiachim, who gives his age at 106, is found dead at the foot of the stairs after a large report is heard, and at the same time a Chinese is caught by Mr. Thwing while in the act of stealing a vase of great value from Jehoiachim's room. But Jehoiachim isn't killed till page 124, and the main issue is whether Thwing will marry Hermina. Also, Thwing unexpectedly is on his way to becoming an avant-garde poet. On arising he occasionally—unwisely—writes down his dream poems before they vanish:

> All the birds whimper and my bed goodbye, the engines
> beat and the wind blows rain, rain, rain in vain on the
> clanking man whose tall candles bleed and the bushes laugh
> on the whanged scarlet of my sullen shore and the heaved
> melons burst on the hissing sea. (4)[1]

Sort of like first-draft Hart Crane on a very bad day—exceptionally drunk, perhaps. Thwing meditates upon it: "The unconscious, he thought, that was it. That great sea, into which we pass in our sleep. Sure, that was it. And in the morning, just on the shore of waking, he would find them there—like little lagoons left by the tide" (61–62). After sending them out and suffering rejection, he follows the advice of a rejecting editor and sends them to George Henri Brezon, patron of *New Age*, who loves them, and doesn't love certain other poets, the "social" ones: "I don't think there's a damn thing in that whole English group," he says, mentioning Auden by name: "Really... the bankruptcy of the whole sociological movement was apparent to any man with a grain of intelligence even before it opened up" (227).

When Thwing, Pooh-like, writes his poems—Winnie wrote "hums" by "letting the hums come"—De Vries no doubt is working off certain resentments acquired during his tenure on *Poetry* magazine, then as now the journal to which most aspiring writers "send things first." Certainly the verse, if it is to be called that, has no other function in the novel, save that it serves to introduce the zany Brezon; as it turns out, Brezon is one zany among many.

Brezon has a cousin, Alapert, who as an employee of a large publishing house had gone insane proofreading Proust. But that's all we hear of Alapert. Mr. Soller, the next-door neighbor, keeps sheep, having gotten them from a farmer cousin in payment for something or other, and is fattening them up for butchering. A roomer, Dr. Zoro, makes herbal medicine; it, exploding, is what passes for a shot as Jehoiachim is killed (no great loss since he's 106). His product, Doctor Zoro's Herb Roots Barks and Berries, is put up in the room he shares with Jubal. Of his roommate, Jubal says he has a neurosis: further, he fears it may become dislodged and float through the bloodstream till it camps in his heart.

A rooming house is a good place for such a collage, and there are more scraps of people: Claud M. Darney, who "had perpetually the look of somebody who has just swallowed his gum" (12), had "come to Chicago in a flutter of publicity as the son of the upper Michigan farmer whose hen had laid three eggs with distinct letters on them, C, M, and D, the initials of the son" (12). Claud can't keep a job, though, till Thwing gets him on in a cloak room, where he sleeps. A similar problem is Hank, dumped on Thwing by Archie, a case worker for Boys' Court. Archie, Hank's cousin, is not seen again, and Hank's function, if any, is to introduce Thwing to Lola Wells, "one of those women who try to look exotic and succeed only in looking sleepy" (194). Inexplicably, Thwing gives her the ring he's bought for Hermina. But nothing comes of it. Hank *is* a prototype of Pete Cheshire, a failed con-man who appears in two of De Vries's early but in-print books.

Hermina has three brothers. One is Odin, working on a Ph.D. in something like psychology, doing a dissertation on something like using a lie-detector to see how children react to movie serials. When Thwing, trying to get out of marriage to Hermina, tells her he has paresis, the machine catches him. Brabant, a second brother, has played for the Cincinnati Reds, but his advancement is blocked because he has accidentally killed a pigeon with a hit ball. Brabant desires Hecuba, another roomer, but again the thread is dropped; precipitously he marries a girl from Fargo, in Fargo, and exits. The third brother edits a digest of digests. At a party, peopled mainly by friends of Odin, there is a former missionary who can talk Choctaw. At the conclusion, when everyone else says good night he says "Ninak Chukma!" (90).

A stolen Ming vase (there also is a dog named Ming), taken by a stage Chinaman, Hang Lee, is lifted only because Jehoiachim died owing him for laundry, and Chinese like such art. Still, Thwing gets a threatening phone call from his brother-in-law, Hang Moy. Nothing comes of that either. But a thunderstorm and lightning in the room brings Jubal to confess that he traded the vase—given him by a drunken Thwing—for a blue sash Jehoiachim had. So there was no theft at all, except Thwing's of the vase, while drunk, and there was no murder; a suspicious bump on the sea captain's head was the result of a mosquito bite, his death caused by an accidental fall. Hermina becomes more and more nervous until Thwing marries her. That ends things.

Is this proto–De Vries, or a trying out that was later abandoned? Both. Insofar as style goes, the future brilliance shows in the quips and little gems of description sparkling here and there: on arising, Thwing "... stood there with one leg drawn up, looking down, like some diverted and musing heron" (5). He watches "skinny little chits ... with breasts like apartment-house doorbells" (5). Lola's "mouth was like a shrimp cocktail." Of someone who is straying, "well, marriage has driven more than one man to sex" (144). In a favorite bar, Rago's, he meets a fellow-sufferer, the for-twenty-eight-years-married Buxton B. Thwackwurst, "tall, scrawny-throated," another Thurberman, but of no importance to the plot. At Rago's Thwing observes

... the girls still there who snap their purses shut with the same hand they have the cigarette in, and pick the shred of tobacco off their tongue with their thumb and middle finger also with the same hand they have the cigarette in. They come in and go out, sliding their bottoms on or off those little muffins of upholstery on top of those tall chromium stools. (94)

Such is the stuff the *New Yorker* is famous for, the delicately crafted snips and bits that sensitive people notice but seldom have occasion to put into words. They read the *New Yorker* to have it done for them, and beautifully done it is, although it is also a fault: much of the writing appearing in that journal has the quality of excellent hors d'oeuvres which are good as far as they go, but who wants a meal of hors d'oeuvres? People who don't believe there is a main course, maybe. However that may be, the scintillating pen is there.

One line that De Vries does develop—clumsily—for the next few novels, before dropping it, is the Mystery Story motif. Since the New

Testament can be seen to be the prototypal Mystery Story and since so many overtly religious people have used the genre (Dorothy Sayers, Graham Greene, G. K. Chesterton, for example), it might be that this tack shows a streak not usually identified with De Vries, one that he later either erased, or camouflaged.

The custom of creating characters for the sake of a joke is one he has never abandoned (Hermina's brother Ludwig, editor of a digest of digests); nor has he changed his habit of throwing out tantalizing turns of plot, turns that lead to blank walls (either Hecuba or Lola would have served as the failed-sex-pot type, but he has them both). Similarly, when Thwing meets Jehoiachim the first time, the sea captain nonetheless is familiar to him since "He had dreamed about this man a short time before" (18). A promising thread is dropped there, but there it lies, unpicked up, unwoven into the pattern of the story: there is no significance to the dream, no prophecy, no meaning. Yet it is a commonplace that nothing in Art is to be wasted, thrown away, even if novels are allowably more amorphous than stories, plays, or poems.

The explanation for this meandering is available, however. Asked about possible comparisons with Thurber, Benchley, Lardner, Lewis, and Marquand, De Vries said,

I don't derive from any of them. I would say my main influences spring from two sources: Debussy and Sibelius. From one the emphasis on the individual nuance rather than the melodic whole, the chord being its own justification quite apart from any duty to a supporting continuity. From Sibelius, Carte Blanche to be as free-form as I please.[2]

More than once, in both his fiction and in interviews, De Vries has approved of Colette's evaluation of Mozart as being "a golden sewing machine." Music is, in fact, often commented on by De Vries's people; generally they like the impressionists, and invariably they detest modern popular cacophony. Often the banal lyrics are parodied.

Which brings up another characteristic motif of De Vries's, not overwhelming in *But Who Wakes the Buglar?*, although covertly present (and a very peculiarly *New Yorker*ish mark it is!): the man of sensibility, damned to life among the mundane. Perhaps this distaste for the ordinary comes from a reaction to Calvinism—a system complete unto itself and intellectually rigorous enough, but lack-

ing in the aesthetic: in short, it offers the theological gourmet a
casserole. Whatever the source, surely of De Vries and the *New
Yorker* it could be said in paraphrase what Frost said of Americans
and America: it was his before he was of it, he was possessed before
possessing. His people are aristocrats of the soul condemned to suffer
the calumny of the bourgeois who own the culture, but who accept
him not.

Either it is that way, or it is that way turned inside out; someone
who is basically a clod somehow finds himself living among the
elect, often causing embarrassment of which he is himself unaware.
In large part this situation is developed for the sake of humor, but
it is significant that in either case it is the juxtaposition of the
widely differing outlooks that makes the drama happen. And this is
incipient in De Vries's first book.

More fully developed is his Weltanschauung. George Thwing,
spokesman here for De Vries, is an agnostic, basing his opinion on
the light-in-the-ice-box analogy: "You could never know if there
was an after life till you were there, never knew upon what your
eyes might rest after death, until you died yourself. But he was
equally skeptical of the atheist" (178–79). In response to this he
takes a Humanist stance, adopting a wait-and-see attitude:

Mr. Thwing stood looking out the window. The sun shone, some birds
flew among the trees, a blanket hung airing on a near-by line, and life
simply was. This was better than night, he thought, the tenuous refine-
ments of starlight; the sun simply rose, neither idiot nor wise, and was
morning, a simple and luminous affirmation, and, like an orange or
two times two, neither right nor wrong. In the country, roads went to
meet other roads, cattle to meet other cattle, only just come home at
night and no questions asked. Thus, each after its kind, one two three
four. And only man is vile. Morning. Each after its own kind. That's all.
Quite simple when you just don't think about it, when you come to
think about it. Go on, and just shut up. Simple, life just goes on. There's
the whole thing, face. Limpid as jello. (220–21)

In nearly four decades of novel-writing, that outlook has not
been much modified.

In the biographical sketch on De Vries in the *Wilson Library
Bulletin*, the *Saturday Review* is quoted on *Bugler*: "It may well be
that this book will become known ... as the first wild bleat of a

young voice which was soon to blossom...." It didn't happen that way, though: "His next two novels...had only a small public and dubious critical reception."[3] Is that why De Vries never went back to the sort of prose fiction that usually passes for "serious"? No, it was the comparatively successful *But Who Wakes the Bugler?* that was zany, and it is to that sort of writing that he has never returned.

The big difference is simply that he got married. The out-of-print books all end with marriage; from *The Tunnel of Love* on they pretty much begin with it. This is a generally un-American situation, writing about married love. In fact, the only way it seems possible to do so seriously is by lacing the work generously with levity: this is what De Vries does. It may be significant that these first three novels, thought by De Vries to be "not good enough," he dislikes because he is too mature for them. Their "dubious critical reception" may be due to lack of maturity elsewhere.

Insanity

Although we are told of funny things done by Brian Carston in the past, none of them happens during the course of *The Handsome Heart*, of which he is the central intelligence. According to Dr. Grimberg, psychiatrist at an asylum from which Brian has escaped,

He would knock on people's doors at night and exclaim to whoever answered, "Alice!" or, "Henry!" "My, how you've changed. I don't recognize you any more." As though he were a relative whom they hadn't seen in fifteen years—and then excuse himself for having the wrong house. Responding when somebody else was being paged in a hotel lobby and seeing what would come of it. (103)[4]

This he tells Edith Bracken, twenty-three, a Vassar graduate and virgin—somewhat apologetic about being the latter—and in love with Brian, whom she has met while visiting her Uncle Edgar at a state hospital somewhere in Michigan. Brian has hitched a ride back to town with her and her aunts, having passed himself off as an orderly. Grimsberg tells Edith that Brian has delusions his brother Charles is plotting to take away his money and put him in an institution. Edith asks whether it isn't pretty much the truth that Charles *is* plotting that way, a possibility Grimsberg apparently had not considered.

In addition to this setting, which invites consideration of the phenomenon of mental instability, there also occurs incest, murder, and suicide, as well as a walk through the halls of high finance. Obviously, it is a very serious novel. And although suffering from the usual De Vries vagaries—characters popping in and out, a plot that meanders—it is also one of his best works, for a number of reasons. For one thing, it is told not just from one person's point of view. We hear it mainly from Brian, but also in part from Charles, and also from Edith. This provides a rich mixture of attitudes, suggesting a more unbiased look at the world than what we usually are served by De Vries. For another, there are fewer gratuitous personalities; and, lastly, no one is patronized—all cultural levels are present and treated humanely.

Mainly it is a study of neuroticism, one of the ghosts De Vries had to exorcise. In *The Handsome Heart* he does so fairly well although there is no novel of his in which someone doesn't have to be put away or in which there is not at least mention of such a possibility. Some things you never get rid of, and in this instance it may be as well for his readers since the initial analysis of the problem seems also to be De Vries's enduring analysis of the problem: Brian, discussing instability with Edith's aunts, is asked by one of them, "How shall we explain that fascination madness has for us?" Her sister says "Maybe we laugh at it to protect ourselves, otherwise it would be too horrible" (21). That explanation will do as well as any, both for the fascination with madness and the humorous treatment of it. But De Vries doesn't glamorize such people, as certain other writers have, claiming that insanity is an appropriate reaction to a cruel world; on the contrary: "The neurotic is a piper for whom there is no hour of day or night when he may not call the family to dance. They must burn the chairs to keep him warm, break the windows in order that he may breathe, and watch him cut down the tree because he wants an apple" (5).

That some of those incarcerated also free-associate "poetry" would seem to indicate another ghost not yet exorcised, although such products seem appropriate enough in the asylum. Mainly the "tragedy of these people is not that they are haunted or harrowed or damned (so are the sane), but that they are wasted" (7). They don't do even that small portion which is "man's task and privilege" (ibid.). They neither labor nor rest, but are in limbo. Brian describes life as an orderly to Edith: "It's like a play seen from backstage. It's a theatrical world, a too real world, overvivid, reflecting life, just as the stage does, by eaxaggeration; only . . . you see the people close up, all paint and streaks, so it looks grotesque and a little ghastly" (28).

Each player says his lines, but to himself. "It's scrambled, but what's scrambled are legitimate emotions," says Edith (28). At that point she doesn't know who she's dealing with, of course, though she soon learns, And when she learns of it—after stopping just short of complete surrender to him—she very quickly warns him and aids him in an escape, during which he speculates: "Fleeing, he sees nightjars cruising for bugs, thinks it's a little ridiculous. Why would anybody want to make something and then make something else to do away with it? This ran inevitably down a blind alley bricked off bluntly with the theology books on his uncle's shelf" (45). The unnamed uncle does not figure in the novel otherwise, so it is to be assumed he is invented for the sake of having an excuse for some knowledge about theology to justify the observation. The observation itself is sophomoric, although it should be remembered that the questioner is young and presumed to be unbalanced.

In an empty cabin in the woods, he sleeps. Awakened by the owner, a rough but vain man, he is allowed to stay. He claims to work for a leftish journal, the *Southpaw*, and goes on inventing tales till the uninterested man cuts him off. The man eats heavily: "Toilers are never epicures" (45). Such throw-away lines and situations do two things: after more basic literary matters are attended to—plot and characterization, say—the quality of writing is classified most easily by these "lines between the lines"; and they portend greater things to come. This ability is shown also as Brian thinks of his sister-in-law in his brother's nest, "purring among the furs and silverware, face smooth as ivory, breasts like cups of cream, the thousand little veins crying for conception" (50).

Already he had *New Yorker* tastes, this son of immigrants, and it seems every author early on has to write something about incest; but before Brian can get to Irene he kills a man who is trying to kill the cabin owner who took him in. Both have been working at moving corpses to make way for a road project when a fight breaks out over gold supposedly hidden in the bottom of one of the coffins. The digging itself suggests an abortive sort of resurrection and, in this case, an attempt to bury the murdered Novak fails when the night watchman makes a spot check. There was no gold, anyway, only a petrified young woman whose dress disintegrates when the lid is opened, "leaving the form stretched out white and marmoreal, the hands folded upon the breast" (65).

Then, with his escape to Chicago, Brian lives in grand style in a hotel after wiring ahead to insure that they'll expect someone elegant. He likes the city, another un-American quality of De Vries's people: "This was not the brutal and metal city of the books, but the human hive in which he felt rooted and restored, in which he felt protected, containing as it did some dim promise of orientation" (71). As for the sister-in-law, Irene, she is a type common enough in the American novel—the highly desirable bad girl with whom the hero has fun but doesn't marry. In this case, that of Brian as parvenu, she embodies the delicious possibilities of life at the top—rather like Daisy Buchanan for Jay Gatsby. Like Daisy, Irene proves to be amoral, and looking out for Number One.

Woodie, a fellow inmate, similarly escaped, joins Brian in Chicago. Previously unmentioned, Woodie appears suddenly, functioning as someone for Brian to talk to; and at one critical point he posts a letter to Edith, to get her to come save his friend from Irene. He has fled marriage, too, as well as the mental institution: "Marriage, that worm in the apple of love," says Brian. Woodie agrees: "Yeah. Sex is a game. Some want to play for keeps, some don't. Women usually want to play for keeps" (73).

Before Woodie appears Brian gets a job running a candy-vending-machine business for a man for whom he used to shovel snow, a man now arthritically crippled. The hotel manager, observing him at his new job, wonders about it all: "O world, O life, O time. Strange, strange; what is this all about? What are we and where do we go? He dropped back in bed, pulled the covers up, and lay there a long while looking through the window at the patch of hurrying sky" (100–101). Already the tendency to parody is showing, although earlier Brian Carston (his real name) has admitted to being much moved by Thomas Wolfe.

There also are instances of precise characterization, so precise and deft as to suggest parody; when there is no further development of the role, as in the case of Charles Carston's secretary, there results a certain grotesqueness: "Jefferson came in, a short, blunt, hard-stepping secretary with dark eyes big as grapes, flat heels, hair skun back, a somewhat fusty creature hailing from Nebraska and given to odd expletives such as Chiggers! and Fut! She had legs like parentheses" (107). She is, incidentally, the first of many women with "skun back hair." When De Vries finds a description apt, he uses it.

Charles has reached the point of success where his banker comes to see him, not the reverse. As for Irene, he sees her as an excellent possession—which is fair enough, since she sees him as simply the better catch: she hasn't married the one with money, she has abandoned the one without it: "And what else is there to do? Isn't the first thing she needs a home for the family she's been built to bring into the world?" (116). De Vries's view of women is, then, traditionalist: primarily they are child-bearers and nest-builders, a view that biology would seem to support but which many contemporaries dispute. If the latter view prevails, De Vries's work may date unduly.

There is on the part of these women resentment with the role assigned them, although they tend to take the assignment as originating with nature instead of society. Brian and Irene watch gulls on the beach; Brian calls them stupid, noting that anything one puts in the gull will sit on: "—stones, doorknobs, anything—and he'll sit on them solemnly till hell freezes over." Irene corrects him by saying "*She'll*" (117). When Edith arrives to fight for Brian, she fights hard for him: "A man has a rival, a woman an enemy" (137).

Charles has had Irene followed, knows of the affair, yet she makes love to him as if nothing has happened. His response, however, is "...a pure animal misery: dry tongue, loss of appetite, the bowels numb in the night's darkness. All grief is physical" (140). There's no "melancholic languishing" to it. Meanwhile the loans are being called in on a building he's foolishly constructing, and the stock that was his collateral is failing: "It was the old story, the myth of a holding company, a kingdom spun on paper. It was a delusion" (149). His solution is cyanide. Irene's is to wash the cup on which the almond scent still lingers; then to go to Steve Crandall, blond and available and announce she's going to stay the night (162). There is no preparation for this action, none at all, but when she cleans up and gets in bed and waits that takes care of *her*. Edith and Brian will marry, although she fears she is his second choice. Nonetheless, she'll do it:

To love and marry is always the willingness to stake everything on an

act of faith. Risk, no less than prudence, is justified of her children. However careful the reasoning, there is always the willingness to take a
chance. (168)

Thus it appears to be a fairly typical romantic novel, having a
troubled hero and a fair and a dark heroine, culminating in marriage.

Grimsberg the psychiatrist advises a plea of insanity, even though
Brian is sane, because he's uncertain of what the prosecution may
pull in the trial over Novak. The trial is a bit long; we see too much
of the gravediggers Judo and Morgan, and new personalities appear
and are developed even in these waning pages. This last is a habit
that De Vries has never changed, and although it does lend a touch
of *tranche de vie* it is not ultimately successful: the "slice of life"
style supposedly is valuable for creating verisimilitude, an atmosphere
of reality. But this atmosphere doesn't develop in De Vries's novels
because he does not use the other techniques or attitudes of that school:
his characters are not naturalistic, and there is a general progression—
albeit a meandering one—from beginning to end. In short, a plot.

It is, therefore, disconcerting to find new people popping up in the
last fifth of the novel. That's the portion of the book where we
expect to see a summing up, with a giving of the lesson. Which—a
lesson—there happens to be in this book. In this case, Grimsberg gives
it. Telling Brian to claim insanity at the trial, he says:

Perjure yourself? That's all relative. What Truth is or whether there is
any such thing in an absolute sense or personified in a God, or what have
you, I don't know—and neither do you. But there is a scale of human
values by which man lives, a hierarchy so to speak, within which there
is much uncertainty and great variation, in the light of each individual
case. (205)

Grimsberg, as a psychiatrist, is an acceptable person to give such
a summation, and since he at least has been introduced early on, his
appearance does not seem *deus ex machina*, and his philosophy is
credible. It is De Vries's philosophy, of course, and his later works
repeat it.

The Handsome Heart ends on the farm, with Beevers conducting
his orchestra, an orchestra invisible to the rest of us. Grimsberg says

Beevers thinks he's Toscanini, but adds that so does every small-town conductor: that's what makes the small-town conductor's existence possible. The only difference is that Beevers has taken a shortcut.

Indeed, the same could be said of De Vrees in choosing as his persona Brian Carston, an escapee from an insane asylum who turns out to be quite sane. It would have been a far stronger work had Brian not been so stable after all; for why else are we started off in the milieu of the unstable? So, readable though *The Handsome Heart* is, it seems largely to be a missed opportunity. The subject—confusion about reality—ultimately is kept at arm's length. By and large the illusions are perceived as being what they are, illusions. But an illusion perceived is an option no longer but only an illusion, and we are left with dull reality, commonplace, mundane.

To draw an analogous illustration: sacraments in the Calvinist tradition. The bread and wine, for example, remain bread and wine; they do not transubstantiate in the Calvinist Eucharist, nor is there a spiritual reality in any way incorporated in them: they only symbolize what they themselves are not. The Other remains Other, and the world is the world. Very matter-of-fact. It was earlier remarked that Calvinism is the bourgeois expression of Christianity and that it was deadly toward Art; this is why. Plato denigrated Art for being a copy of a copy of Reality; in his thinking, even nature itself was a copy, and art was one step removed from that. Even so does the Calvinist think, and thus the artist raised in that tradition—even if he is renegade to it—labors under a heavy burden. The illusions are only illusions, and the world is as it appears to be. This is a very good foundation for science and business and engineering, however.

Grimsberg, whose job consists of the sorting out of illusions, comments on the serviceability of some of them:

Falling in love, for instance, is embracing an illusion, the illusion that one's woman is the most wonderful creature in the world. This is a serviceable delusion, and indispensable to society, which would of course abruptly come to an end without it. So marriage, our number-one social institution, begins with an illusion. (213)

Maybe it does, and maybe it doesn't. (Notice that it is the *man* who is deluded, above, not the woman: do females know better,

and merely go along with men's delusions, or are they the prestidigi-
tators who create the delusions? A bit of both, thinks De Vries.)
Whether marriage is based on an illusion or whether it is a mystery
makes some difference, obviously, as to how one will write about
it. One more novel, and De Vries would be willing to consider the
subject seriously. Humorously, of course, but seriously.

Just Shut Up and Get Married

That's how *Angels Can't Do Better* begins, with a prefaced quotation from James Thurber's *One Is a Wanderer*: "Just shut up and
get married, just get married and shut up." And it is a good introduction since this, too, is the story of a young man's finding himself and
then marrying (De Vries's women would seem to find themselves
through marrying), giving up meanwhile the world of politics. It is
a much less schizophrenic novel than its two predecessors. Although
Peter Topp is somewhat divided, he's less split than Mr. Thwing;
and he has no double, as Brian Carston has with his Charles. He is
simply a young man who knows that if he chooses the option of
marriage he'll be closing the door on a number of other possibilities;
it's not a matter of having a theoretical complaint against the institution as such. Marriage is simply seen as female victory and male
capitulation—a view he would later modify and speak to at some
length.

In this, De Vries's first novel after joining the *New Yorker* staff,
absurdity is as usual in the saddle and riding mankind. But unlike
the absurdities of writers like Kafka, the logic is not that of the night-
mare: Peter Topp (whose name we first learn on page 60) is quite
aware that he is being ridden. Thus the absurdity is perceived for being
an illusion, and we can relax a little. An illusion perceived is an
option no longer. We are, in fact, told at the outset that absurdity is
the topic when De Vries defines it as "the gulf between intention and
appearance—a hat worn on the side of the face like a poultice, scratch-
ing a bit with one hand and leading the Philharmonic with the other,
statesmen standing on balconies for forty-five minutes making like
a dog eating flies out of the air" (2).[5]

In short, the De Vries cocktail can make you giddy, but there's
always the acrid lemon twist of sanity that keeps it from making the
drinker sick. In *Angels Can't Do Better* the town, Chicago, is jammed

with birds—starlings—or at least the ward Topp lives in is. Since Topp is the ward-heeler, this is a matter of some importance. This was in 1936, and when the book ends, early in World War II, they still are there. Inbetween times, Topp has to decide whether to follow his father (and grandfather before him) into the ancestral chair of Political Science at Lebanon College, nearby, or whether to go into politics. Contractors who put up inferior buildings at Lebanon do so by paying off politicians, and he decides to try to stop it. So it's politics, with academics in tandem: "I saw life as blurred, scrambled, patternless. Morons with earlaps eating up all your ham sandwiches, key men of great institutions dying at inopportune moments, people electing thieves to rob them, and one's father dancing indifferently in the hall" (14), Peter comments.

What he means is that no one came to his political organizing meeting except one fellow who ate all the sandwiches, the president of Lebanon College is dying, the councilman who likely will defeat him is a crook, and his father absurdly slaps his mittens together in the hall to keep warm. Pastor De Bruin also shows up at the party-formation meeting, although mainly in order to "labor" with the elder Topp; the pastor is the sort who won't let a man quit the church. Rather he must be excommunicated. The father's unbelief—matched by the son's—doesn't prevent their Dutch-fashion throwing of proof-texts at each other, each gobbet wildly out of context. Neither the father nor De Bruin, however, is of much importance to the progress of the novel.

Rago is. An old-time politician-racketeer, he has torpedoes who do his dirty work for him. He "seemed hard at the same time that his body seemed soft; he was not at all fat yet his flesh was of the kind that if you poke it it stays poked" (22). His secretary, Judy Marsh, eyes like "blue jumping beans," becomes a romantic interest of Peter's, malapropping as she goes: asked if she's hungry, she says she's ravished. Also there is Lucy Mayhew, daughter of a Lebanon alumnus whose construction company (with Rago's connivance) will bilk the college. He fears her: *She would be forever doing things for my own good"* (43). But he cannot separate himself from her before his Lebanon appointment comes through. Also there is Bessie Murdock, left over from undergraduate days, a girl who for good reason owned many sweaters.

With Bessie he goes to restaurants, where she lets it drop that they're newly wed; free drinks and dinner invariably follow. She rationalizes the imposture on the grounds that it lifts out of the hum-drum the lives of the buyers, too, gives them a chance to celebrate. But the word marriage immobilizes Topp: better to be free but lonely, or companioned but in-lawed? He can't face it. "Man," he says, "is bound on the east by economic necessity, on the west by sexual obligations, on the south by social responsibilities, and on the north by unfinished business" (55). Then he pleads that the world is "uncertain." Bessie informs him that it has ever been so.

The campaign progresses; he has a cousin throw rocks through his windows, notes wrapped around them warning him to lay off his crackdown on gambling. But the campaign is not terribly important in the novel. Blessedly, it is not a Political Novel, one of those works of art designed to get salami taxed at the Brenner Pass instead of somewhere else. Politics, to be sure, was an early interest of De Vries—so it furnishes in part the background structure of *Angels Can't Do Better*—but he knows well enough to use it for the sake of his art, not the reverse. There is time, for instance, for observations that transcend political trivia: looking at a flock of overalls drying on a line, he sees that "Inanimate objects take on a monstrous presence sometimes in overwrought moments..." (65), an opinion worthy of comparison with Auden's "Musée des Beaux Arts."

Birds function throughout as a leitmotiv, one pathetic starling in particular: "It was one of the most miserable spectacles I have ever seen. He was sitting in the nest, his head just visible, looking out with the sourest, most disgruntled and ill-tempered expression I have ever seen on a face. Maybe he was sick. But I thought better of that: it's a nervous breakdown I said to myself. And I caught the image of severance from the many" (97).

Whenever Peter can't face up to marriage with Bessie, he focuses his telescope on the starling. When the bird seems to crack up finally and attack the window of the room where Topp is, he realizes it's only his own reflection that the starling is fighting. Even so with himself. Judy finds a wealthy man; Lucy's kisses "are a bestowal, not a participation" (83), so Bessie it is. The election is lost; the war is on. Pfau, a sage old man from an apartment down the hall, recom-mends, finally, marriage—although he suggests that the partners "should live together for several months, maybe a year, before mar-riage, *without congress*" (150). Peter Topp says that's asking a lot, and Pfau agrees. Writers (and perhaps the rest of humanity, too) tend to assume their own problems of the moment to be those of the world as well.

And the world has troubled them: "Half the world is nervous," Peter tells Pfau, "and it's spreading to the animal kingdom. We must try to love one another" (110). But he will face up to marriage, to war: "Civilization is the record and result of man's not scramming..." (111). As he is driven off on the bus to army camp he waves goodbye to Bessie, his "version of the Woman who haunts, in some fashion, the dreams of every man apart: the immortal She who taunts and blesses, the gift of the covenant, the treasure where the heart is" (181).

Chapter Three
Exurbia

The Tunnel of Love

A fairly good way to find out quickly the slant of a magazine is to glance through it and read the cartoons. The *New Yorker* is famous for theirs, of course, and it is to be remembered that De Vries's job there for some time involved working on the rough basket—looking over the cartoons as they first came in. It happens also that Augie Poole, the character of central concern in *The Tunnel of Love*—first a novel, later a play—is a would-be cartoonist. What this three-dimensional game of checkers adds up to is this: if one understands *New Yorker* cartoons (selected by De Vries, submitted by Poole, who is created by De Vries) then one has an insight into the book.

And what does the typical *New Yorker* cartoon reveal? Most often it is about a person who considers himself an aristocrat suffering because he is caught in a world dominated by the bourgeois and having to make the best of it. The narrator of *The Tunnel of Love*, Dick Pepper (such is his surname in the play; in the novel he has none), shows well this mentality when he reacts to an overheard conversation:

> ... I wished that damned woman at the next table would stop ... delivering one of those "ices" monologues to a female friend. "So ices if you think you deserve a better job, go in and tell him ices. Ices you've been in the bathroom-fixture game long enough to have that right, and if you don't blow your own horn nobody will. Right ices? Ices nobody ever got anywhere hemming and hawing—take the bull by the horn ices to him."
> "Let's get out of here," Ices to my own companion. ... (p. 157)[1]

Well, it is tough in a democracy if one has good taste—maybe it's tough anywhere, but in a democracy masscult is the norm. Still the reaction De Vries makes is not the one, say, Evelyn Waugh was tempted by and then fell prey to, that of elitism. The affluent and cultured exurbanites are themselves subject to analysis and dissection, although—again happily—not in the clinical sense or method of Sinclair Lewis. The people of Avalon (in the play, Westport) are atheists, but, like John A. T. Robinson, sometime Bishop of Woolwich, they're conservative atheists. They don't go to church much; if they do, it's for a lap supper. The clergy, when they appear, are of a sort that go about taunting street-corner evangelists, reminding them that the Gospels don't harmonize.

It is the late 1940s or early 1950s (middle 1950s in the play) and Dick Pepper is doing pretty well as Art Editor of the *Townsman*. He's thirty-five, the usual age of a De Vries hero, married to Aurora, who has changed her name to Audrey; he has four children, none of whom likes his name, and the dog isn't too thrilled with Nebuchadnezzar, either. Augie is a near neighbor and a great gag writer but a terrible cartoonist, one who fears separating his talent from his dross because then he would no longer be an "artist." His wife is Isolde, a minor actress who gave up her career, such as it was, for marriage to Augie, such as it is. She wants very badly to have a child, but can't.

Her mannerisms suggest Joan Fontaine to the narrator—a sort of half-smile—although her pleasant aspect does not mean tolerance: when she finds out the baby they are at last about to adopt is in fact her husband's bastard, she tosses him out. Paralleling and framing this story is that of the narrator's near-affair with Terry McBain, twenty-five, who is being funded for a year by her father while she tries to write. Pepper thinks she's pregnant even though he's not slept with her (he was very drunk that night), but he gets out of it all right. Again, then, there is the phenomenon of the double, or near-double, male parallels of the traditional bad-girl and good-girl pairing, the one who does and the one who doesn't. Pepper, even when very drunk, doesn't; Poole, at every possible opportunity, does.

Cornelia Bly, his pregnant mistress, fades from the story once her condition is established, thus assuring that the situation will be of more concern than the participants. Or, rather, that the participants will be seen in relation to the situation and not in relation to each other: the child's father and mother—Augie and Cornelia—are separated. In lieu of her, however, we do see her three professionally liberal brothers: Hubert, the literaturist, lives on successive scholarships; Emory is the fundy-taunter; and Carveth is in music and is married, but his wife is on a dig or some such in Africa. So Cornelia would hardly be expected to care about her condition anyway.

Dick Pepper conducts his assignations in a dream place on the Maine coast called Moot Point, allowing him to have his cake and eat it, too. It's what one does while riding to work, but he keeps his silliness there and doesn't act it out the way Augie does. His dreams are similar to Augie's, but he sees that their soap-opera character needs a soap-opera setting. Hence, Moot Point. By the end of the novel there's a six-lane highway in front of it and Moot Point has gone to weeds.

Before that happens, though, we see the workings of an Eastern exurbia—to use August Spectorsky's term for people who are highly enough placed that they can live beyond suburbia, needing to report in to the city more or less only when they want to. Their ways are seen by Pepper, a midwesterner and graduate of Northwestern, a school that dreams sometimes it has been misplaced, that it should have been dropped down 800 miles farther east. Thus Pepper has one foot in, one foot out, of being "in," in the jargon of the time. Liberals, Intellectuals, Artists, Romantics, Fornicators—all the sorts (or different aspects of the same sort) our age takes seriously he lampoons. He includes himself in the silliness: when his wife says how level-headed he is, he resents it: " 'Why don't you ever build me up,' I asked her, out of what she no doubt took to be a clear blue sky." Whoever heard of a level-headed artist? "Sure, make me out a cheerful moron" (53).

At a party "a small knot gave off twitting Sid Walters about the clarity of his verse" (88). Similarly, Pepper likes the Dylan Thomas line, "Altarwise by owl-light in the halfway house." Then "Just as I was getting drowsy, I sensed something nagging the back of my mind; something about the line. I didn't know what it meant" (125). Augie, as fatuous a spokesman for the artist as any philistine could hope for, is given all the rope he needs: "Western culture! The way it mauls and mangles the individual to save him for society. It's time we turned it around and organized society to let the individual live—yes, let him indulge impulses that don't hurt anybody. Soon enough we'll all be dead, or what's worse, old. When are we going to get civilized and let the whole man live. The French—" (86). This he says at the same party, on a "typical Avalon evening studded with intellectuals who listened only to jazz and read principally the avant-garde funnies" (87).

When a helpful second eye was added to a full-face painting done by Cornelia Bly, added without her consent, she sued; a critic from *Bloodshot* testifies in her behalf and she is awarded 25¢. After he gets her pregnant, Augie shakes his head distractedly and says he blames himself. Dick, leading him on, says, "Blaming yourself. I'm sorry." Augie is unaware that Dick's tongue is quite literally in his cheek—or probing a molar, rather—and answers, "Who else is there *to* blame? I don't know what's the matter with you sometimes. Put yourself in my shoes" (102). He doesn't mean it: who except someone who didn't believe himself to blame could claim responsibility for what so obviously is his? Anyway, Cornelia had planned to live on the $10,000 she expected to collect from the painting-changing flour company and to keep the baby; when the award is less than she'd hoped for, up for adoption it will go.

Originally guilty for not feeling guilty, Augie has explained his sleeping around in order to justify the guilt: "It's the only way of getting back to guilt."

"Why should you want to get back to it?"
"Because I feel I have it coming to me."
"What for?"
"For sleeping around." (68)

Happily he is able to transfer his guilt to his sleeping with his wife; then he feels guilty about cheating on Cornelia (96). Since most people of Augie's mind-set think one should feel guilty only about feeling guilty, probably this lapse is to be understood as suffered for the sake of the joke. It would hardly square with his notion of the artist as someone superior to society, for one thing. That's why he mustn't sell his cartoons: "once he took a nickel for them his status would be confused and polluted, not to mention the unlikelihood of a gagman's ever eluding those bourgeois moral laws from which the artist enjoyed exemption." At a party peopled mainly by artists and intellectuals, Dick Pepper points out that publishers also are at odds with their culture:

"The editor," I repeated, snapping the match away into the sand. "You know. He's at odds with the culture of his time too. Very often. So are the auditor and the architect, for all I know, but I can speak for the editor. I can name you several, all top men in their field, who wouldn't take a plugged nickel for ours."

I pestered them systematically with this heresy for the good part of ten minutes, a long lecture for me. I went on to say that I didn't know of an editor worth his salt who was really integrated with the prevailing mores, that at least two editors of my acquaintance had imperfect domestic backgrounds and even histories of sexual digression, as well as other of the stigmata or creativity.... (132)

The party-goers feel superior and need the taking down; what they refuse to admit is the commonness of their condition. As Saul Bellow has Charles Citrine say in *Humboldt's Gift*, "I couldn't understand office jobs ... or clerking or any of the confining occupations or routines. Many Americans described themselves as artists or intellectuals who should only have said that they were incapable of doing such work."[2]

Part of the same mind-set (among those who care not for the middle-class way) is an exaggerated sense of the worth of those who are as far beneath the bourgeoisie as they, the elite, are above it. Consequently: folk-worship. Many of the Avalonians want Pepper to go to folk dances.

One of the most persistent was Sid Walters, the clear poet. Sid's obsession with things of that nature formed, as is often the case, part of a generally political concern with society, and conversely, my indifference to them has been vaguely deplored as somehow indicative of scrawny thinking and bourgeois leanings. [Pepper's aversion] ... dates back to a milking of certain Avalonians, myself included, received at the hands of a minstrel with a guitar, who wandered into town off a freight car and thence into our hearts with the story that he was an ex-convict, a detail which granted for him an extra status among a small but discerning minority. (208)

The fellow feared work, it turned out, and jumped hotel bills, but that was all. Status had been given him because Society didn't like him. The algebra of such reasoning is that Society is bad; therefore those called bad by Society are (two negatives make a plus) good. Similarly, those called good by Society are bad (a negative and a plus make a negative). Pepper will have none of it; he recalls a song the fellow sang, to the effect that "I was a stranger and you took me in." Should he ever return, Pepper will sing it back to him.

The narrator then rejects the romantic view of life, saying that the "greater cumulative toll" is taken by the "small irritations of life—than its major woes..." (29). He would much rather pay "in one good snakebite" instead of the "thousand perennial gnats," even as the heroic sorts would have us conceive it—as a fierce battle against an horrific snake. But it isn't: it's gnats, gnats, gnats. Thus when Augie muffs a conquest at a particular party the reaction of Pepper is one of despair: the girl is lovely, but for him is mainly "part of the world's weary wasted stimuli" (55). His regret is not for Augie's failure, but for the attempt that led to it. Augie is, after all, his alter ego.

Probably that is why when Pepper has assignations (with Terry McBain) he muffs them totally—Augie's one failure was an anomaly— or at least ultimately. In part the disappointment is there for the sake of the humor, to keep it harmless, but mainly it is so because he is the opposite of Augie. And McBain is deliciously well turned out: "Terry was dressed in a navy blue faille suit of provocative sibilance and a blue and yellow ascot that, under the eaves of a floppy yellow hat, set off her amber skin and blue eyes." Another time she appears in "Swiss batiste. . . ." And again in "a brown suit and had a silk ribbon in her yellow fleece." Another time "We met in the Baltimore lounge, and this time she had on a salt-and-pepper tweed suit and a 'courageous' little hat of butterscotch color with a pompom on it" (141, 144, 154).

Very few men notice the texture of life or of clothes so acutely as that, and most don't know what faille is, or batiste, and would hardly know whether calling such a hat "courageous" was appropriate or not. Although it is possible that everyone on the staff of the *New Yorker* does, the generality of men do not. Such observations leaven the loaf considerably, as when a barman sees Dick Pepper arrive at his establishment already well prepped: " 'I see I got competition,' he said, wiping a glass..." (237).

Anyway, in due season Augie "realizes he isn't wielding a rapier, but only laying about the kitchen poker—," as Dick says to Isolde, who misunderstands anyway (180). Actually Augie "reformed and settled down and became a breadwinning husband, because he was scared into it" (224). And although Pepper remarks that had

Augie not sinned on the scale that he did, he couldn't have reformed as much as he did, it seems likely that Poole is unaware of having done either. He is a modern secular chap, "a kind of Everyman, combining the good and bad in us" (225). The illegitimate babies sown actually help the salt-of-the-earth types by giving them someone to adopt. (This was written before abortion on demand dried up that source.) "Augie was just his own source of supply" (225). Probably it was the possibility of that irony that suggested the situation to De Vries in the first place. Augie has gone into harness: "So Augie was gathered into the orbit that claims us all at last. So the damnation is that there is no damnation; the peal of doom is a penny whistle, the Good Humor bell calling the children at evening. So the years glide along. I never go to Moot Point any more. There is nothing doing there. A new six-lane highway goes by the door, and Moot Point is a silent ruin" (245).

The dramatic version, adapted by Joseph Fields in collaboration with De Vries, opened at the Royale Theatre on 13 February 1957 and ran through the year. A successful entertainment, it had Tom Ewell and Nancy Olson in the parts of Augie and Isolde Poole, and was similar to the novel, except where the need for conformity to the limitations of the stage exacted its demands. The people seemed to be continually at the bar.

Comfort Me with Apples

Again we are back in Connecticut, in a town called Decency, although that doesn't mean De Vries is a regional writer—he just happens to live there. What is a little unusual about *Comfort Me with Apples* is its concern with middle America; in this case, as it happens to exist in an area being exurbanized, Chick Swallow would like it well enough were he a boulevardier—although he hasn't it quite in him to bring it off—and the novel is his story of coming to terms with himself. As Louis Hasley notes, most De Vries people "are married or shortly embrace that state. What happens before marriage is not of the first moment. The real stories begin after the ceremony."[3] That's what happens here, and we're told it will be so in the very first paragraph: "If an oracle told you you would be a shirtsleeve philosopher by the time you were thirty, that you would be caught in bed with a woman named Mrs. Thicknesse, have your letters used for blackmail and your wife threaten to bring suit for sixty-five dollars because that was all you were worth, you would tell him he was out of his mind (3).[4]

As well as being a fair synopsis, it's not a bad get-'em-in-the-tent pitch, either. Chick and his friend Nickie Sherman, son of a Jewish tailor who presses seams into pants sideways, are apprentice boulevardiers, as late adolescents are sometimes wont to be. They shine at the Samothrace restaurant, owned by a Greek who has Americanized his name to Nachtgeborn. Swallow dates the intellectually very ordinary Crystal Chickering, daughter of the Lamplighter column in the *Picayune Blade*. (Why the useless similarity between her surname and the diminuitive for his given name?) She is a delicious animal who, like many De Vries females, mismatches her metaphors a lot: she's cool as a cucumber at him, or mad as a March hare when he doesn't phone; sauces, she says, are rich as Croesus. One would think the author spent a long time teaching freshman composition, when really it has more to do with De Vries's estimation of the female soul. Interviewer Richard B. Sale said to De Vries once: "You give the impression in your novels of [women] not sharing the philosophical perplexities of men, of having made their peace with the cosmos." He replied:

Any peace with the cosmos is a negotiated one, on its own terms, and you can jolly well like it. There are lots of ways of doing so. You can get out on your knees and *plant* some cosmos, which will give you a very satisfying flower. Or you can make your peace with it by throwing empty bottles at the stars, which we all of us do on occasion, women too. Incidentally, why do we have to choose between cursing the gloom and lighting a candle? Why not a little of both? I do a little of both, and I'd be hard put to say which makes me feel better. But by and large women's cosmos is human, not galactic. In the end, they bring everything back down to earth where it really belongs, like Molly Bloom in *Ulysses*. They don't deal in things like categorical imperatives and windowless monads. They don't know what the hell you're talking about, and they'd be damn fools if they did. Has there ever been a woman philosopher?[5]

There hasn't, not on the level of Kant or Liebniz, certainly, not even in a century when women have done very well in other arts and letters. So there is probably validity to De Vries's analysis, and anyway he means it as a compliment. Unlike Molly, Crystal does not have her own chapter; thus we see her only through Chick's eyes, so we have to look sharply indeed to see her as she is and not only as he sees her. Actually, she's bringing him along throughout most of the book, even when she yields herself up to him the summer before college is to begin for him. Unhappy in his own home and frantic with worry for a couple of weeks, he's so relieved when she tells him she isn't pregnant that he asks her to marry him.

They wait till after his (hurriedly skipped over) college years to wed, when Chick takes over his father-in-law's job: the elder Chickering hits a homer at a soft ball game, has a heart attack, and dies on third. (Aristotle notwithstanding, humor is almost always in bad taste: the philosopher said "aberrational without harm" was what was funny, but the aberrational always injures someone. Of course, one of the "functions" of humor is to define the aberrational, point it out so that it will be avoided—those who ignore the warning will be laughed at.) Swallow has a hard time making a sow's ear out of his silk-purse wit, but he manages to the satisfaction of Harry Clammidge, the editor. In time Clammidge suggests an advice column, but that and the problems that accrue from it occur later.

In the meantime, Nickie—who likes undercommunicativeness in women—asks Chick's sister to marry him; what he doesn't realize is that Lila simply has nothing to say. To save Nickie from such a blunder, he and Lila are invited to dinner at the Swallows', Chick being careful to set up the house in deplorable taste, then serves food "Chosen with a view to their very names striking terror in the heart of a *boulevardier*: beef stew with dumplings, peas and carrots, cottage-fried potatoes..." (49). After he's screwed a light bulb into the mouth of a plastic alligator from Florida and thrown about tasseled cushions from Wisconsin Dells, "cocktails were tendered in glasses bearing the legend 'You don't have to be crazy to get along with us but it helps' " (50). After dinner Chick puts his feet up, loosens his belt, and undoes the top button of his pants. He feels he's having his head bashed in with bad Scott Fitzgerald when he overhears Nickie tell Lila (who lives with Chick and Crystal) that he'll get her out of there and they'll never let that happen to them.

But while Chick increasingly is deciding he's well enough cast in his role, Nickie refuses to give up his aspirations and pretenses. He works on a rhyme scheme more subtle even than those of early

Auden, calls it half-assonance, but has no job. Because Nickie is a "keen analytical mind" (70), Chick decides he'll make a good detective. Thus once again we see the above-it-all fellow who nonetheless does his mundane job while his more or less double is slack and irresponsible; one would be tempted to say the Calvinist was lecturing the Cavalier, but though Chick is bourgeois, he's no Puritan. He's being attracted to a slightly older woman, Mrs. Thicknesse; Clara Thicknesse—unlike Crystal—does have a brain. Science, she says, "is a pack rat, which . . . leaves something in return for what he steals from you but of considerably less value. It has taken our soul and left us a psyche—a zircon for a diamond" (89). Crystal, busy being a housewife and mother (the kids are there but we never see them), is not capable of such.

There is work for Nickie, as it happens. A series of robberies has been committed, by one who calls himself "The Smoothie." The Smoothie turns out to be Pete Cheshire, assigned by the court to Chick's care as part of his parole. Given to wearing ties with actual trout flies hooked into them, he's a clear case of militant vulgarity. He turns twenty-one halfway through the book and, speaking "with a quid of food in his cheek" (114), tells Chick and Mrs. Thicknesse that he longs to be a businessman. It would require the least amount of change in his life-style. The adults "agreed that a business of his own was probably the only solution for him because he was obviously unemployable" (116); but he needs a liquor license for his projected restaurant, and with his record it's iffy.

Pete does confess to Chick that he feels guilty: it struck him of a sudden—but while he was robbing, not after. On the way out, in fact: "by that time it was too late . . . having the boodle and all" (97). The guilt obviously is faked, so even though he's an unsuccessful con man Pete at least is a modern and thoroughly secular one. Guilt is a concept that doesn't mean much to him. For that matter, it doesn't figure prominently in Chick's world-view—until Pete finds out about his dalliance with Mrs. Thicknesse, that is. Then, seated with Nickie in the Greek's restaurant, he says, "I thought it fitting that here, here at the Samothrace where Nickie and I had so often conceived of life as an intellectual feat, we learned that it is in fact a moral one. We had been clever so long that it was now necessary for one of us to be good" (148).

If the Smoothie is caught, he'll squeal on Chick and ruin his domestic life; if he's not caught then Nickie won't be rewarded by being allowed to go plain-clothes. Parodying Montaigne's "Hypocrisy is the tribute that vice pays to virtue," Chick decides that "Morality is the premium paid Respectability for benefits accruable, and computed on the actuarial tables of social . . . uh . . . uh . . . well, what I'm trying to say, I guess is that conscience is a lightning calculator as much as it is anything else, including a small voice" (133).

Nickie is willing to throw caution to the winds, which makes Chick suspect Nickie also had "a debit he was trying to crucify himself out of," probably so that the self-sacrifice would be seen as being of great worth and "*so much more indicative of moral fiber than the peccadillo it exposed was of moral frailty*" (147). Morality is of a piece, De Vries asserts, and no plea bargaining is to be allowed: he knows the human heart too well for that. When he laments the loss of his youthful notion—shared with Nickie—that "just about everything was possible," Nickie says, "Well . . . it looks as though it just about is, doesn't it?" (148).

The illusion of his being special has led Chick into this fix; his banter with Mrs. Thicknesse was excused that way. When she says that the early autumn air was like wine, he replies that such is what accounts for the nip in it. "Nothing much, you understand, just the small change of intellect we were jingling, not its gold coins" (109). Together they listen to Sibelius. He imagines himself living at Wise Acres (successor to Moot Point). Their tea they drink from Limoges cups. Their superior sophistication justifies flouting conventional mores.

These mores are a trifle deadening. Clammidge, editor of the *Blade*, thinks Chick likes it there and doesn't perceive that he's gagging every time he utters something like "Say *Stability* and you've also said *Ability*." Clammidge tells him to write it down before it's lost: "You may not be suffering from a real depression—just a recession" (130).

Asked whether he likes it there, as a whole, Chick says, "As a hole it's fine" (130). Clammidge, pleased, says the Swallows will be asked over to dinner shortly; present will be "all the social heavyweights in town, including the new Episcopal minister and his wife. . . . I guess we all become climbers in the end" (130–31).

"The climber is a creeper, I wanted to say" (131). But he doesn't, although he complains in a men's-lib sort of way that he has sold his birthright for Crystal: "For her I had suffered my talent to be buried, my wit to be pickled in platitude, I had taken a job" (112). So there is a measure of balance. Anyway, Crystal has improved with Chick's tutelage. She's a Galatea to his Pygmalion; thus when he tells her that "Our morals, like our bodies, are better for a little relaxing" and she doesn't laugh he asks, "You don't like my little joke?" "Joke! Don't make me laugh" (201), she puts him down.

So there has been an improvement, shown when she threatens to sue Mrs. Thicknesse for alienation of affections in the amount of $65; she doesn't want to overcharge her. Chick, protesting that it'll make him a laughingstock, is told, "Then you'll know how it feels" (217). But his affair has been only seven-tenths of one since he and Clara never actually slept together; statistics show that seven out of ten married men have affairs at some time or other, and now he's had his seven-tenths (199). Indeed, his slight case of the real thing ought to amount to an inoculation against the real thing.

Technically, then, he hasn't actually had an affair—in the same way that a large number of American unmarried females used to be virgins; although they might have necked and petted profusely they were technically intact and proud of it. There's no parody intended in this case, though; it's only that in adultery failure is funny while success is not. "There is no comic mileage in peace and harmony, any more than there is drama in it."[6] What De Vries is saying is that he chooses to treat human stress, but comically.

It is curious, then, that De Vries's novels are as fluid as they are, since comedy usually is much more tightly plotted than is tragedy. For instance, with the book three-quarters done, there enters Sherry Budd (wearing a neckline nowhere near her neck), sent by Pete Cheshire's tutor, a fellow named Lammermoor. Her intent is to blackmail Chick after getting something from him—anything—useful for such a project. Telling him of her early life with her father, she says "blee-me, it was no fun." Catching her dad with another woman, she wonders, "Shy tell Mother? Shy?" Finally she asks Chick to "Hypmatize me" (227).

She brings Chick to court for philandering, but Nickie exposes her fraud by showing that her diary entries are false, all written on the same day. As a reward he's given a scholarship to the Police Academy run by the FBI. Chick, Nickie and Pete have thus played off against each other, oddly grouped though they seem to be; still, they do have one point in common, one link: "You could call it the romantic ideal, the idea that life can have style" (275). Sherry is dropped and for a time Nickie blocks out Lila, refusing to recognize her because her gaucheries embarrass him. But that is temporary, and when he succeeds at the police department he resigns from it: "He quit the department and got a job driving a truck for a diaper wash. I could see his own private wheels turning. Working in an office, or at any white-collar job that made some kind of sense, he would be just another chap who hadn't lived up to his promise. Driving a laundry truck was an indictment of society" (220–21).

Writing this in the early 1950s, De Vries seems to be predicting well enough the mind-set of a large group of drop-out Nickies in the 1960s. As well as being accurate in the prediction, his analysis of the reasons seems well taken also: for Nickie it's a lot of fun to talk Shakespeare and Kierkegaard while wearing a uniform that has *Tidy Didy* stitched across the back of it. The next summer he and Lila, Chick, and Crystal all go to Europe and then return on the *Queen Mary*. And with fewer than ten pages to go we meet Beryl (Googoo) Hoyt: "Middle-aged, handsome, she represented a class distinct in our culture: women who get about" (272).

Married or between marriages, when these women marry money they appear to have had it all their lives; they have two children or none, they shop for men unerringly, have nephews of marriageable age who rise up on the balls of their feet when they walk (273). She serves no purpose in the book, apparently is there only because she is a type De Vries finds fascinating: she has class—money and sophistication, that is—and is of a vintage (early forties) decanted fairly often in his novels. Variations of her type occur again and again; nothing comes of her proximity in this instance. Chick is tamed and widening at the waist and his hair thinning, the few strands left he combs down the middle into a herringbone. All is well, although one wonders how the vacation was afforded. Such matters rarely come up in De Vries's world. Marriage is what matters.

Asked by Israel Shenker about this persistent concern, De Vries said that:

"Woman isn't alone in displaying an altar ego. . . . Even adulterers can't help playing house. I had lunch the other day with a friend, a practiced amorist. Toward the end a harried look came into his face. It seems his wife understands him all right, but he's being nagged to death by his mistress.

"When a man has a good connection, he'll formalize it. When he gets a wrong number he should hang up and try again, instead of constituting a couple who kill themselves daily until death does them part. There are fleeting bonds worth their weight in gold, and marriages that you wouldn't give a dime for."

The article goes on:

> Mr. De Vries sees this problem of freedom vs. responsibility as central to civilization. "The simile the Orientals have always had for it," said this mandarin for all seasons, "is the one about a man being on a leash— perfectly free within the circumference permitted by the leash.
>
> "I have another metaphor which is my personal motto: 'Nail fast the trellis, and let the roses sprawl where they will.' "[7]

It is sometimes easier in fiction to make things (and people) turn out as they should—according to formula—than in nonfiction. But, allowing for that cavil, *Comfort Me with Apples* exhibits the formula's application pretty well. One other thing it does is show a lingering taste on the part of the author for something like "detective" writing. When Nickie sets to work on the Smoothie case—knowing Pete Cheshire is guilty but having to prove it—he notes that he is going backwards, from solution to clue:

> .... deduction was reasoning from generalities to particulars, induction from particulars to generalities. In the light of which facts mystery writers, going on about the "deductive feats" of their protagonists, were misusing the word on a scale unparalleled in the history of poor English: what they meant was induction. This is probably the only case of pure deduction in the history of crime detection. . . . (164–65)

In part this anomaly is there just because it *is* an anomaly, the sort of thing that amuses De Vries; Chick says it reminds him of a vaudeville act "where the fellow played a violin by tucking the bow under his chin and scraping the fiddle across it" (166). That's so, but it also indicates a certain touch of the dogmatic in the author; writers of genuine detective fiction (not mayhem, but stories where a puzzling crime is solved rationally) are typically people who see the clues of life as revealed but rational—that is, dogma. W. H. Auden, who had a taste for that sort of escape reading, has written learnedly on it in an essay called "The Guilty Vicarage." In this game the hidden is revealed. Most often the practitioners are Catholics or high Anglican—Chesterton and Sayers, for example—and this may account for De Vries's limited allegiance to the form. Also, his writing is far above the level of formula; but so is that of Graham Greene, in much of whose work that detective element is present. So it probably comes down again to De Vries's one-foot-in and one-foot-out attitude.

It is a beautifully balanced attitude, a position some have chosen to describe in other writers as "tension"—being pulled two ways at once. Whatever it's to be called, it's a good stance for a writer who wants to move his audience while seeming to eschew propaganda. Actually his position is as arbitrary as any, and all art is propaganda for something or other; but it doesn't need to seem so. De Vries manages the cover-up very well.

The Mackerel Plaza

There are two sorts of clergy in the novels of Peter De Vries: those who are fools, and those who think Christ was. The Reverend Andrew Mackerel is of the latter sort, although there's more to him than just that: probably his name was chosen for the sake of a one-liner—in seminary he was known as Holy Mackerel—but the mackerel is also a fish, a New England fish. Thus we might look on him as somehow symbolic of what is happening, or has happened, to New England (Calvinist) Christianity. ("Fish" in Greek is ἰχθύς , the first letters of which form an anagrammatic confession of the early Church: Ἰησοῦς Χριστός Θεοῦ Υἱός Σωτήρ —"Jesus is the Christ, of God the Son, Savior.")

Such symbolism shouldn't be pushed too far with De Vries's characters, although Andrew Mackerel and certain of his parishioners— the ones who put up a green and orange phosphorescent public billboard that reads JESUS SAVES, mortifying Mackerel—these two sorts between them represent a fairly common phenomenon in Calvinism. Since the pattern of this phenomenon is repeated from time to time in De Vries's writing, it is worth looking into. It is the matter of Unitarianism (historically) or Laodiceanism (generically) being spawned by Calvinism (which is itself both generically and historically a spawn of Paulinism). In part it is to be explained by the Calvinist separation of Reason from Tradition in the name of an exaltation of Revelation (Scripture); then, having taken the Bible from the Church, it is fairly easy to take Jesus out of the Bible.

It doesn't happen in the first generation, of course: in America it was mainly an eighteenth-century phenomenon, although it occurred earlier in England. Also, it may be noted that Neo-Orthodoxy is a perennial—witness the popularity of Karl Barth within living memory. It might also be noted that the Death-of-God theologians were all of them formerly Barthians. The danger seems to be one that Barth himself very early recognized: after his work (1919) on *Letter to the Romans* (considered by many the coffining of nineteenth-century liberalism), in which he emphasized Paul's emphasis on the great distance between God and man, he turned to the Johannine (1:14) text that says, "... the Word became flesh, and dwelt among us...." Thus he would escape the trap he has himself set.

Those who fall into the trap are many, as, for instance, John A. T. Robinson does in *Honest to God*, when he scoffs at the notion of God's becoming flesh as an act resembling a man's dipping a finger into water to retrieve a gnat. Barth objected to the simile: first of all, the distance between God and man is infinitely greater than that between man and gnat; and, anyway, to be parallel, the man would have to *become* the gnat. Those who ignore this warning (as does Robinson) must end up looking on Jesus (if at all) as Someone Who Votes Our Way.

Even is it so with the Reverend Mr. Mackerel, the widowered minister at People's Liberal, a place so mod that divorce is a sacrament and the worship area—an embarrassment—is small and in a corner. His departed wife, Ida May, believed even less than he, but is about to be memorialized with a plaza to be named in her honor: hence the title. Of her he says she "had a mind like a steel trap, an antiseptic, sardonic modern mind" (170).[8] The plaza to be named for her (and, latterly, for him) is a popular area with the town leaders because it will also open up for commercial development any remaining vestige of scenic beauty.

Whatever mourning he may have undergone for her has been completed and Mackerel shows the degree of lust normal to a De Vries narrator—that is, quite a lot of it. Indeed, he invents stratagems to

curb it: "I often find relief...in the notation of a bad feature or dis-
illusioning trait. It's something that I imagine most men do to some
extent, at least unconsciously..." (8). The female in the novel, Molly
Calico, who first elicits this need for control, turns out to have no
flaws. She also happens to be the one he's phoned to complain about
the atrocious billboard. A minor official, one who carries about a
copy of Parrington's *Main Currents of American Thought*, she is
able to tell him who got the variance to put up the sign: one Frank
Turnbull. Mackerel reels: "A member of my own congregation!
A man exposed each Sunday morning to what were taken to be
among the more urbane dissertations available at that hour in Avalon, and this was the fruit of it" (12). He leaves to call on and
discourage from doing so "a woman bent on visiting hospitals and
organizing hymn sings among the patients..." (12–13).

From this we can see that Mackerel is not quite Phyllis McGinley's Reverend Doctor Harcourt, of whom she wrote in "Community
Church" that he

> ...in the pulpit eloquently speaks
>   On divers matters with both wit and clarity:
> Art, Education, God, the Early Greeks,
>   Psychiatry, Saint Paul, true Christian charity,
> Vestry repairs that shortly must begin—
> All things but Sin. He seldom mentions Sin.[9]

Now Mackerel knows as much as Dr. Harcourt, but he's different.
Because he's a comic *reductio ad absurdum* of Harcourt? No, because he's not a fraud. McGinley's man is an atheist, but he's a
conservative atheist. He's in the liberal suburbs, but he isn't liberal.
Mackerel isn't conservative. This does not mean that he isn't serious
or is not to be taken seriously. As Richard Boston writes, "It is
astonishing how much confusion is caused by the overlap in meaning between the words *solemn* and serious."[10] Is it really necessary
to point out that a writer need not be solemn in order to be serious?
Does it really need *proving* that "true comedy" has nothing in
common with "superficiality"? Yes, it does, since the two long have
been confused. One test, however, of any art is whether the work was
accurate in its forecast; for this reason contemporary artists seldom
are included in literature courses: one has to wait a space to see if

the weather did indeed turn out that way. As De Vries himself has said, "My needs are modest. A good artist predicts as well as reflects, and all I ask is that they say, 'We know now what they couldn't see then. He was six months ahead of his time.' "[11] In the case of Mackerel's so-mod-that-divorce-is-a-sacrament church, De Vries was ahead by two decades, almost: the Methodists, at least, now have a ritual for "divorcing" couples, one they hope will keep in the congregation people who usually drop out with separation.[12]

Molly Calico, lovely as she is, seems to have had four of those divorces. *Seems.* Mackerel meets her in bars in Chickenfoot, an industrial town somewhere near his Avalon—near as Bridgeport to Westport—in bars happily lacking in parishioners of his. These assignations help the minister forget his backsliding Turnbull, the man who put up the JESUS SAVES sign. Turnbull believes Jesus saves us "from our sins," that if we aren't saved from them "we'll go to hell" and if we are saved from them we'll go "to heaven." Thus does he answer to Mackerel's catechizing, eliciting from the cleric certain musings: "Can this man be educated? Or is he beyond salvation?" (17).

Although he's not really important in the book, Turnbull is hardly a flat character: he smokes heavily, he likes to talk of previous sins (particularly of a liaison he had in Naples in 1926 or 1927), and he offers opinions that balance out those of Mackerel. Turnbull says he thinks "what's wrong with our world [is] no sense of sin. Guilt feelings, sure, that's very fashionable. But a sense of sin, no" (18). Thus the man serves not only as a foil to Mackerel, but also to establish a balance and a tension. It is such counterpointing, says William Walsh, in *Encounter*, that produces "writing, which has the surface eloquence of Santayana, is never too creamy or too pat— one senses something turbulent, violent, agitating underneath—and it is why this funniest writer since Oscar Wilde (though one with an immensely superior intellectual equipment) is so serious. One hears something tearing at the satin sentence elaborate, the cry of one who wants to judge society from the standpoint of good and evil when these categories have been reduced to mental health and psychosomatic disorder."[13]

The sentences *are* satiny, and filled with the *New Yorker*ish hors d'oeuvres—"Flakes so huge they resembled small doilies fluttered dreamly down on [Molly's] hair" (24)—but this quality, although delightful, is superficial, as are the jokes that throw one off guard. In the bar in Chickenfoot, a hard-hat threatens Mackerel when he obviously doesn't like a puerile religious song, "My Skipper" ("I Believe"?), the fellow has selected on the juke. He prays in church "that a kind Providence will put a speedy end to the acts of God under which we have been laboring" (28). Other prayers conclude with the request that He "give us relief from the troubles and calamities under which we have been groaning, for Christ's sake!" (28). De Vries maintains his balance, he just doesn't want the readers to do the same.

Molly is a type of De Vries's who helps to maintain this usual sense of vertigo: a cocktail brain (cf. the Parrington), she malaprops often, offering her eyeteeth for a beautiful smile, uses *like* when she means *sometimes* or *for example*, and ends declarative sentences with question marks. To justify their going on seeing each other she joins his church; anyway, Mike Todarescu, one of her exes, is also a member of People's Liberal and directs its Little Theatre. Then, in the background, there is Mackerel's housekeeper, Hester, the departed Ida May's sister, given to tucking a fresh black-edged hanky into his breast pocket each day. Hester, her hair severely parted although in the main not unattractive, seems appropriately named; she serves without pay; Mackerel puts her wages in escrow. Prophetically, Mackerel suggests she's trying to step into her sister's shoes.

Yet her interference in his life is mainly held to seeing that he keeps to Ida May's various memorials, and that life goes on. Molly's mother, who resembles a harmless character in a children's book about cute animals, calls Andrew by the names of several fish other than Mackerel and serves to offer occasions for De Vriesian opinions not otherwise admissible. When she proclaims that "Poetry went to the dogs under the Taft administration," Mackerel agrees, saying that "they only write for each other. Well then, why publish it? Why not just send it to one another in letters?" (58). This is true of anyone in such a book, however: Turnbull's preppy son has had privately printed a volume entitled *Some Notes Toward an Examination of Possible Elements of Unconscious Homosexuality in Mutt and Jeff.* The father is worried—needlessly, it disastrously turns out—that the same elements may be present in his son. De Vries's is a mind brimful of wit, of ideas; as an artist his chief task is to see them deftly poured into wineskins—human wineskins—whose seams it won't burst.

So it goes. "Balls," says Mrs. Calico, apparently apropos of nothing, but eventually, it seems, in reference to yarn. When Hester is called a prude, Mackerel quotes scripture: "He that is without sin among you, let him cast the first stone" (75). When he and Molly attempt to begin an affair—in lieu of the marriage they can hardly negotiate with the Plaza as yet unstarted—it goes awry: in the fleabag hotel room where they register she needs a sedative, then oversleeps, one eye glued shut when she awakes. As for Mackerel, he "resembled a wire photo" of himself (114). It's less than romantic. Says Jellema, "The barb goes something like this: *worldliness is not half so satisfying, fascinating, and addicting as the Calvinists make it out to be.*"[14]

Molly, who has to explain her absences to her mother, is infuriated that Mackerel must account to Hester: she perceives who it is that Hester wants Andrew to marry, even though Mackerel has been given obvious enough clues. Hester tells him—after he's accused her of worshiping her departed sister—that she had read Korzybski (instead of Scripture, just as he'd asked) "and Korzybski speaks of 'time binding,' the ability of man to pass from generation to generation that gives man his distinction above other forms of life. If survival isn't true, then let's make our own!" (127). Then he notices for the first time that "She was naked except for skirt, blouse, underthings, stocking and shoes" (135). (When another similarly scantily attired female appears to him he's delighted to overhear banality issue from her "soft, pulpy pink mouth"—he's off the hook, his desire dead.)

He's hooked differently, though, when he protests that Ida May was not a saint, that she didn't jump into the water (and drown) in an attempt to save Frank Turnbull from the apparent danger of an out-of-control motor boat. She fell, through her own fault, but now Mackerel is accused of pushing her. Then he is jailed when he heckles a street-corner preacher. Worse, Knopf rejects his book, *Maturity Comes of Age* (someone really did publish one called *The Faith to Doubt*) but he is bailed out to preach, with odd results: "The instant I entered the church I saw how far my reputation had fallen. The place was jammed" (198). When he's too ribald in the pulpit even for People's Liberal—they've just sung "Funiculi Funicula" as a hymn—Dr. von Pantz, who runs the PL mental health clinic, has him put away.

Von Pantz, orthodox enough to believe in the devil, tries to *save* Mackerel (since he can't possibly be *cured*) by asking him to make a decision for Christ. No soap: pie-in-the-sky won't do. There's still the matter of the murder charge, until the only evidence that could possibly be used against him is destroyed by Hester (a rough parallel to *An American Tragedy* helps give form to *Mackerel*). Turnbull's reading of the same data makes Mackerel a hero anyway, so nothing comes of the charges.

The novel concludes with a double blast: prayers are asked by all "the bores, dullards and bigots in town" (259) for rain to end the drought afflicting the area, and God gives them a deluge—an act of such utter bad taste that Mackerel's faith in a decent deity is gone; and he agrees to marry Hester, whose body next to his is "like a bursting star" (259). She says he's as Calvinist as his father—at least in his anti-Calvinist stubbornness—and he concedes that *her* mother's view may be correct, that all religions teach us "To be as humane as is humanly possible" (260). Anyway, the loss of faith such as his was like "losing a wooden leg in an accident" (257). The Plaza will be built, and he has, in Hester, his *belle isle*.

Probably this is his best book before *The Blood of the Lamb*, and maybe after.

The Tents of Wickedness

The Tents of Wickedness, among other things, is an example of what can happen when a well-read man of wit chooses to write fiction. The result of such a phenomenon is analogous to a ride in a dog cart pulled by some scores of Chihuahuas: there will be much yapping amid possible loss of direction, and, when the author is as clever as De Vries, a lot of fun. Richard Boston, after noting that "*The Mackerel Plaza*... effectively parodied the beliefs and disbeliefs of Dr. John Robinson's *Honest to God* some years before that book was actually published," proceeded to commend *The Tents of Wickedness* for having "anticipated Women's Lib by nearly a decade...." After noting the "twists and turns" of the plot, he says that "there is a dizzying and dazzling range of parody that covers Marquand, Faulkner, Thurber, Fitzgerald, Proust, Joyce, Kafka and many other nineteenth- and twentieth-century masters. Not only are the parodies deadly accurate, but their presence in the novel is always ingeniously justified by the demands of the plot."[15]

This sort of urbanity is rare in the United States, the land of the practical—hence of the antitheoretical—and our major novelists have suffered accordingly. According to David Noble, an intellectual historian, Americans have as part of their mythology the notion that their land is a "New World Eden":

The American democratic citizen is a new Adam. . . . Where all is perfection, there can be nothing novel in the life of any individual. It follows, there is no place for the novelist in this Eden.

The American novelist, then, beginning with James Fenimore Cooper, cannot write within the traditional conventions of his European contemporaries. He is precluded by his nation's romantic self-image from being an analyst of social and individual comedy or tragedy. Our novelist must be a metaphysician and theologian. He must always begin with the question: Is it possible that Americans are exempt from the human condition?[16]

De Vries has not entirely escaped this handicap, although perhaps because of his immigrant parents he has an edge over most American writers. He does *not* find Americans to be exempt. The result is rewarding reading for a discerning audience, and a lack of concentrated attention from critics unused to such urbanity. Unused to such serious comedy, they assume his work trivial.

In this the last of his Chick Swallow–Nickie Sherman novels, De Vries seems aware enough of his status among critics inasmuch as he quotes in a frontispiece Sydney Smith in *Letter to Bishop Blomfield*: "You must not think me necessarily foolish because I am facetious, nor will I consider you necessarily wise because you are grave."

He knows the score with his central character, too, who is not Chick or Nick but one Beth (Sweetie) Appleyard. She is a type found in much American writing—and not infrequently in De Vries's—the inviolable, yea, even a *theological*, virgin. She is our Eve, our Daisy Miller. Or Daisy Buchanan. Or Temple Drake. To her father she is "an Emily Dickinson without talent" (35) and to De Vries a royal pain in the ass. She surfaces here as a baby-sitter (somewhat overage-in-grade) for the Swallows as they go off to a party at the Groteguts'. Her mundane task for the evening is no more than to see that Mike and Fillmore are bedded on time, and that Blitzstein has water. We see no more of the children than that: pueriles in literature are of no serious interest to adults, except for those Romantics who account for Evil by seeing it as a Product of Society. Such thinkers imagine humanity *good* by *nature*; hence they can account for misfortune no other way than to blame it on Society, and they look to children as (being youngest) the Best People—or at least as those Society has as yet not had time to corrupt. This view of humanity is strongest among those Romantics who either had no children or who, having them, left their care to others—Rousseau and Wordsworth, say. Sweetie is also of that mind-set. Society is wicked; marriage, therefore, is wicked, since that institution is basic to society.

This attitude of hers is not all unusual in American letters: in a 1949 UNESCO poll undertaken to find out from leading scholars of our literature just which of our books were most important, only one novel (*The Rise of Silas Lapham*—hardly in first place) was listed in which a leading figure is successfully married.[17]

In a typical De Vries novel what happens before marriage is prologue and usually his works start out with people already joined; thus it appears that here is another strike against his being considered "serious"—he who looks (ultimately) favorably on that institution must by extension so regard other institutions. Anyone who does that also by implication has asserted the priority of Society over the Individual. Such an outlook is nothing less than un-American. It disputes the American Adam.

De Vries addressed himself to the issue facetiously, as usual, having Crystal Swallow complain to Chick about a certain coffee-table book: "Why must novelists keep romanticizing prostitutes? I mean must we still have that? And the way they keep referring to it as a profession. Marriage is regarded as a trade" (44).[18] That there have been such books is undeniable; Faulkner so romanticizes in *Sanctuary*, Hemingway and Steinbeck do whenever possible, and on a popular level have been such books, plays, and films as *Butterfield 8, Irma la Douce, Never on Sunday,* and *Sweet Charity.* In part the phenomenon of good whores may be explained as intriguing along the lines of the "man bites dog" novelty, but only in part. Crystal continues, says the author's style is "heavy as lead," and complains that too much of the seamy side is presented. "Why have they always got everybody in the sack?" She concludes that "Maybe they don't know the facts of life" (45). James Jones's beginning novels probably are the ones Crystal has in mind.

Beth is opposite to Crystal in all this and is presumably more interesting, or would be if De Vries didn't keep presenting her as ridiculous. Once, during the most furious of her "aesthete" days, "she threw herself into the open piano and embraced its strings" (19). Chick knew her in "those days, and [although] committed to beauty in all its forms, he had felt this to be a trifle overshot, the hum of the ravished wires unsettling. Urbanity had begun, in his case, to set in, and his tastes to shift rather toward those that would bear the scrutiny of the boulevards" (19). Thus their ways had parted. Beth had been unable to tend to the mundane: " 'Humperdinck,' she would say with a helpless gesture, if it were a record she was listening to, or 'Millay' if a cloud of poetry in which her spirit was afloat" (20). If asked to help with the dishes, that is.

Sweetie's syndrome is such that she is also given to using the paranoid *they*: " 'So they've done it to you' she said. 'They've put you in a blue serge suit and tie to match, and shiny shoes to go to work in. They've given you a swivel chair to sit in from nine to five, behind a desk piled with papers for you to do things with before they take them away again to other people' " (24). Again, "So they've put you in a tweed cap with little teensy checks and set you behind the wheel of a Buick and said, 'Be one of us. Conform.' They've given you a house to keep up the payments on and an office with a typewriter to sit behind—you, Charles Swallow, who used to read Shelley to me—and set you to work turning out platitudes for morons" (39). Of a female contemporary of hers she says, similarly, "They've put her in a frilly apron and locked her up in a chintz prison. A little jail with pretty chintz curtains on the kitchen windows, and there they keep her very well. They've put a broom in her hand and the last I heard she had four children" (40).

This would put off all but the most desperate, and although Chick is feeling rather trapped in his marriage and in his job as an advice columnist for the local paper he feels more comfortable in his condition after hearing Sweetie speak for the other side. Actually her father has bred her up to this sort of thing: himself a failure, he worked for years in his attic on a life of Woodrow Wilson, ran a "literate campaign for mayor of Decency but neglected to mention garbage removal and all that, owned a movie house that showed good stuff and accordingly went broke. But he invested money inherited from his French grandmother and the bauxite mines in France paid off. [This French connection becomes important later on when Beth's only kin die flying there.] The investment had prospered, permitting Appleyard the life of cultivated leisure to which he felt by nature entitled" (27). The man believes that his daughter is a bit retarded socially: she is, after all, Chick's age, and here she is still at home. "She's a 'good' girl for bad reasons, where the reverse might have some virtue to it. My daughter is ruined far worse than if she had been ruined!" (78). Reasonably, he wants someone competent to deflower her. Chick demurs. No, says Appleyard, "I've given this considerable, and very earnest, thought, and I believe it makes sense. Take up where you left off, and get it right. I'm a father asking you to seduce his daughter. Is that such an unreasonable request? It happens every day..." (79).

In some people's novels it does. It is at this point that Swallow "had begun to fancy himself rather a Marquandian sort of hero. For one thing, he had this profound sense of the past. It more than greatly enriched his own life: to it he owed the fact that he was alive at all" (3). By this joke De Vries lets us in on the truth, that he claims no sense of the past at all. If by this sense of the past is understood something Faulknerian, he knows himself well: his novels are always contemporary in setting and are peopled by youngish marrieds. He even parodies Faulkner, there being the question of what happened between Chick and Sweetie those years back in the coal bin:

The children locked in that conspiratorial dark while overhead and then outside the coalbin door the footsteps come, and the hand that had wielded the fly swatter and might wield worse reaches for the latch, the feet and hands blended in that amalgam of familial power, that matriarchial Menace of which this is the one single feared avatar; and then the door swinging slowly open and for that suspended second the two still quivering in the still unblasted dark; and then the detonating light, revealing the shocked materialized old face beneath the upraised arm and the fingers like fried bananas still fumbling the light cord though the light cord has been pulled, the bulb itself dancing in frantic antic something-or-other overhead, disclosing, for her, the shocked one, the two innocents naked where they stand." (30)

Crystal is amazed:

"Naked?"
"Not in the physical sense..." (30)

Sweetie, a poetaster, does some parodies herself. Emily Dickinson, then Auden, but not intentionally. There follow Frost and Eliot, Elinor Wylie, Wallace Stevens, and one she can't place—Dylan Thomas, as it turns out (86). These are De Vries's parodies; he was once editor of *Poetry Magazine*; they are accurate, fun to read, and good enough to make believable Sweetie's later getting them published under the title of *The Mockingbird*. They also serve the added purpose of pointing up a fault in Sweetie's personality, and thereby offering sage advice for others as well: "This girl needed characters to ape, not verse forms—influences on her *conduct*. For if the principle of imitation is all it seems—and religions call believers to perfection by no other—then progress is a series of successful plagiarisms, and the good life a long, translucent parody on which God the Father will grade us at last. All the world's a stage—in our development" (118). Such an attitude is markedly Classicist, one based on erudition, scholarship, and reverence for the lights of the past; no writer with notions such as those could possibly hope to be taken seriously in America.

Then Sweetie goes too far—to the Village. Her father wants Swallow to go look for her. " 'What! Like Lambert Strether in *The Ambassadors* sent to spy on What's-his-name in Paris?' I saw the miles of relentlessly combed Jamesian syntactical fleece stretching away into a dubious future, and rejected it out of hand; unwisely, perhaps, since I was groping for a literary formula that would get us all out of this mess, some *mystique* as potent to stop the spell as the Faulkner had been to start it" (125). He goes. Sweetie is holed up on Bleecker Street, and introduces him to Bill de Chavannes and Ursula Thorpe. Sweetie is living with Danny Dolan, who has the "diamond-shaped eyes of the Irish," as have other hibernians in De Vries's fiction both before and after him. Danny, a would-be Hemingway sort, says, "We're a rotten bunch" and hopes that makes him belong (128). When the rest go out, Ursula asks Charles whether he sleeps with anyone other than his wife. Told that he doesn't, she wants to know "Just what are you trying to prove?" (133).

It would seem from this that the novel is proceeding in straightforward enough fashion, seemingly justifying the opinion of Louis Hasley that "the structure of a De Vries fiction is simple and uncomplicated. Events are usually in chronological order, loosely organic or even episodic, and too frequently undermotivated."[19] Were this evaluation so, it would be a little unusual for High Comedy, most of which is rather tightly plotted: the task of any plotting of course is to secure the illusion of reality while at the same time succeeding in this by not calling attention to the strings and grids by which the author's people are made to move through the author's world; plotting is equally important in goat songs as in revels, but in comedies it seems more important than in tragedies. This is so because of the differing attitudes of the gods in the two—in comedies friendly, in tragedies hostile—so that in the one the (finally) reasonable man acquiesces to things-as-they-are whereas in the other heroic man defiantly swings his sword against the waves. Thus in the latter it *seems* that plot is the enemy, and *external*—a foil, as it were. In comedies plot *seems* integral—it is the System, however friendly, against which silly man kicks and thus it appears false. Anyway, Hasley is wrong.

There is, for one thing, the parallel plot of the troubles Nickie Sherman is having in coming to terms with the ordinariness of life: Nickie is intelligent and high-strung, a would-be boulevardier, disappointed that the claims of society are prior to those of the Individual (members thereof). He says, "I hate having my life disrupted by routine," claims to "have only once heard Gluck made interesting, and that was by a conductor who misunderstood him" (54–55). As the son of a pants presser, Nickie has come to his malaise from a different route than has Sweetie; he is, nonetheless, just as silly: his urbanity and her artsy ways are both insufferably holier-than-thou, and De Vries likely intends them as such. By comparison, Chick and Crystal Swallow seem healthy. Which may be the point to the novel (and of quite a few other novels of De Vries's), that to be bourgeois is for some people one hell of an accomplishment.

Nickie has, after all, a wife (Chick's sister) and two kids, one with a malocclusion that will need attention. It is fun to have his wit—when he meets Chick at their old hang-out, the Samothrace, he says, "Nothing is so alien as the once intimate, once we are parted from it—" (61). But his wit must be subdued; when De Vries divides the novel into two sections he introduces the second with a quotation from Ben Hecht's *A Jew in Love*: "Convention has always more heroes than revolt" (115). The problem seems to be that Nickie is "like half of a pair of scissors" (112), a very bright fellow who would use his brilliance to solve crimes (and thereby divert himself), but "life offers no Raffles to use [his brilliance] on" (112).

Then, fortunately, a crime he has predicted is pulled off by "The Smoothie"—jewels are stolen by (they assume) Pete Cheshire, a low-life for whom such dangerous acts are *his* way of intensifying existence. Reflects Swallow, "life is a tragedy perpetuated by the passion that relieves it" (113). Nickie is thus a sort similar to the Smoothie when he becomes Johnny Velours, acting out a part in a play he and Chick had written years before. Velours is a boulevardier—at last!—a charming and high-level crook. He charms Lila (his wife), who falls in love with him again. And he with her. "He's asked me to marry him," Lila tells her brother. "I'm so happy for you," she is told. Lila adds that "He's promised to go straight" (161). But he steals a Jackson Pollock from a twenty-room house, the alarm system of which the police had thought perfect: the challenge was too much for Velours.

Meanwhile, Sweetie has decided to become pregnant although she has no desire for a husband: by then she had known enough men in the Village "to know that's not for me. Or I'm not for it—what's the difference? But why *should* I go in for it? Why can't a woman satisfy her maternal instinct without undertaking the institution society attaches as a condition? Why really?" (135). He has no answer, really: a man around the house, that sort of thing. But who would father it? Even then—unbeknownst to Sweetie—her only relatives are going down in an airplane into the Atlantic; Danny is being lost at sea from a rubber inflatable horse. And just as she had chosen him to father the child, Charles declines. He notes that her new literary set imitates lives as their favorite writers depict it even as surely as Beth imitates poets (137). Thus the artists do seem to be, as Shelley said, the moral legislators of mankind; it happens that Swallow doesn't care for the sort of morality they legislate.

He does agree to father her child, although only to get her to lay off Nickie—or Johnny Velours as he now is to her, and even to himself—the two have become hopelessly confused in Nickie's mind. Since she was to go off to New Mexico—Taos, probably—this act of Swallow's would keep the two quarantined from each other so Nickie could have the "needed time to resolve his conflict, Sweetie to wind up her affairs and be off for New Mexico and whatever D. H.

Lawrence existence she had in mind for herself there ..." (147). Thus with dispassion that would have pleased St. Augustine (next to St. Paul, Calvin's favorite author) he inseminates Sweetie (Augustine's problem with coitus seems to have been the temporary loss of control of the will at climax) and afterwards drowses under her sun lamp (152). When he gets scorched by the experience he buys a lamp of his own and sneaks with half a red face into his own house and claims to Crystal he's done it there in their bed, trying to clear up his sinuses (152).

Sweetie has, as usual, made the exotic seem banal and the ordinary appear very pleasant: just before their mating she has offered a poem in which are listed the marital difficulties of Coleridge, Dickens, and Gauguin, concluding, "These things attest in monochrome: / Genius is the scourge of home" (151). Then she adds Byron, Wagner, Shelley, and the women—George Sand, Isadora Duncan, Edith Wharton, and so on. He counters:

"Well, I was just thinking about Bach. . . . Loyal not only to one wife but two, with twenty children all told. Not just an ideal husband but a loving pater-familias. Then there's Mark Twain, Thomas Mann, Conan Doyle who adored his family. . . .
"You're pulling my leg."
"No, you're pulling your own. I think it's wishful thinking, this idea you artistic types hug, that you can't be one of the folks. It's a self-justification, a kind of goofing off. Why take pride in being a lousy human being, for Christ's sake?" (151)

The answer is not given in so many words by Beth, but the logic of her thought is precisely of a piece with that complained of by Crystal in regard to the proliferation of literary sentiment in favor of prostitution and against marriage. That is, if one starts with the assumption that Society is Bad and that Man is Good, then one must proceed to the notion that the phrase "socially acquired evil" is a redundancy: since Man is Good, where else can Evil come from? What Society calls Good must be Bad and what Society calls Bad must be Good. Therefore, Marriage and all that appertains thereto is Bad. This thinking is cousin to that of the Soviets whose Communist theory allows that in the Future Perfect (Soviet) State there will be no prisons: wickedness is a social product, and the perfect state will have no criminals, obviously. This Communist myth calls in fact for the State to "wither away" once the redundant "bourgeois-acquired" wickedness is unlearned, although until such time as that it will be necessary to give "all power to the Soviet." De Vries's rejection of this myth may account in part for his being George Will's favorite author.

The local criminal, Pete Cheshire, confesses to the theft of the Pollock painting, which angers Nickie; Cheshire hasn't the talent. Even if it's a bogus confession, though, he is off the hook legally; but he wants credit for defeating the burglar alarm. "Either way, I can't lose," he tells Chick, who adds, "Or win." Nickie agrees: "Yes, we shall see who's the cleverer. I—or me" (163): Johnnie Velours at stealing it, or Nickie Sherman at catching him.

Sweetie meanwhile is pregnant, unable to sell her house—and uncaring about it—and thus unable to move to New Mexico, and mayhap she'll not inherit her father's fortune: "A child on the way and no money. Oh, Chick, what'll we do?" (166).

"We?" Chick notices she has at last discovered the value of husbands. To make things worse, Crystal is coming around to something like Beth's way of seeing things: she's off to discuss "The Ordeal of Modern Woman" at her club. Swallow is by now aware of the complaint: "You mean those two cars, automatic dishwasher, beautiful house in the suburbs but Something's Missing? That ordeal?" (170). That one. Crystal affirms it: "The fact that she has all that after being educated for something else—ignoring your sarcasm." In more cogent fashion than Sweetie has managed, she recounts the nervous breakdowns, the alcoholism, the unwanted affairs, all because

the whole *lifeline* of a woman today is ridiculous, in an awful sort of way. A woman is educated to be an intellectual companion for a man, a creative mother to her children, and a cultural force in the community . . . and after getting her degree, or even degrees, wakes up one morning and finds herself a housemaid to a stockbroker and a chauffeur for three kids. She spends four years at Bennington in a leotard, and there she is, stuck in a—a—"

"Chintz prison?" (171)

She likes her metaphor, and pencils it into her notes. Sweetie's having said it first does make it a bit stale for the reader, as no doubt is intended.

Sweetie the while considers suicide, and Charles soon sighs, "Well,

I've done all I can to talk you out of it" (176). But he finds he's "not emotionally up to things" one might "condone intellectually" (177). Hence he takes to looking in on her when he ought to be with his legitimate wife and children and cat, and he is "able bitterly to reflect that conformity is after all the broad highway— it's the way of the transgressor that's strait and narrow" (177).

Drifting on the oars at a picnic Sweetie hints at a divorce for him, and he favors drowning her, as in *An American Tragedy*; but they're in a rowing machine in her basement, and it won't do, so he suggests an abortion. This he justifies on Dreiserian grounds, saying that the "alternative would be a miscarriage of justice, and that's a hell of a lot worse. Life is too full of it, as our best writers have been telling us. There's no rational explanation to any of it, we're all puppets of a blind fate, chips bobbing on a meaningless sea. So what difference does it make if we prevent another cipher in the human swarm...?" (185). Although his arguments precede (and predict) those of the most banal editorial writers by only fifteen years, Sweetie doesn't buy it. Anyway, even as they were caught in decades past, someone is coming down the basement stairs. It's Colonel Bickerstaff, sibling to a woman who was interested in Sweetie's late father.

The Colonel is a WAC, one who works on a literature degree in her spare time, and speaks remarkably like Hemingway. When she later eyes a brunette at an adoption agency we learn she is also Lesbian. Charles is abandoned by her: "Christ but the war between the sexes is complex, I said to myself. I finished my beer and left my table to some people who felt like eating. Then I paid and went out and walked back to the motel in the rain" (202). And back to Crystal, on whom he urges Shaw's *Getting Married*, trying to draw her out and show her that such attitudes lead to being like Sweetie. Finally he "slid to [his] knees, whinnying, my hands lapping her cool curves. I called what they sought 'a fringed exclamation held in a sweet parenthesis of loins'" (210). Thus won, she receives him back; anyway, she has herself just spoken publicly in favor of unwed motherhood.

A psychosomatic illness urges this reconciliation along; and amid Joycean bits and pieces overheard from a washerwoman in a laundromat, he turns into a pig: thus Kafka and Homer are paralleled at once. He's excited: "This is it! We've made it! We're in! Tell Cowley, tell Warren, get everybody on the wire, we're in, do you hear! A Homeric parallel! At last! Get Wilson on the wire, get Hyman and Daiches and Jarrell! Shoot it to the newspapers and magazines. Wire Prescott and Rolo and Gissen and Hobson and Hutchens and Hicks—" (255–56). Like Nickie, he's not guilty by reason of insanity. Sweetie went off with child to San Francisco, where—as seen from her subsequent verse—the "rearing of a child must have taught her a lot. Taught her that the conformity we often glibly equate with mediocrity isn't something free spirits 'transcend' as much as something they're not quite up to. That convention calls for broader shoulders—and, for all I know, more imagination—than revolt"(267). The child, it develops, is of semi-anonymous parentage after all—Sweetie only panicked and tried to make Swallow think he was the only possibility, so that he would support her emotionally and maybe even marry her.

In an appendix we learn that Beth has married, with the "West Coast sales manager of a retail shoe corporation, and has moved to the suburbs of Los Angeles" (269). With the marriage she got his two children by a previous marriage, so that she then was quickly the mother of three.

Thus the labyrinthine plot leads to a place similar to that Chick entered—but on a higher plane, where the air is clearer. The people live pretty much as they did before, but now they understand that it is not at all bad to do so. The wit is constantly flashing and the *New Yorker*ish descriptions are exquisite: Nickie compares marriage to "turning somersaults on a net, with a trapeze to catch you if you fall" (210). Chick describes Swallow's boss as "thick-figured, thick-fingered, thick-necked, thick. He wore a hand-painted necktie depicting a scene of the kind more normally seen on bass drums . . . a woodland prospect featuring a waterfall, which spilled the length of the cravat, knotted so that it would" (51).

This is good stuff, but it requires close reading. It is, above all, highly intelligent. Probably because of this Jellema thinks the two Chick Swallow books are almost destroyed by the narrator. Then, oddly, he writes that the "novels are, I think, saved from the excesses of Chick Swallow's cleverness if the reader will only keep in mind that it is Swallow, not Peter De Vries, who is writing the book."[20] That is a most peculiar opinion: point of view is the hardest problem for most writers to solve—who will tell the story so that it seems most verisimilitudinous. (Literary criticism depends, like sociology, upon restating the plain in obfuscating terms.) Swallow tells it because De Vries *always* uses the first person—such a maneuver prevents condescension on the part of the writer and encourages intimacy on the part of the reader. But it's still De Vries telling it; and if it gets away from anyone, it's from De Vries that it gets away. Even Pirandello must have owned a blue pencil.

Still the criticism is apt insofar as it protests the dizzying cleverness: life just isn't like that. And as it happens that's just what De Vries is saying here, mainly through his rejection of the boulevardier view of life. In particular he does this with Nickie Sherman, but Swallow isn't too far behind. In the end, both are reformed. And, at the same time, a clever man has written a clever book for clever people— *Eine Kleine Nachtmusik*, say.

As the 1950s became the 1960s, the world observed by De Vries changed: married women began not to think in the plural *we*, merging themselves with their husbands, but chose the singular *I*; divorce became ordinary, affairs casual. The Chick and Nickie books ended— maybe they had gone as far as they could; maybe they would begin to answer unasked questions. The human comedy was just as amusing, but those who justified their silliness were beginning to do it from somewhat different premises.

There really were few possibilities for Nickie-Chick anyway. Their development into a sort of dual or schizoid Mr./Fr. Brown character (Chesterton created his detective as an Anglican priest who became, when his creator did, Roman) who goes on solving victimless crimes really wouldn't do: they would have to age, both of them, and Nickie finally would have to grow up or else be put away. Anyway, De Vries is no Catholic or Anglican with a taste for dogma; dogmatists are collectivists rather than individualists, and supernaturalists rather than naturalists: they believe that complex riddles of human existence can be studied and solved by the application of reason and revelation, discovering divine patterns thereby. De Vries's heart and soul (and mind) are not of that persuasion. If he's a supernaturalist at all, he's an individualistic one: such people are mystics, not dogmatists, and they don't write detective fiction.[21]

For these reasons, De Vries moves on. His next book deals with the changes already evident, putting the matter into sharp contrast by bringing three generations together at once. Although the point of view from which it is told is that of omniscient author, the novel centers on the oldest pair: they have seen the most changes and have the best perspective on what has passed. Enter a new decade.

Chapter Four
Another Part of the Forest

Through the Fields of Clover has for its focus the fortieth wedding celebration of Ben and Alma (Moo Moo) Marvel, both about sixty-five years old; it is 1960 in Hickory, Massachusetts, on the Spitachunk River. There are reasons for not waiting—as the title of the book suggests they ought to—for the golden celebration: in ten years the principals won't be as vital as they still are, their children will be older than middle aged, their grandchildren will by then be getting their first round of divorces, and there will by then be assorted great-grandchildren. Already it's confusing, a sort of one-family Yoknapatawpha County.

They had four children, Ben and Alma—daughter/son/daughter/son (even as De Vries had till then that number and order, although his were younger)—and each has had at least one divorce. Elsie, the oldest, although frigid, is married for the third time. Her problems—for which she blames her mother—are said to have come to a head "when on her wedding night she had been forced to commit an unnatural act: sexual intercourse" (160).[1] That was with Louis Squalante. Her second was Harry Marvel, Jewish, a comedian who looks like a Hashemite king of the decadent period; with him the "same crime was enacted" (161), although he did manage to get two children on her. One is Lee, incipiently Lesbian, who lives with him; the other, Chester, given to Elizabethan euphuistic flights of prose, who lives with his mother.

Marvel has trouble with *ing* endings, tending to add an extra *g* to the following word (*living glanguage* or *checking gup*), but he is a type that De Vries obviously likes, the connoisseur of the female smorgasbord. He worshiped Elsie

with all his five senses, a contingency for which she was...unprepared. "You smell like fresh bread.... [Your breasts are] Jujubes." He worked his way steadily southward into more tropical zones. "Wet catalpa blos-

62

soms! Pine needles in the sun! Tomato vines! My absolute and all-around flower!"

She was disgusted. She bore him two children, and a good deal of resentment.... (162)

When she used a quip from a cocktail-party book on sex that it took two to make a woman frigid it worked on Squalante, but Marvel turned it around to assert that it also takes two to cure her. Elsie believes that "Woman is the victim of a culture which requires educated attainment of her while obstructing its fulfillment and keeping her at best an economic asset and at worst a physical entity, or what's-on-the menu as Harry called her body, the frenzied consumption of which seemed at times an extension of his life as a gourmet" (162). She, with a lot of help from her sister, is spokesman for (and example of) the Ordeal of Woman question that is one of three motifs De Vries plays through the novel.

With number 3, Art Trautwig, it was again the "malefactor (male factor?) breaking and entering in the same old way despite all the expectations aroused by a desultory courtship...." Now she's "rounding that equinox no woman can be blamed for hating. Regret for her womanhood was then compounded by the knowledge that she had never really wanted it..." (163). Art is the vent for her resentment felt toward all men, although their skirmishes (she says she married beneath her, he says so did he) occupy little space. Of more interest is her daughter by Marvel, Lee, who becomes increasingly involved with an illegitimate half-breed Chippewa who writes for her father. Prufrock—that's a translation of his Indian name, Rolling Stone—is probably as inverted as she, and is as intellectual as she is arty. Obviously, they're made for each other. Prufrock, with help from Marvel, is spokesman for the Why People Laugh question, a second motif.

Lee happens sometimes to be in the area for the summer anyway, once working backstage on a "drama of the Dust Bowl by a promising young exponent of the new 'twisted' theater, touted as a sort of Tennessee Williams without hope, in which ... the mother ... had had one breast caught in a potato-digging machine" (36). Moo Moo thinks her granddaughter's troubles stem from the divorce, but Lee demurs, saying "most kids my age have something like this. Parents divorced or separated" (38). She, at least, does not blame her mother; she does think her brother speaks Elizabethan English perhaps as a result of their parents' troubles. Moo Moo blames Elsie for the divorce: instead of a roast in the oven for Harry at the end of a hard day's shooting there was a statue from a ceramics class. It is her son Bushrod, however, who speaks for the third motif, the question of whether certain untoward acts are more accurately labeled *Sick* or *Bad*.

Always helpful, Moo will line up Lee with Malcolm Johnsprang, a stage Southron trying very hard to be a stage Yankee (*Time* magazine is *Tom* to him). Malcolm also wonders if the family is dated: "Freud did show us how complicated a little nest of neurosis the family is. Maybe it's got to go" (48). Roderick Jellema thinks De Vries's targets in the book are not family per se, however, but "all the new, ridiculously inadequate formulations about love, sex, child training, religion, adjustment and psychology that have *already* made a mockery of marriage and the family."[2] Probably this is so. De Vries writes about nothing if not marriage and family, often along with insanity and/or humor.

Johnsprang's own father wigged out when "He was riding up in an elevator in the county co't building one winter morning when with his teeth only, not using his hands, he lifted the derby off the head of the man in front of him and set it on another man's head" (50). (The situation—a sort of comic epiphany—is one De Vries likes, and thus uses more than once; it is a shorthand joke, an "economy of insanity" even more intense than he usually offers. Such asides have the advantage of requiring no new characters to complicate the plot further.) Lee cares little for Malcolm, though, noticing that his "lips on hers were like a touch of cool, spotless bologna . . ." (52). She does find him to be an "interesting bore, an intelligent ass" (53). Prufrock, who collects asses, recognizes in Malcolm the Real Thing. He likes him. Lee is just as disinterested in Prufrock, observing his kinetics, his diction: "These boys say 'actually' too much. . . . And spread their fingers across their chests like we do, and what else? Yes— they move their eyes without moving their heads" (59).

Still she does find herself on a rock with him at the edge of the sea at neap tide. Her knee has been slightly cut and his hand is on it; she urges it higher:

It slipped along her skin to softer flesh, to where both thighs came

together. ... After some time, his hand ascended clumsily into silk ob-
structions, whose folds his fingers explored till his palm rested at last on
the curve of all legend. Then they remained absolutely still.

Lee was performing with herself the experiment of which she accused
him.

In her few previous skirmishes, she had always bridled at this point. ...
Now she could describe herself as feeling nothing. This was progress,
in that it was at least void of distaste. [They kiss.] He tried his best to
Feel Something. So did she. Neither knew each was trying to do this,
to wring something from the other, and so they lay kissing on a rock,
two lovers in a seascape, clasping and clutching one another the more
passionately because neither of them felt a goddam thing.

An old man watched from a cottage window, his heart torn with memories of his youth. (79–80)

That this is funny is not to be denied, yet one wonders why. It ought
to be pathetic, yet we laugh: as says Lew Pentecost, a friend and rival
of Harry Marvel, "... we have to bear in mind that humor is a
release for people's cruelty" (69). This opinion concurs with that
of Freud, who pointed out that harmless jokes are not funny; Bergson, in substantial agreement, said that laughter requires an anaesthesis
of emotion. Also in support is Richard Boston, who in *An Anatomy of
Laughter* asks those who dispute the contention that laughter is cruel
to recall childhood: "the mockery of the playground is more cruel
than the physical violence. As Hazlitt [said], someone is almost always the sufferer from a joke."[3]

Then who is this joke told on? On Bill Prufrock, on Lee Marvel,
or on the old man? On all of them, and on us: Bill and Lee are trying
each to use the other to find out something about himself and herself,
although no real harm comes of it, and things are not at all as they
seem; this last point is made most clearly by the old man who obviously misrepresents as joyful what more often are the sorrows of youth.
Probably he does not properly recall his own youth, either. Because
there is a germ of truth in his lie, Lord Chesterfield was being at his
sophistical best when he denigrated coitus because "the pleasure is
momentary, the position ridiculous and the cost damnable." Obviously
the act *is* overvalued, and it is certain that on a physiological basis
what we call pleasure is intimately bound with pain, the former consisting mainly of the rapid cessation of the latter (food is good when
one is hungry, not otherwise—and so on). What is more to the point

is the strong likelihood that the same thing is true on a psychological basis; that is, although laughter is not ordinarily the expression of physical pleasure, it may well be an expression of sudden release from psychological pain. Louis Hasley has written that "Wit has undoubtedly been the [De Vries] way of coping with disappointments, agonies, and frustrations."[4] And for what wit, pray, is this *not* true? Wit is a defense against pain.

The pain that modern man seems most to suffer from is the general conviction that *It's All Meaningless.* Certainly it is central to this novel, inasmuch as the clan is gathering to celebrate the solidity of something that is terribly fluid. At the start, Alma tells her husband, "You and I, Ben, stand for something. I see us doing that. Forty years together in this day and age!" (6). Ben wisely decides to withhold from her the information that they are and always have been incompatible: "He had never told her" (7). He does ask her why they should "summon people for miles around to crow about something they simply no longer believe in? People don't care any more about their sisters and brothers, let alone their cousins and their uncles. There's been a social revolution going on for just about the forty years you want to commemorate. The family is going and the clan is gone. Come to bed" (23–24). As Willa Cather said in *Not Under Forty,* "the world broke in two around 1922," and those younger than the stipulated number of years wouldn't comprehend her offering. She apparently drew the line with those born around 1896, and few from that decade remain. Ben and Alma would have been born right about then; thus they were just in time for Chaos.

Prufrock, urging Mercury on, says the "art of Complete Chaos is a delicate and difficult one. Who in our time has the courage and talent to explore for Humor the possibilities inherent in utter Meaninglessness?" (87). Not Mercury, but Prufrock does succeed in getting him an engagement to speak on the psychology and philosophy of humor at Winooski College; it's a bust—elephants don't lecture on zoology. (De Vries, asked by the theological faculty at Princeton to talk to them a few scheduled times at a rather good fee, declined, wisely; his essay on Thurber is good, but it's a genre different from the one he usually works in, and requires different tooling up. He's better off showing than telling.) Harry is able to observe that "even a non sequitur must have a grain of logic to make it go," but he's quoting Prufrock, without giving credit: "That's what makes nonsense—the grain of sense inside it" (87). Thus, an "economy of insanity."

Alma has her pet inanities, too, if not insanities: she wants to join the Mayflower Society but to do so requires an appropriate ancestor. Neil Sligh, a researcher, tells her that Archibald Spry, till then her hope, got back off at Plymouth, England, when the ship turned back to accompany the *Speedwell* for repairs. But, for an increased fee, he'll keep quiet about it. Alma fears not to pay for it: "Ben was an intellectual; he would find an ancestor who had deserted the *Mayflower* uproarious—refreshingly antiseptic in a belt of patriotic cant. And as for Cotton!" (121).

Alma's rationalization is that she wants to be a member of the Mayflower Society only to be rid of them, rid of a local and overbearing specific one in particular—Mrs. Wetwilliam, the sort who goes about one-upping everybody. Alma does manage to reject the grande dame by pointing out that Puritans and Separatists alike had fled persecution mainly in order to set up a worse sort of their own. As for the New England heritage, "Who knows that the sense of guilt that ravages modern man, mucking our attitude toward sex and what not, isn't directly traceable to it" (211); besides, the Catholics got here in 1608; the others not till 1620. Actually the Anglicans arrived a year earlier, but since they're socially acceptable De Vries doesn't mention it.

That takes care of Mrs. Wetwilliam, whose reason for being in the book is to furnish an occasion to mention the whole matter of the New England Calvinist heritage. Her disposal by Alma is a little strange in that Alma usually is not so cogent in her presentation of arguments; she malaprops—speaks of a jeremiad of champagne, admires Proust's command of the English language—and is thus one of De Vries's common types. She reacts more than she thinks and in predictable, if good-hearted, ways. Still Hasley considers that "unity, complexity and verisimilitude of character portrayal" are at their best in this book (and in *The Vale of Laughter*). Possibly it's because there are so many characters working here that they are consistent; they *have* to be.

The researcher is dispensed of by some research of Malcolm's, who finds the man is a fraud; but Sligh does have the virtue of keeping a mother in a private rather than public mental hospital. When Malcolm informs Alma that Lee has been dating a queeah—Prufrock—

she decides that Sligh, whom Lee has also seen, is worse. When Sligh plays his last card and apologizes publicly for seducing Lee, Alma calls him wretched names and says he'll marry her if it's the last thing he does.

Mercury, given the same information about Lee and Prufrock, cares little, considering Prufrock safe for just that reason. When Malcolm left, "Mercury closed the door after him, half wishing the world were a better place to live in. Of course if it were, according to the intellectuals, there would be no Laughter, so in a perfect world he would starve to death" (116). The insanity of the world produces the laughter which protects one against insanity. De Vries makes Mercury not mentally unstable but physically so: unlike the witty Dr. Johnson—who was never very sure of his sanity—he is frequently and hypochondriacally in the hospital. When Sligh is announcing his triumph over Lee, Marvel is in the hospital for an emergency appendectomy and misses the culmination of the family gathering.

Bushrod, the Marvels' second child and first son, is there, as is his second wife, Clara. She "was one of those women who are content to be reflections of their husbands, having no identity of their own. As the wife of a tool and die manufacturer she had held opinions of a reactionary stripe, which Bushrod had promptly reversed on marrying her a year after her first husband's death" (136). Typically a humanist, Bushrod hates people: that is, he hates them as they are and loves them as they might be *if only they would live the way he wants them to.* In fact, he has come home only because he is convinced that there is anti-Semitism in Hickory; and, once Bushrod gets there, there is. Asked by Axel Aronson if he is Jewish, Bushrod becomes indignant. As for Axel, he, acting on his friend Larsen's advice, decides the mad letter Bushrod sent him is the work of a crank, despite the fact that it came on Civil Liberties League stationery, from the Washington, D.C., office. A liquor license is being denied Aronson for reasons of zoning, nothing else. His accent isn't, as Bushrod initially decides, a variant of Yiddish, and he's not opposed, as Bushrod rationalizes, because others think him Jewish.

As for poison-pen letters, when Bushrod asks him, Axel says, "Yust yours" (144). When Larsen decides the phrasing of the letter "suggested an unstable and possibly even deranged mind . . ." (141), he isn't far off, although this mind-set is fairly common among the enlightened. A part of the pattern is the notion that if their son Beaumont tries to burn down the gazebo, as he does, he should be rewarded with something sweet: "We don't punish in the old-fashioned sense any more. We remove the cause. . . . What the child is trying to compensate for, or release his hostility about" (151). Since Beaumont is quite fat, it is apparent he is quite hostile; when he later steals a watch, he gets early dessert. This reasoning follows from certain theological assumptions, preferring to use in cases of aberrrant behavior the word *Sick* instead of the word *Bad*.

In common parlance these people use *Bad* to mean behavior that a decent fellow might be capable of in an off moment if he thought no one would catch him at it; *Sick* is reserved for use to describe behavior that is so awful that a decent fellow wouldn't do it even were he sure he could get away with it: thus the more enormous the horror perpetrated, the more Sick the perpetrator. Why isn't someone who does something truly outrageous called Bad? Because such would imply the person was *free* to be Bad. Thinking that labels acts as *Good/Bad* instead of Healthy/Sick assumes: (1) that one knows the difference, and (2) that one is free to choose. That is, one assumes something like theism, involving a God separate from His creation (although constantly operating in it) who allows the choice of Good or Bad to His subjects and informs them of His standards for deciding which is which—approximately, at least. Those who think in terms of Healthy/Sick presuppose differently: (1) there is no freedom, there being no Creator separate from creation, and (2) there is, in any one instance, *One Right Way* of doing things, and those who are intelligent and educated will of course see what it is. Then if someone who is intelligent and educated persists in seeing things differently, he could hardly be called Bad because that implies not only the possibility of choice but also that there is something to choose from. Since there is neither freedom to choose nor a multiplicity of choices (there being but One Right Way), the word clearly is inappropriate: Bad implies a deliberately and knowingly made wrong choice. Since there is One Right Way (which any educated person of intelligence can perceive), he who denies it must be *Sick*. Thus the Soviets put in asylums those intellectuals who dissent.

This reasoning may be correct: in fact, Socrates' defense at his trial for corrupting the youth was very similar; to wit, he argued that he would not intentionally corrupt youth since he would then have to live in their corrupted company, and no rational man would do that, while, if he *un*intentionally corrupted them, that which he did by honest mistake he ought not be penalized for. Since there is no final proof for or against a Creator, the argument could go either way. De Vries chooses to poke fun at the atheist side of things because that side is the most fashionable in his day and place; and what humor has for its target is *reason* (*not* *un*reason). As Marvel (or Prufrock) said, there has to be a germ of sense in it to be funny. If there is no germ of sense, it's not an economy of insanity—it's insanity itself.

The reason that reason needs laughing at is that reason is never quite so reasonable as it makes itself out to be: America, as noted, is not the land of theoretical excellence; thus when one says John C. Calhoun is our greatest political theorist to date maybe one isn't saying much. However that may be, his mind was considerably greater than others produced here, and he used it to defend slavery. He was *very* sane. Humor thus is not a defense against insanity only; more important, it's a defense against sanity.

Continuing down that line of thought, Bushrod and his wife favor having few children; he has two by his first wife—they get lost on the train to the reunion but do finally arrive—and he and Clara have Beaumont, who is enough for any couple. Clara's sister "believes in Planned Parenthood" and has no kids, but another sister has six. For her husband, Bushrod recommends a vasectomy. Then, in the same breath, he asks, "Where's Dad?" (153). In a similar vein, when an array of lights Ben has planned to surprise Alma with is suddenly turned on and surprises Bushrod instead—kissing Ruby, the black maid—it is Bushrod's wife who is guilty. He accuses her of prejudice, but magnanimously accepts her pleas for forgiveness and accepts her back. Alma, distressed, wishes her husband had whacked her son more when he was small. In fact, she'd like Ben to whack him then. When Ben says no, that wouldn't be mature, she flares back, "Oh, mature! Is that all anyone is ever to hear these days? Why can't they see children as bad anymore, instead of maladjusted or insecure or whatever, and give them a good whaling instead of more confidence . . ." (240).

Ben points out that they didn't raise theirs that way, they beat them—and look at them now. Temporarily, at least they both seem defeated, consider that perhaps the family *is* the villain, and ought to go. Their youngest child, Cotton, confirms this. Asked by his mother why he doesn't go to church, he answers, "There is no God." She responds, "Don't split hairs with me, dear. You know that's not the point, but whether reverence is a fine thing. *Values*, the kind your father and I have had for forty years. They hold people together," she objects (17). That capital is spent, and Intellectuals—even *manqué* intellectuals, like Cotton—are asking *Why?*, and asking it about the most basic institutions. This is serious. Society functions most smoothly (if stupidly) when Basic Values are commonly held, but not questioned. Then one can get on with other matters. Thus Intellectuals (Those Who Ask *Why*) and minorities are not liked; the latter, because they too inadvertently question what the majority would rather take for granted—except for the perverse, that is, who might prefer minorities and intellectuals just *because* they question the majority status quo. Marriage, however, is something more than a cultural variable; it is a constant in all cultures. If it goes, there is little left; it is not a healthy thing for the man in the street to go about asking, "Why is there something rather than nothing?"

Cotton poses this question, telling his father that "Every man reaches the point when he realizes he were better off unborn. By that time he has reproduced himself" (167). Although Ben fully agrees, Cotton is too dogmatic a soul to perceive the joke. Similarly, Cotton blames the deity for the evils in the world, but adds, "When will people realize that we have only our own two feet to stand on, our own human courage and grace to see us through?" Again he misses the irony of his father's concurrence. Cotton is one who knows what isn't right: because the senses give only assimilated data, for instance, he distrusts the senses. He's the other half to Bushrod, who knows what's morally right for everyone.

The best marriage of those yet going for the Marvel children is that of Evelyn, their second daughter, and Johnny Glimmergarten, her second husband. He is "advertising manager of a large Chicago store, and miserable in it." Thus he's well suited to speak on the Woman Question—he doesn't like his lot any more than many women like theirs. Still, he and Evelyn "were famous on the lower North Side and along the lakefront Gold Coast as a glamorous couple, a term that would never have crossed their lips" (220). When she walks away from him at the party he notices that "She's got the prettiest little tail in Christendom, and she knows it" (221).

For Glimmergarten, the most important part of being human is one's identity, part of which is sexual. Being true for both men and women, the "trouble comes when the parties to it, in order to secure their own, tread on the other's. The result is a sex war.... [and] Prisoners. Women's imprisonment we know. It is of old. Child-bearing. Shaw reminds us that she resents the burden of creation being so unequally divided. Hence the Nag, the Battleax.... More and more she wants her cultural life, and to get it, more and more must man assume the abandoned chores.... Eighty years ago Nora walked out of the Doll's House—where to? Nobody knows, least of all Ibsen" (217). Previous generations had their ogre, too: for Victorians, the father; later it was the mother, now the wife. Evelyn, overhearing, sweetly asks if she's a castrater (219).

De Vries, interviewed and told he'd been seen as one who wrote on "the Ordeal of modern woman," demurred: "I think the term is a misstatement. It should be 'the modern Ordeal of woman,' for it is but an acute inflamation of a chronic woe." Then he quotes Shaw to the same effect as does Glimmergarten. But he thinks

that is only half the story. She further resents the fact that the life she has produced is organized and ordered by the sex having least to do with its creation. The urge to correct this manifest inequality shows itself on those petty levels familiar to us as the nag, the battle-ax, and the back-seat driver, but on worthier levels we see her spreading her wings in art, government, and business. Woman is educated for the latter, to find herself oftener on the local zoning board then in the halls of Congress, her pictures staring down at her from a bedroom wall oftener than hanging in a national gallery.

Now, the odds are exactly the same for the male of the species, but her disillusionment has been parlayed into this ordeal with a capital "O" from which man is excluded, and with a powerful lobby of anthropologists and journalists putting her case for her. But isn't it about time this lobby were dissolved and women recognized the general human ordeal, with her husband as full partner? Maybe he is trapped in an office when he wants to write, just as she is in a kitchen when she wants to paint.

What we need is not submission of the one to the other, but a joint submission of both to the hard facts of life, or we shall soon see a counter-lobby with the slogan, "Equal Rights for Men" (or perhaps more appropriately "Equal Wrongs for Men") and then the jig will be up. It's nearly up now, I'm afraid. There's so much sand in the matrimonial gears that the old machine can hardly function any more. And each spring, down from Radcliffe and Bennington, swinging brief cases and paint kits, comes a fresh crop that can hardly be expected to ease matters.

The problem of the sexes is coexistence, and it is the same for the two great political powers: Not to let rivalry become enmity. I would advise all newlyweds to make a sampler of that and hang it over the kitchen sink. This way the husband will see it as often as the wife.[5]

Since De Vries has a disconcerting tendency to quote in his novels fictionalized versions of comments he has made in reviews, it is not surprising when Glimmergarten fantasizes that "Everything in our time is phallic, Henrik . . . except the male. He's in the kitchen washing dishes while his wife is off listening to some lecturer explain the sexual symbolisms in Dylan Thomas" (255). Then, in his interviews he quotes his novels. Given, further, that in each interview he quotes other interviews he has allowed and given that in each novel he uses material from other novels—Glimmergarten considers suicide by vacuuming out his innards, a trope also appearing in *The Tents of Wickedness*, his preceding novel—given all this, De Vries's constant reader is swamped with experiences of *déjà vu* so often recurring and interlocked as to be vertiginous.

Then add to that mix the discovery that many of the often cross-referenced thoughts are themselves mind-boggling, and the ground becomes spongy indeed. Glimmergarten offers this one: "Infidelity has no doubt stabilized more unions than it has undermined" (216). The claim is at least oxymoronic since it offers unfaithfulness as a major support of faithfulness. More comfortable is Moo Moo's blocking out of Elsie's too confessional style with an electric egg beater: the more graphic her daughter becomes and the more she spreads the guilt, the more determined Alma is not to hear. It disgusts her and finally she blows the whistle: "It's all too easy! Because if your generation wants to blame us for everything, we can blame our parents, and they can blame theirs, and nobody will ever take any responsibility for anything" (203).

This, known as Determinist's Delight, she repeats to Dr. Patchkiss in his New York office, he being the psychiatrist her daughter Elsie (Case Nineteen in a book by Patchkiss) had visited. She, the mother of Elsie Trautwig, saves herself from telling too much to

the very leading but supposedly nondirective shrink by confessing to
a failing: she has a compulsion to "make a white ball bounce from
one word to the next" (270). On every word she hears. Thus she
gets Patchkiss doing it, and she escapes. Driving back home to Hickory, she

heaved a sigh, thinking of all they'd been through, of all the Twentieth
Century that had been brought to their old door. What was happening
in and to the world, including supposedly rock-ribbed New England
Massachusetts?
    "What are we coming to?" she wondered aloud.
    "Connecticut," said Ben Marvel, who had been watching the signs.
(275)

Ben and Alma are as bewildered as the rest. They have been "progressive and advanced relative to their generation,"[6] but the times
have slipped away from them. They lived on the capital inherited;
now it's bankruptcy for their kids. Actually one would think that
captial (like the metaphor itself) had been spent a long time before.
De Vries is laughing at a dead horse, maybe, to put it the way some of
his malapropping women would.
    In an epilogue De Vries suggests that perhaps Lee Marvel and Bill
Prufrock—both still virgins—may marry. She blames her frigidity on
her mother; he says he can't have any "emotional relationship whatsoever" (256). The "curse of our time," says Prufrock, is the inability
to love: "We're breeding too ingrown an individual" (256). Well-
named, he says. "The exquisitely self-conscious, hypersensitive, super-
distilled but gummed-up first person singular. Curse of our time.
The two I's ... that can't make a We. And it's going to get worse
before it gets much worse. The wave of the future" (257). And
"Thus he wooed, in an age of Criticism, under the apple trees" (257).
Still, they may marry. Or she may renew a half-begun relationship
with a Lesbian; or he may meet Cotton in New York, and their relationship may deepen; or maybe Lee and Bill will marry. The horse
may not yet be dead and may yet bear laughing at.

Chapter Five
Absurdity

The Blood of the Lamb, published in 1962, is dedicated "To Jan, Jonny and Derek." The previous novel had been sent off "To Emily with Love," the beautiful little blonde who appears on the dust jacket with her father (she being the only De Vries child ever so honored) of *Comfort Me with Apples*, 1956. By 1960 she was dead from leukemia. As does any artist, De Vries organizes and makes sense of the world—turns it from chaos into cosmos—by means of his craft. In any case to do so is a challenge, and in this instance the challenge must have been very painful indeed.

The format is the familiar one in which an up-and-rising son of immigrants moves from the Celestial City to Vanity Fair, works in a verbal occupation, and has troubles appropriate to his time and station. The ordering of the novel is the normal one for De Vries, which means that the birth of the daughter, Carol, does not even occur till the book is half over. Yet it is her death—impending and then actual—which informs the book, shapes it. This means that the focus of the work must be not the life and death of a child per se, but rather the effect of that life and death on Don Wanderhope; he is the central character, and not Carol.

Really nothing is very different for him than it is for the narrator of other De Vries novels—except that the subject is death, Death, *Death*—and because of that one goes in farther, and down deeper, and stays there longer. Death is the occurrence, the advent that causes even the most "come of age" modern soul to ask Ultimate Questions. Small wonder, then, that one so unmodern as De Vries asks the question with intensity. From a biological or from any rational point of view, the explanation of death as the coupled partner of sex is valid enough. But man, said Pascal, is the animal who knows he will die—other animals may know it at death, man knows it before. And that makes things different. Why should there be all this hurried confusion of death/life/death/life? Why cultivate beautiful but temporary blossoms? Because there's nothing else to do, probably. Still when one of the blossoms is your own child and when the blossom is nastily and prematurely destroyed, then the arrangement *does* seem ridiculous. It's not one's own death that is such a bother, since no one does know he will die (never having experienced our own, how could we?) except abstractly and by extrapolation. Anyway, it is the death of others that is most painful. Everyone that Don Wanderhope loves dies.

One grants that it would be absurd to assume that no one should die until old and full of years, or to assume, say, that a tree might never fall on someone. To assume otherwise would be to posit a world in which Nature would be no more than a painted backdrop for a high-school assembly hall, and Society no more than a collection of actors uttering prewritten lines.

That existentialism generally does so view nature and society in no way commends the theory; certainly that is not how nature and society are. What does commend it is the possibility that Scott Fitzgerald was correct when he wrote that "in the deep dark recesses of the soul it is always 3 a.m." That's existential time. But 3 P.M. is worse. Napoleon probably was wrong when he said that 3 A.M. courage was the rarest in the world: Romantics love that sort of thing; and marriage proposals most often are made at night. No, bald daylight is worse; 3 P.M. is worse. That's when Jesus died; that's when Carol dies.

Although many of the deaths in *The Blood of the Lamb* parallel and approximate the same event in his own life—the girl with TB, for one—De Vries has other children, and his wife survives, but for reasons of artistic concision he leaves these out. It is more poignant that way, although this is not only because it focuses the tragedy that much more on poor Don; it focuses it that much more on Poor Everybody. Life rolls like a steel ball through a pinball machine's gaudy guts, inevitably headed for the anus of death at the bottom, although some succeed for a long time in flipping and bumping the ball in play, maybe even running up a high score. Even so, eventually the ball will plunk through the hole. Maybe that's the metaphysics of pinball—why the machines—thus approximating life—are fun to play. Pinballs, then, like all art, simplify and clarify Life.

So De Vries's three surviving children are omitted, not that their presence made the grief less. When Don and Carol are moving to a new house farther out of the city, they pass a now ex-neighbor whose "hyacinth-haired" son had died awhile previously: "I wanted then to stop the car and rush back and tell him what nonsense I knew it had been to remind him that he had three other children" (153).[1] He waves instead, but the man does not see.

That is getting ahead of ourselves, though; De Vries begins as usual with the narrator's patronage. His father, Ben, never intended to settle in America—only to visit—but he became so seasick on the way over "that a return voyage was unthinkable" (3). A doubter, although on the very lowest intellectual level possible, he chose a believing wife, one with a ministerial brother. The dominie's theology is hardly more advanced than his brother-in-law's skepticism, so the quibbles remain trivial until Louie, Ben Wanderhope's older son, joins in. Louie, nineteen, a medical student at the University of Chicago, is able to throw out "ontogeny recapitulates phylogeny," a damning concept for biblical literalists. When his uncle completes a sermon on the years since creation—his figures aren't far different from those of Bishop Ussher—he uses as a paperweight a rock collected by Louie's mother; it happens to be a fossil from the Paleozoic era.

The reasoning, apparently very much off the point, seems to be that if the calculations of the Bishop Usshers are wrong, then Total Depravity is wrong. At least that is the doubt De Vries seems to be working at engendering: if mankind is not depraved, then it doesn't deserve what befalls.

Ben, Louie's father, isn't far different from the father in *Angels Can't Do Better*, one "labored" with by a Pastor De Bruin. De Bruin "was not very effective but he considered it his duty to come, and would sit in the house for hours, taking deep breaths and looking at the carpets." Like Ben, that father also is assailed by the "twin devils of drink and doubt," but is more sophisticated than Ben. Pressed, he offers his Creed: "I believe that the sky is high, that blood is a river of miracles multiplying questions faster than you can answer them, I believe that faith is a kite in a cloud, that it is insolent of you to scatter the dust of your platitudes across the incomprehensible riddle of the Universe, that death is neither a question mark nor a semi-colon but a period, that bugs are in earnest. ..."[2] In other words he speaks for most sensible De Vries people; nothing has changed. De Bruin won't let the man quit the church; they must excommunicate him instead.

De Bruin's heritor in *The Blood of the Lamb* is Van Scoyen, who gently asks Louie on his death bed, at age twenty, if he has any doubts. Ironically, Louie says he has none. He repeats this with a smile to Don, who worships him. Later in the night, with Don and his mother watching, Moeke's first-born dies of pneumonia. Although the pious would say He, too, lost a son, the younger brother's reaction is to ask why God didn't pick on someone His own size. That of the mother was different. "She rose and, taking something from the dresser, began to brush his golden hair" (30). (When De Vries's own mother lost her first-born, a daughter, she sang no more in church; but then she was the skeptic half of the pair to begin with.)

Louie lives on as Don's model, and he too courts in the bushes of Hamilton Park, quoting Joyce and others to willing girls, but always having trouble pronouncing his *th*'s. He would escape a life where his father cleans his teeth with a washcloth, but not to a life with Maria Italia; the daughter of a widowered organ grinder, she's not good enough for him: "Girls like Maria did not measure up to my standards. Neither did I, but I would" (36). Although they have been careless, nothing comes of it; and when Officer Murphy catches them *en déshabille* and casts them from the park, they drift apart: "a wedge of shame—like that of Adam and Eve—had been permanently driven between us" (40).

He enrolls at the university, paying part of his way himself, his father paying part. Even as De Vries's father moved up from ice and coal hauling to furniture storage and moving, Wanderhope's father moves up to garbage—a line of work in Chicago that is disproportionately Dutch. Since he works with his father on the truck he fears he'll be recognized on the campus—it's part of the area they service—but no one notices a garbage man, and he's safe. They do notice, but don't know him when he goes into bars in the chic area (Hyde Park was chic then) for a snort. That is, his father goes in, as was his custom as an iceman, and the amused patrons "could slum for a moment on their own home ground, how amusing! Hateful people, of whom I would soon be one" (46). He likes his father, despite his "being the reverse of all I planned to cultivate in myself..." (47).

Proceeding to the dump, they inadvertently dump themselves in a pit where it "took no more than a touch of the poet to see in the palls of smoke and sluggish fires a dismally burning hell" (48). Gehenna is scriptural enough, although Samuel Beckett's *Endgame,* when it appeared, held no charm for De Vries. Don does react rationalily as one in such a situation could be expected to; but his father, no foxhole atheist, begins quoting and misquoting the Bible, in particular the opening verse of Psalm 121. He sinks from sight and reappears haloed by a cantaloupe rind, eventually to be rescued with his son by other dumpers who happen to have a rope. Don's reading of the topography is that this is what hell is like for those who are bad stewards of their talents.

Making the best of his, he cultivates people who are socially ele-vated and even gets into the home of one whose mother thinks he's old New York Dutch. The family is ersatz, though, and a disappoint-ment, their veneer of culture no more than that. So he returns to the Dutch community of his own and dates the niece of the man who was late his father's partner; Greta Wigbaldy's own father now was doing well building homes, one of which—the Model—she suggests they use for trysting instead of the lakefront beach or her parlor or her father's car. Don is nervous, but not Greta: "This was only one glimpse she gave me of the throughly practical morality of women in matters 'of the heart,' once they are committed" (68). Of course they're caught, only shortly after having their way with each other.

There's time only for them to scramble into each other's under-wear and get back beneath the sheets before both Greta's parents come in showing the house to prospective buyers. Mrs. Wigbaldy's English is not yet perfected, and she denounces Don by calling him "Prude!" and any number of more or less appropriately rude titles (rat, slut); then she informs him he'll be her son-in-law very shortly. When Don discovers that actually he and Greta share certain illusions —learning, that is, that they love each other—he decides it wouldn't be so bad. She, however, dreads marriage, at which confession he embraces her: "Darling, Greta. I never dreamed we had so much in common" (75). They'd fumbled so much at each other's body that they'd not got acquainted before. Had Doc Berkenbosch not discov-ered a slight case of TB they would have married then and there.

In order to go to a church-run sanatorium at a ridiculously reduced rate one—or, in this case, one's father—had to be in good standing with the local congregation. But Don's father has backslidden after his garbage-dump experience, and the threat of triply increased fees looms—until his reconversion. As for Don, the thought of putting a thousand miles between Greta and him bolsters him somewhat.

Dr. Simpson, of Scots Presbyterian background, is a wry sort who "prefers to make the jokes himself," whose sensitive eyes mock all but himself. Listening to Don's lungs, he says, "Well, I can hear a little music in there, but I don't think it's playing 'Nearer, My God to Thee'" (87). This line De Vries says was said to him in a like situation. Simpson suspects that TB is 90 percent mental, up from the 50 he used to think; in the ambulatory section the typewriters never cease. Simpson dislikes these people, and has a Thursday-night collection over to his house—"Young Men Who Don't Write" (88).

Some of those there are most seriously ill; among them is a Rena Baker, a slender blonde girl only recently promoted to ambulo. When Don sees her, something shoots "along the surface of [his] heart like ice cracking on a pond" (94). Thus he is well set; he has the urbanity of salt-and-pepper-tweeded Dr. Simpson and the pulchritude of Rena. Others incarcerated there include a professor of economics who has "conspicuous consumption."

While Rena is pious, her roommate, Cora Nyhoff, is bigoted and, besides, has an interest in protecting Rena that has an unhealthy side to it. Unlike in his affair with Greta, Don gets to know Rena before beginning to fumble; she wants him to pray for her, but he declines on the grounds that he'd be asking Him "who arbitrarily does us dirt" (104) to relent. "We're supposed to deserve it," says Rena; but although he denies this is true of her, she claims to be a sinner. He says she's giving herself airs. The week following offers a day of mystic beauty as the snow obliterates all temporality outside her room; and, she cooperating, he explores her body till she arches in delight. Only the arrival of the supper cart ends their love for the day.

Two days later her room is stripped, and he learns she's in surgery. When she's still not back after dinnertime he goes for a walk outside— "the snow hard as iron underfoot. The stars throbbed in the clear air" (107). He knows she is as dead as the moon, she "who had warmed me" (108). Then "There was a cry from an animal down in the brush beside the icy brook, where nature was also keeping itself in balance. 'Thou shalt not kill.' This was advertised as the law of someone who had also created a universe in which one thing ate another" (109).

Thus he reverts to a favorite trope, one that tantalizes because it doesn't carry the question—except by implication—to its conclusion. For if lesser beings eat one another and we eat them, the question becomes why should they and we be here? As Heidegger puts it, "Why is there something rather then nothing?" This is a most excellent question that all people should ask once, and not again: one should be well aware of the fundamental absurdity—it would be unhealthy to be otherwise—but one should not dwell on the absurdity since that would be even more unhealthy. In no way from this fundamental absurdity does it follow or not follow that there is or is not a God, although it does question His sense of humor.

Dr. Simpson brings him in from the cold, tells him that Rena has indeed slipped away quietly—a mercy, because she stood no chance. When Don, admiring the objectivity of science, asks whether Simpson believes still in a managed universe, he's told of the doctor's own loss: "I had a son once, whom I had to watch die of leukemia. He was seven. Stevie. He was such a boy as you see riding dolphins in the fountains in the parks. A dolphin boy. A faun. I watched him bleed to death" (109). He doesn't care for the melodramatic Chopin and Wagner sorts they sometimes get there: "Death is the commonest thing in the universe" (110).

There follows a brilliant summation of the attitude of the serious man who-has-thought-much-on-a-subject to the shallow questioning of a novice: Don asks Simpson whether he believes in God. Simpson looks as if he wishes heaven had spared him that.

It took me some years to attain his mood and understand my blunder. He resented such questions as people do who have thought a great deal about them. The superficial and the slipshod have ready answers, but those looking this complex life straight in the eye acquire a wealth of perception so composed of delicately balanced contradictions that they dread, or resent, the call to couch any part of it in a bland generalization. The vanity (if not outrage) of trying to cage this dance of atoms in a single definition may give the weariness of age with the cry of youth for answers the appearance of boredom. (111)

Simpson declines to specify beyond saying that "You believe what you must in order to stave off the conviction that it's all a tale told by an idiot" (111).

Letters from home meanwhile tell him that his father is grotesquely losing his mind, grotesque being, he says, the "intellectuals' definition of . . . a blend of the tragic and the comic" (115). His madness is the sort that allows such acute observations as "Ninety per cent of the universe is missing." Since, as De Vries notes, the gravitational force existent ought to have nine or ten times more matter to go with it, this could be said to be so. Also, as nothing in art is wasted, this tells us again that the sea of our ignorance is immense; it follows therefrom that one who is honest can be neither certain nor faithless.

Perhaps for those reasons he has little time for the "Marxist-oriented" intellectuals of the Great Depression. His immigrant parents and his job as a garbage man gave him instant heroic status among such a group he associated with briefly back at the university, and "well it might, for I was the only one in the bunch who had ever done an honest day's work in his life" (122). That dismissed, he encounters Greta Wigbaldy on the same grounds as his father is on; she has broken down because of an affair with a married man, an affair that led to a child she left at the "home" where she gave birth to it. Wanderhope, of course, asks her to marry him.

Things go well enough until Greta converts to another denomination—a "no Creed but Christ" group—which at least didn't endorse infant damnation. It emphasizes guilt, however, and Greta is disturbed that Don analyzes things differently. Eventually she undertakes acts that will justify her feelings of guilt; she drinks and she fools around. Don meanwhile has finished a college degree, gotten on with the local branch of an eastern ad agency, and their daughter, Carol, has been born. Then they move to the main office in New York. Greta's behavior is largely the same; and, after one failed attempt, she achieves a suicide. Don and Carol and Mrs. Brodhag, Carol's nurse, move to another suburb.

Then, at a stag party at the agency, tales are told of peaks of experience. Wanderhope hears a colleague define being saved as being "restored to the human race" (163). For himself he decides that the "greatest experience open to man is the recovery of the commonplace" (166), this after he is told that an illness of Carol's is nothing serious, and his beautiful fairy child will not turn into a gnome.

Polished bar glasses, not noticed till then, take on a glory, as do dogwood blossoms, and the smell of smoke in cheddar. It is at this time that he tidies up some correspondence waiting his attention, among it a request from his college paper for representative alumni to offer synopses of their philosophies of life. Complying, he says religion is of the childhood of the race, and that philosophy isn't much better: "Human life 'means' nothing." Up to that point Auguste Comte would heartily agree, but Wanderhope does not go on to place his faith in Science. Instead he says "Man has only his own two feet to stand on, his own human trinity to see him through: Reason, Courage, and Grace. And the first plus the second equals the third" (167). His, then, is not the biblical grace, which means Gift-from-God, but is of purely human derivation. That creed is soon tested when he learns that Carol's disease is serious indeed: leukemia.

Leukemia was and is an idiopathic disease, of unknown origin. Yet it seems most prevalent on the North American continent in areas just Northeast of concentrations of urban-industrial pollution; winds in this zone blow mainly from the Southwest. This suggests that the incidence is at least in part man-made. That being so, why is not some of the resentment deflected from the deity to man? Maybe because if there is a God, He is responsible for creating man. Don's complaints are therefore against the One he holds basically responsible.

Dr. Scoville is a good man, obviously admired by Wanderhope. As for questions of God, he doesn't ask them—no time for it. Mrs. Brodhag, an old-fashioned sort of Congregationalist, does have time, and on occasion stops at the nearest church to pray. One of those occasions takes her to St. Catherine of Siena, where Wanderhope finds a shrine to St. Jude; there he prays, or curses. Thus Catholic churches enter the picture, they offering a Gestalt with more artistic possibilities than do the Protestant ones: there is the art, for one thing, and the comparatively precise theology for another.

To balance his thrust there also is introduced Stein, a secular Jew whose daughter Rachel is a friend and fellow sufferer of Carol's—lifelong friends, Stein sardonically terms them. He believes in nothing—not church, not science; cancer he says is itself a "souvenir from the primordial ooze. The original Chaos, without form and void. In de beginning was de void, and de void was vit God. Mustn't say de naughty void" (181). These two racquets are the ones between which Wanderhope's shuttlecock mind bounces until the end. (Another

doctor, one he meets when taking Carol to see her confined grandfather Wanderhope, believes not only in God but in man, a belief
that he finds a lot harder. Thus there is balance on that count.)

But mainly the world is Carol's, and he works at making her days
normal. From a movie she's gone to with Omar, a local resident, she
discerns the metaphysics of comic pie-throwing—that after the first
is thrown, the thrower waits for one to be thrown at him, indeed, he
expects it. Then he ritualistically wipes it from his eyes; it's a *ceremony*.
It is a ceremony that Wanderhope also will go through.

Mrs. Brodhag warns him that he's buying Carol too much, that
she'll get suspicious; he even buys a two-hundred-dollar tape recorder
so he can get her piano pieces on it. Although she complains occasionally of pain, Carol otherwise gives no hint that she suspects the
gravity of her situation. Wanderhope, shaking his fist at the stars,
asks only that "if you won't save her from pain, at least let me keep
her from fear!" (204). He debates the while with Stein, forced by
the situation to be the Defender of the Faith against the other fellow's
bitter probes. The arguments are quips, mainly, but are well crafted,
succinct, balanced, and justified; after all, "Airing the absolutes is no
longer permitted in polite society, save where a Stein and a Wanderhope meet..." (215). These two obviously symbolically named men
are allowed to discuss what the rest of us stay away from, because we
"live this life by a kind of conspiracy of grace" (215), pretending
life is worthwhile—a thin-ice pretense that we break through in time
of crisis.

The crisis hurries on: Carol is stigmatized on hands and breast
by needles and probes, her hair falls out; she has gone from fairy
to troll. It is the "Slaughter of the Innocents. Who creates a perfect blossom to crush it? Children dying in this building, mice in
the next" (225). Then comes remission, then an infection that hits
hardest those whose blood can't handle it. Wanderhope has come
to bring a cake to Carol because it's her birthday, but left it in
St. Catherine's, where he'd gone to pray. Seeing Carol, he "knew
it was time to say good-by" (234). When the nurse steps outside
he prays: "The Lord bless thee, and keep thee: The Lord make his
face shine upon thee, and be gracious unto thee: The Lord lift up
his countenance upon thee, and give thee peace" (236). At three
in the afternoon—at the same time as did Jesus—she dies.

Wanderhope wishes taking leave of her were like Hemingway's "saying good-by to a statue," but she looks instead "like some mangled flower, or like a bird that had been pelted to death in a storm" (236). He gets drunk at a nearby bar, then remembers the cake. In the by now carefully set up scene he balances it for a moment, then hurls the cake onto the face of the corpus: Christ has pied him, now he Christ. "Then through scalded eyes I seemed to see the hands free themselves of the nails and move slowly toward the soiled face. Very slowly, very deliberately, with infinite patience, the icing was wiped from the eyes and flung away." And he hears a voice saying, "Suffer the little children to come unto me . . . for of such is the kingdom of heaven" (237).

His attempt to recover at his daughter's grave the piety lost at his brother's is not successful; when he plays the tape to hear her recorded pieces he gets as well a message from Carol in which she quotes with approbation his credo sent to his college magazine: Reason, Courage, and Grace have sustained her, she says, and she knows about her disease. Although a bit precocious, it's convincing; and Wanderhope flings away his crucifix, flings it into the trees of the woods where they had walked. The world is hateful, and progress only enlarges our stay in it. Grace is ours, but to give rather than receive; and compassion is gained as one realizes "how long is the mourners' bench upon which we sit, arms linked in undeluded friendship, all of us, brief links, ourselves, in the eternal pity."

There is no cosmos, only chaos; but we're all in it together.

Reprise

Seven years and three novels intervene between *The Blood of the Lamb* and *The Cat's Pajamas & Witch's Milk*, but it would appear that the set of paired novellas was required to get rid of the as yet unexorcised demons. In one of them there is the death of a child: *that* is the demon. A couple of the same characters figure in both works, a technique that allows us to see the characters more acutely for being able to see major character A intimate with major character B, and B with C; this is particularly effective with an author who writes in the "third-person limited," as does De Vries. In that point-of-view technique the reader sees only what the Central Intelligence

sees—the A or the B, but not both—but since it's in the third person we
assume it's objective rather than subjective. By multiplying the points
of view we can see just how subjective "objective" can be.

De Vries has said that the books are paired in part to show how
different people react to adversity, whether they sink under it or
manage somehow to sail on. Hank Tattersall is one who sinks. As a
member of the English department at Chichester he has occasion to
speak on the state of contemporary writing, and to quote literary
figures (Eliot in particular). He was an undergraduate at the same
school; and at a twelfth or so reunion he runs into Lucy Stokes, a
fellow undergraduate and an old flame. Indeed, her husband is the first
half of the Wurlitzer and Wise advertising agency and is scheduled
to speak at a banquet on campus. Lucy's niece, Mayo, one of the
buzzard's-guts school of writers, has had a course or two with Hank,
so Lucy knows some of his recent history. Hank has been unaware of
the relationship of the two women.

Wurlitzer has the brio usually associated with the best of ad
men—bright but shallow—and this suits well his dropping of a
series of bons mots that De Vries must have been cataloging while on
the Westport commuter: "The discoveries of psychology, augmented
by the illuminations of literature, have left us little to admire in
ourselves. . . . It's now reached a point where no self-respecting man
has any use for himself" (16–17).[3] Wurlitzer laments that the front
porch is gone, everyone having retreated inside to study his personal
interior. Nothing there for Tattersall to disagree with.

Trying to make more of an impression on Mayo now that he knows
her connection to Lucy, Hank takes her to a concert of "plaid" music.
Although De Vries often enough deprecates the cerebral classicists
(three or four times he uses Colette's jibe at Mozart's "golden sewing
machine"), favoring instead the visceral romantics, he has no use for
the alimentary moderns. A violin is used to beat a rug, a flute is
blown underwater. Nothing happens, really, with the ethereal Mayo,
she whose typewriter needed washing out with soap, then or later.
He does have such revenge on her as anyone who has taught a Creative
Writing course would love to take in similar cases; and with a colleague's novel he reverses the pages to achieve the complete dissimila-
tion of time the would-be author only partly achieves otherwise.
Mayo, thin-skinned as any, does not take it well.

Thus through the honesty urged by Wurlitzer and by Mayo's take-over generation, Tattersall embarks on his self-destruction. With his wife, Sherry, who adores him, Hank goes to a party at Wurlitzer's and is persuaded that there is more room for the absurd in advertising than in academe. Asks Hank, "Are you tired of detergents that never get your wash really white? Light up a Salem" (58). After a series of such non sequiturs, Wurlitzer wants to hire him. The world itself is ridiculous, Tattersall explains, expanding and contracting at intervals of 82 billion years. Why bother? Why should there be something rather than nothing? Thus he endorses nihilistic existentialism for advertising, too, to get it in step with the rest of modern thinking.

Then Mayo, over whose case he bleats (Maaw! Maaw!), gets an acceptance from a publisher for the wretched novel Hank has damned. All the while, Tattersall lectures his classes on comedy; his definitions help explain De Vries's work. In *The Blood of the Lamb*, Wander-hope's choked laughter was once mistaken for its near cousin, sobs; in this one Tattersall says that the "relativity scientists of the day tell us that the quality that most nearly resembles Everything is—Nothing" (62). He agrees with the Aristotelian view of "laughter as being provoked in man by something that falls just short of that which would have excited pain. . . ." Humor he says deals with what isn't funny, or wasn't at the time—bad food, hangovers, and so on. He approves also of Socrates having said "that the talent for tragedy was the same as the talent for comedy. Tragedy and comedy have a common root, whose name at last I think I know. Desperation" (62).

Mayo's success makes him desperate indeed. He begins with more frequency to play the role of American mug, as earlier he had been Russian peasant, English toff, even college teacher in salt-and-pepper coat and falsely maloccluded teeth. Adoring Sherry, who from time to time has remarried him for the sake of second (third, fourth) honeymoons, goes along with it. Underneath it, though, he's honest; he points out, in Negro dialect, that the Dean is a fraud for claiming his neighborhood is color-blind since it costs so much to live there that only a very few affluent blacks can move in. And if he fails at accurate self-assessment, there is his Doppelgänger who writes to him and tells him what's what: for one thing, men want to be thought of by women as the cat's pajamas, and for another he doesn't really want Lucy, but just wants Lucy to want him. And when the students demonstrate against parietals, he will have to take a stand. When the Dean asks advice, he suggests relaxation of the rules. Then he and Sherry share a joint—a new experience for both of them—and they go on a laughing jag that leads, after an exchange of sexual favors, to his analyzing laughter; Schopenhauer laughed at tangents because he thought laughter "our sudden perception of the incongruity between an abstract concept and the actual reality" (76). He imagines her nude body triangulated in all sorts of lovely ways and planed with many tangents. They marry again, and a party at a nearby table sends them a bottle of wine. But she knows he's going to try to lose his job by siding too strongly with the students when the occasion arises.

He doesn't, though. After joining them in a protest march and after defending a student whose sexual liaison was of such long duration and of such faithfulness that it outdid most modern marriages, to the delight of the Dean he resigns. Then he goes to work for Wurlitzer. Academe and humor are hardly compatible for an entire novel.

As an ad man at the Double W agency he is, for a time, the cat's pj's indeed; he's not successful at selling the idea of absurd and totally pointless commercials for a street-singer show a company wants to sponsor but he is asked to sing on it. Mayo, now employed at her uncle's agency, is writing also absurd but acceptable copy, but not Hank: "...he sensed that the trend of his life was irreversibly downward.... The story of his life was like a book with ever shorter chapters..." (119). Before he can be fired, he quits Wurlitzer and Wise. But he has a thirteen-week contract as an Italian street singer. He is renewed twice, then canceled. His Doppelgänger by now is calling him "the greatest single pseudo-sado-masochistic self-castigator around..." (129). He agrees.

Given the pushcart as a souvenir, he uses it to peddle fruits and vegetables. Sherry meets with Wurlitzer and Mayo, and they decide he's calling them all hucksters. He obviously is, but some people make the most of it. When he turns to freelancing mottoes for varying commercial uses, the blackness of his humor deepens. Soon he's hiring out as a day laborer, but "To be a misfit in a tale told by an idiot is after all hardly the worst of fates" (136). What does seem a little curious is his lack of an obvious motive for failure; his renouncing of the vain pomps and glories of this world seems to come entirely from his intellectual conviction that there are lots of frauds around.

Thus he plays roles consciously, effortlessly but mockingly doing what others take most seriously. Few "normal" people can take much of that; it makes them aware of the tenuousness of their own hold on sanity. When he becomes Handyman Hank, Sherry leaves him. Now he's honestly blue collar, living in a boarding house. Thus whatever madness the world embarks on is no fault of his, unless he be held accountable for mental suicide. Mrs. Yutch, his vulgar landlady, makes her bed available to him, but he refuses her: "He was out to prove the purposeless squalor of human existence, but he could not both deplore it and be guilty of it" (156). So he's clean: "He was now off everyone's back but his own" (156).

Mrs. Yutch chokes on a piece of meat and dies laughing at some ribaldry of Hank's and leaves him with her mongrel dog, Lazarus, and her mongoloid son, Raymond. This fate is an excellent justification for Tattersall's view of the world; to Raymond he speaks on several of the more erudite clichés of literary, musical, and theological criticism, and he accepts the gurgling replies as equally cogent commentary. He bakes their chicken *Haute Loire* in a bedpan and turns Lazarus into an alcoholic.

Into this squalor eventually enters the inevitable social worker, Mrs. Seltzer. She realizes he's biting down on an aching tooth, but tells him that "Whatever happened, you brought it on yourself" (172). Anyway, someone has always done something even more surrealistic. It's tough on romantics, she says. Then *she* lectures the boy, although only after her third glass of wine: "...the truer it is that Everything Stinks the less one should call it to others' attention...." Referring obviously to Hank, she damns those who "gorge themselves on Nothing.... They can't suck enough out of that Existentialist tit" (178). Such a person "will commit as much suicide as possible without killing himself" (179). She weeps as she eats the chocolate mousse Hank gives her.

Then comes winter and a snow that reminds a tired Tattersall of purity; returning home one day keyless but with the alky dog, he puts the mutt through a dog door to fetch Raymond to let him in. Instead the dog toddles to his own bed to sleep off a drunk, even as Raymond must be soberly sleeping. Raymond is unwakable. Tattersall realizes how serious is his situation once his own head is in the dog door,

where he stuck it to call the idiot. And he can't get it out. The
Doppelgänger takes a Parthian shot and, in a back-to-the-womb position that even Nicodemus knew was hopeless, Hank Tattersall dies.

Tillie Seltzer (née Shilepsky) is the central intelligence in *Witch's
Milk*, a role played by Carol Burnett in the film version, *Pete and Tillie*
(to Walter Mathau's Pete). The title for the book De Vries says
he got from some physiological information he had about the mam-
maries of infants; those of each sex have some small amount of fluid
in them, and this is called Witch's Milk. To De Vries this means
that we are each of us born with some innate goodness. Why this
should mean that to De Vries or anyone else isn't clear, but it is a
different reading from what Calvinist orthodoxy would suggest. Maybe
that's why.

Pete and Tillie are blind-dated at a party where he's expertly double
talking; Tillie is less than thrilled but does appreciate the difficult
art of nonsense. Actually his telling jokes is an adroit way of keeping
from getting involved in the silliness around him, a good ploy for
avoiding having to give cocktail-party answers to cocktail-party questions; he would prefer to be honestly glib. Intelligent, he's not Intellectual; he will not belabor questions that lack answers. Physically
lame, he is mentally healthy—but likable anyway. They leave together,
in her car (he having none); and it occurs to Tillie that Gertrude
Wilson, whose party it was, is probably talking about them to Jimmy
Twitchwell, her interior designer, also in attendance. Seltzer doesn't
like them either, and as they continue to date she realizes he has a
great many redeeming features; then she realizes one oughtn't need
so many.

He *is* a trifle unaware of some commonplace matters: megalopolis
he thinks a prehistoric animal; Havana cigars he knows he can't get,
but not why; and he asks her her age. But they get along, accept
each other's Courtship Corrections (he tells her not to wear a girdle,
she tells him to cut his hair), and so to bed. Tillie was virginal, Pete
skillful; for further relaxation he plays piano, in particular a frenetic
"Twelfth Street Rag." Then, after continuing "to sleep with him to
prove that she wasn't promiscuous, as a single fling would have done"
(213), she tells him the honeymoon's over and it's time to get married.

This goes well enough, the nonsense talk continuing. She "scrokes
his quonkles," he sinks into her "thrombush." Pete defends his be-

havior by arguing that all language is jabberwocky that has become familiar, says that if one picks any familiar word and isolates it and stares at it long enough then "you will find meaning running like sawdust out of yourself" (224). Tillie perceives that he's an Existentialist and calls him such, although Pete is ignorant of the term: "They just believe man makes out as best he can in a meaningless universe" (225). He can't be bothered with theory, saying he has more to worry about than the universe. Tillie by then is pregnant.

Gertrude Wilson and Jimmy Twitchwell thread back into her life again, mainly for counterpoint; Jimmy is waspishly witty, and Gertrude is a bitch whose husband isn't faithful. Pete apparently is steady—a son-of-a-bitch manqué, he calls himself—although during the courtship Tillie had found what she thought were cleaning woman's hairpins in his bedroom. Pete is the salt of the earth, Tillie decides after Charles is born and they move to a chic suburb that's a little over their heads. "Let the Jimmy Twitchwells be its pepper, mustard and vinegar," (238) she braves it out. Her only fears are occasional *déjà-vu* experiences that nag her and a sense of dread; she too apparently is Existential.

For frequent readers of De Vries, a line or two exchanged between Pete and Tillie, and between Tillie and Miss Lund, an employee of Pete's, also have a ring of *déjà-vu* about them. Lund says "marfact" for "matter of fact," and, asked, Pete denies that she's dumb, "Not from the neck down" (245, 244). This sort of thing one gets used to, even likes: it's similar to seeing cartoons by the same favorite artist in successive editions of a magazine; the *déjà-vu* pattern is as welcome in the one case as it is disturbing in the other. Pete is a good husband, though, and—ultimately a child himself—a good father to Charlie. Then Charlie's blood goes bad: what Tillie saw in *déjà-vu* had happened.

She curses the Trinity, addressing each Person individually, and spares not the mother of Christ (who also lost a son, but presumably got him back). They grieve singly—grief cannot be shared, De Vries reminds us—and give the child all the comfort they can, but in the dead of winter Charlie leaves them. A Congregational minister is not offended at being asked to officiate, even though their claim on him is slight. He even reads poetry they give him to incorporate as part of the service, including a Robert Louis Stevenson poem Tillie liked because it seemed an example "of the petitions that might validly be

uttered by people who didn't really think anyone was listening" (264).
Listed under Prayer in *Letters and Miscellanies of Robert Louis
Stevenson: Sketches, Criticisms, Etc.* (1903), the poem is called "For
Success" and does make references to the Lord, and to Christ; these are
excised by De Vries.

The result is a request that hearts be purged of lurking grudges
and that we be given courage, gaiety, and quiet minds. Pete gradually
begins to regain these, but Tillie does not and she resents the fact
that he does. When asked, he says he sees patterns all around him
that life does make sense: "It's the words we try to do the thinking
with that gum the thinking up. Would you think whether life had
any meaning if it wasn't for the word meaning?" (266). Again she
calls him an Existentialist. Just like Tattersall, he knows the world
to be expanding and contracting at intervals of 82 billion years;
anything is possible.

"Cosmic hypochondria" is the clever summation given by Sidney
Hook to that form of intellectual malaise that Tillie accuses Pete of;
actually it's she who has it, she who believes in a sort of cosmic
pathetic fallacy. Pete is not in the least a systematic thinker; he's
more of a shrugger than anything. Existentialism, according to Hans
Jonas in *Gnostic Religion*, is a modern form of gnosticism, a system
which is fundamentally dualistic, separating spirit from matter and
love from law; thus the individual finds himself lost in an indifferent
and patternless chaos. (Really, Tillie with her frequently recurring
déjà-vu experiences ought to deny this; if there is anything that an
"already seen" experience does not allow, it is a random and unpre-
dictable world. It says instead that this is some sort of cosmos, not
chaos.)

Making love with Pete—letting the dead bury the dead—seems
to her a betrayal of Charlie, with whom she imagines conversations.
She allows her husband evenings in town as compensation; and although he tries to draw her along, she won't have it. When Gertrude
suggests that Tillie could divorce Pete on grounds of adultery, Tillie
defends him: "There are adulterers who are often good husbands
and fathers, and mates loyal unto death who kill each other daily"
(275). The line, one that has appeared in De Vries interviews, is a
good enough example of contemporary gnosticism: law and love are
separable as flesh and spirit and meet, if at all, only coincidentally;

thus one can love well while breaking natural or any other law. To Tillie's credit, she can't quite face Gertrude when she says it.

Gertrude stays active, however, running the Mental Health Ball for charity. Jimmy is mad at her and gets Tillie to go along with her to register the event with the police since one requirement of that act is that the registrants have to give their ages. Gertrude breaks down at the sergeant's desk, a fight with Tillie ensues outside, and both women are put away to rest—Gertrude at a place in the Bahamas and Tillie at a local establishment.

While there she tries to rewrite the Stevenson poem more to her taste: "Give us courage for our fears, the wisdom to survive our follies, and charity to bind up the wounds we inflict on one another" (291). She's not badly off, really, and when Jimmy Twitchwell comes to visit with bonbons and flowers she's glad to see him. He's a witty and erudite sort who speaks in bitchy fragments; he charms Tillie, and he knows it. Following his disclosure of Gertrude's age—fifty-three—he proposes marriage to Tillie. He'll dress her nicely; they'll vacation properly, feed well, return to their house on a hill (he'll build one there shortly on property he already owns), and he'll protect her from women. But when Pete calls and asks her back, she agrees. He has been informed that he can keep his market-research job, but will go no higher; they could use a second income. She'll return to case work.

She recalls a Redemption Center for Green Stamps, a place they ironically assume trades in old souls for new. It's her second chance, too. Not that she will give up her Charlie: "I'll walk the streets of the city with my raving heart, dreaming of my demolished faun. But I'll be on my way to work, the day dedicated to you" (303). At least she had Pete to see her "through the disillusionment of marriage" (303). What she has rejected (with her rejection of Twitchwell) is the aesthete's attempt to impose order through tasteful selection of the bric-a-brac of life; of course everyone of sense wants the best possible surroundings, but much of life is muddy. She will wade in.

Chapter Six

Black Humor

Reuben, Reuben is somewhat similar to *The Cat's Pajamas & Witch's Milk* in that it is tripartite, with many of the characters wandering through all three of the segments. De Vries has said that he thinks it his best effort, although authors' judgments of their own works are seldom accurate; however, there *is* an increase in depth that is gained by the use of three different points of view, and, at 435 pages, there is an increase in breadth. He said he tried to be funny for 180,000 words instead of his usual 75–80,000.[1]

Spofford, who tells the first segment, is a man who has become a stranger in his own land, because the exurbs have spread out to displace him. McGland, a Scottish poet obviously modeled on Dylan Thomas, a man much troubled with terminal satyriasis, tells the second part. Mopworth, a likable English light actor, finishes the tome. Since Mopworth has unwisely wed the granddaughter of Spofford and since she was once intimate with McGland, the book makes a sort of circle. Since the granddaughter, Geneva, is a first-generation collegian (and a pill), it also says what has become of the world of the Spoffords. A play based on the first segment of the novel, and so named, was adapted for the stage by Herman Shumlin and had a decent turn on Broadway, although it was not so successful as *The Tunnel of Love.*

Several of De Vries's critics have noted that with *The Blood of the Lamb* and after—and no wonder!—the hue of his humor has darkened. The same types are there, but their suffering is greater. In an interview with De Vries, Richard B. Sale said, "There are not outright villains in your novels, only bumblers, moderately bastardly folk, or just poor bastards" and, asked if he didn't see any villains in comedy, De Vries replied that man was his own worst enemy, and such was true for his characters: "More and more it's beginning to appear that contemporary literature doesn't need any villains. The heroes are bad enough."[2]

That's not really the issue, though. What De Vries does that few

94

other comic writers do is create what E. M. Forster calls *round* characters and then put them into real situations. The usual method of keeping the humor light-hued is to create—the way, say, that S. J. Perelman does—two-dimensional or *flat* characters. When this happens we have garden-variety comedy. This is what Richard Boston must have had in mind when, applying Bergson's thought, he said "that laughter implies a momentary anaesthesia of the heart. In the world of slapstick comedy our normal waking feelings are suspended. We laugh at Keaton's falls because we know we needn't worry about his getting hurt, that with a clear conscience we can withhold sympathy from him. . . ."[3] In black humor it is different: the people are round and the falls are real and thus when they crash-land it hurts. In *Reuben, Reuben* a child is run over by a bloodmobile, but survives it; an agency of help becomes an instrument of terror. Similarly, most people laugh— even if they like his poetry—when they hear of the manner of Frank O'Hara's departure (run over by a dune buggy on Fire Island).

Why is it funny?

Basically it has to do with what has been called "the death of God," a demise Nietzsche proclaimed some time ago (although sons of ministers are suspect in proclamations of that sort). The first requirement of tragedy is a hostile deity. Comedy requires a deity or set of deities who are friendly, at least ultimately friendly; for this reason the story of Jesus cannot be seen as tragic since the Book has it that He was triumphantly resurrected. God was on His side. And if there is no deity, is Jesus tragic then? No, at least not in Aristotelian terms, since Jesus then would not be a great man but rather some variety of madman, one who claimed to be able to call on legions of angels, to raise the dead, even to rebuild Himself in three days: in short, black comedy. Tragedy requires a great man, slightly flawed, who falls disproportionately to his deserts; comedy requires any sort of man with any sort of flaws—so long as his sensitivity is sufficiently developed that he can feel pain; he falls about as far as everyone does. (High Comedy, that is; it apparently was Low Comedy that Bergson had in mind.) But God is ultimtaely on his side.

Black humor, a sort of amalgam of tragedy and comedy, is the humor peculiar to a season that believes in the death or absence of God or gods. It is the Gospel told from Judas's point of view. (It happens that this is what *Jesus Christ Superstar* is: the authors said they had no particular theology, they just told it as Judas would see it. They didn't realize that such is the prevailing attitude of modern man, thus they had a big box-office success.) This, largely, is what De Vries does; there is no friendly *or* hostile deity—man is his own worst enemy—and thus his buffoonery, earnest though it is, is hideously silly. Like Adolf Hitler doing a jig.

Whoever caught the dictator hopping down from the railroad car at Compeigne just after the French surrender struck gold; he or someone else who came into control of the frames found that by running it backwards a bit and then quickly forward Hitler could be made to appear to jig. The Allies were very careful not to let anyone find out it was a trick—a jigging Hitler looked like a clown, especially since he was in uniform. This lends credence to the claim of Desmond Morris, author of *The Naked Ape*, that man laughs when he realizes "the danger is not real."[4] Or when he wants to think it isn't? Certainly laughter is not the normal expression of pleasure; ordinarily it expresses relief from pain, or it is aggressive.

Even so in Spofford's section, although the threat is not great. The silly people are merely the newly arrived exurbanites in Avalon, people who think themselves to be the salt of the earth. Spofford is amused as well as chagrined: "I got displaced by staying put," he says, telling the story himself. This is a little tricky since he speaks with the usual De Vriesian wit and insight but without the education. He says they have a church so modern they're thinking of making divorce a sacrament and that a Lesbian psychiatrist who wears her hair "skun back in a bun" orders from his place the same thing each week—one capon—and so on. This is clever (if repeated) stuff that needs justification; De Vries justifies it by lampooning the Successful Writers School that has located in Woodsmoke. Spofford has enrolled, but they've turned him down, thrown him out, because his stuff is too good. They've had plenty of "polished but dead" writers; his work is the opposite. That much accepted, he's a plausible narrator.

Now, says Spofford, dungarees are "shiek" in Woodsmoke, because of all the New Yorkers, and he's writing to study how he got made into a D.P. The Springers are excellent cases in point of those that have displaced the natives; indeed, Mare, his daughter-in-law, is grooming Geneva to be ashamed of her family. When the Springers' son's liaison with Geneva is broken off by his family Mare refuses to sell to commuters. (Geneva is in Brazil for a while, a cultural exchange student; with her is a chum, Nectar Schmidt, a girl who "had defined a mother as a wad of contributing factors" [74]).[5] Flahive, a teacher at the Writers School and would-be writer himself, suggests that Spofford learn about these people instead of just hating them. *Then* he could write: "There are primitives in art, why not in literature? You could be above sentence structure like Joyce, you have Lardner's anti-sophistication, and you're mean as O'Hara. Greater praise in my book there isn't" (21).

Mrs. Punck, the plump and attractive mother of Mare, meanwhile moves into the roomy farmhouse. Spofford fears this; he's ignorant, but Mrs. Punck is stupid, although pleasantly so. She isn't the only one Frank Spofford notices, though; Mrs. Beauseigneur, who drives a blue Jaguar, is so attractive in arguing with him that he looks at her more than he listens to her. She pleads that her husband gets off at Stamford and, therefore, they ought to sell to her, as eventually they do—eggs, but no chickens. She reads a "pocket-size semantic quarterly of Non-Aristotelian thought called *But*. On its maroon cover were featured articles with titles like 'The Linguistic Constants in Prejudice'; 'Word Hashes in the Congressional Record'; 'The Ceremonial Hour: the Wittgenstein-Fabrizio-Shuv Hypothesis of the Coffee Break as Neo-Ritual' . . ." (36). He must purge himself of Aristotelian absolutes, she says, and think relatively, of glaciers in the Arctic, of stars boiling at thousands of degrees; in short, there are commuters and commuters. Desperate, she calls Mare *sick* but escapes with the eggs. Spofford doesn't agree, quite, that getting off at Stamford is enough; it's as if "Jehovah might smile at a mortal pleading some technicality before the bar of Judgment—as though hairs could be split over Original Sin . . ." (33).

His friend Harry Pycraft runs a motel and sells off his land to developers, an honest thing to do since the preservationists just want to look at and not work the land. He's convinced that most of the young girls nowadays are cold and few of the boys nonhomosexual. Only 10 percent of the high-school girls are in trouble at any one time, which means that the few normal girls (and fewer boys) are active as hell. The parents are just as bad; he sees them meet in his motel. One matron meets regularly with a Scottish poet whom he doesn't know, but Spofford does; it's the mother of Tad Springer, "whose family was too good for mine" (51).

He reads *But*, thinks of the "eternal flucks," and decides he has to go to Punch Bowl Hollow—her development—to see Pussy Beau-

seigneur again. He makes himself useful to her through his knowledge
of plants, noting the while the cheap job the builders did on her
house. He also reads in a little magazine there a poem by Gowan
McGland, the fellow then trysting with Tad Springer's mom. Except
for the profusion of similes it's a good poem in itself and is a clever
Dylan Thomas pastiche. When he goes home he speaks of the ghastly
summer, of dinner being eaten at an ungodlyish and grotesque hour.
He's catching on.

He gives a gardening day a week to each of three ladies of the
Hollow, in one case imitating a Midlands dialect he's picked up from
a discarded Lawrentian paperback; he has a "nack for imitation"
(67). When he begins to babysit for Pussy Wilcox and others, he gets
to see the innards of their lives, scrapbooks that show when women
gave up on being actresses and got married, easels with unfinished oils
on them, uncompleted divorce actions filed away. From a checkbook he
learns of $200 a week alimony payments that Wilcox is paying to
Wife No. 1. When he sits for the neighborhood psychiatrist he learns
a lot from his basement notebooks. Tad Springer is one of the worst:
sucks eggs, steals. The shrink's kid walks on his heels so he can keep
his toes clean for sucking. He overhears the psychiatrist and wife
fighting. So he learns the enemy is human, too.

When Pussy Beau asks him to help serve at a cocktail party she's
having for Mrs. Springer he buys the wrong sort of white jacket and
manages to pass for a guest; he will learn their ways so that Geneva
can pass "mustard" (87) next time. "The problem was to refine into
more sophisticated, or brittle, talk the humor that in some small degree at least I possessed" (90). He's the same arriviste sort De Vries
so often writes about, except he's starting a little late. After all, he
had to wait till the Celestial City came to him. He does it well, saying,
"He hasn't a prayer," when asked the chances of someone's kid getting into Yale Divinity. Mrs. Springer invites him to come look at
her roses. At last he is inside the inner defenses.

There he meets Gowan McGland, looking, as Harry Pycraft has
said, like either a clean poet or a dirty businessman. McGland happens
to remember Geneva, whom Spofford said had heard him: ". . . hair
in bangs, like a row of question marks . . . [looks] like she just swallowed her gum" (98). He's unusual not only for his sexuality: "Everything is sexual whether people know it or not" (99). McGland happens to know it. He asks Spofford to show him an indecent place to

dine and drink and is taken to Indelicato's (the model for which has since disappeared from Westport). Back at the farm, Mrs. Punck, who asks that Spofford call her Eunice, has moved in. He sees her increasingly as human bric-a-brac, even as he once had been seen. He patronizes her, asks her to repeat her banal aphorisms ("A stitch in time saves nine. Saves *what*? Nine!") but notices that what he likes most about McGland is that he doesn't patronize anyone.

McGland likes Indelicato's because the basement bar has the damp smell serious drinkers like, ever thinking of themselves as mushrooms. They belong to the class of thallophytes "characterized chiefly by absence of chlorophyll" (115). Thus "Fungus: a spongy morbid growth, as proud flesh formed in a wound. Poetry: same thing" (115). There has been too much sun for him around the pools of the browning women of Woodsmoke. Then at a table nearby one of the locals complains to an imbibing priest that they feel like regular churchgoers crowded out of their pews on Christmas and Easter, "—only we're crowded out *all* the time lately" (119). People who think they're slumming are pushing them out of Indelicato's. When a slummer offends Bobsy Springer's honor, McGland reluctantly rises to defend it, covering his teeth more than he needs to. He draws his Boy Scout knife for a weapon, but opens a spoon instead of a blade. The police break it up.

After giving an impossible Welsh address to the police, McGland makes the allowed phone call, asking an Englishman named Alvin Mopworth to do a bit as a State Department attaché. Remarkably handsome and convincing, Mopworth manages the trick. Returning with Spofford, McGland is introduced again to the just-returned Geneva; quickly he invites her to the Springers' for a party. Mare is delighted: what does Geneva think they're educating her for if it's not so she "can look down on us at least a little? Yes—feel ashamed of us!" (138).

Spofford continues to play with Mrs. Punck, threatening to leave her everything in his will if she doesn't sleep with him. But he's only half playing, and he does pinch hit for her Golden Age Club at the Y when the scheduled speaker takes sick. Spofford speaks on modern writing and approvingly of modern verse that "comes straight out with double meaning" (145). The cops are called. As he is leaving that scene for McGland's, Spofford overhears Bobsy call the poet totally amoral, wondering whether he's more of a moral imbecile or only a sexual glutton. She's disgusted because McGland has gone after, and caught, her sister-in-law, too; while C.B.S., her own communications-industry executive husband, would be jealous if he found out, Lucille's, a dentist (they tend to Sadism), would kill him. Spofford can't judge Bobsy, the standards for immorality having sloped upwards somewhat. (Hester Prynne today would get no better than a C+.) Later in the day he almost tumbles Mrs. Punck, their progress interrupted by the inadvertent arrival of Mare. He's compromised, more convinced than ever that the world is "all one great mating cry, mostly out of season" (158). At the least, art, poetry, and music are.

When Eunice's back goes out, a Dr. Rappaport, semiretired from New Haven and covering for the local, is called. Since he hitchhikes to meet his patients—hasn't driven since his wife died in an automobile accident—he's seldom prompt. Of course he and his patient become emotionally involved, complicating things for Spofford; he can never rise to Pussy Beau's level, and he's largely cut off from Eunice Punck's. To make it worse, Tad Springer brings Geneva home so late at night that Spofford can't sleep. He knows Tad has been seeing the psychiatrist for some disorder or other, so that he again breaks into Wolmar's office to see what it is. He's arrested and disgraced—that's what climbers get in De Vries's works—and anyway it's McGland who's seriously after Geneva, not Tad. Mrs. Punck sets off to confront the poet about her granddaughter, and the section ends.

The McGland portion of *Reuben, Reuben* is brief, some eighty pages, ending shortly after the poet hangs himself. Since only Moses can write a book in which his own death is recorded, the omniscient point of view is used here. The task is a formidable one, that of making somewhat sympathetic a fellow who generally is despicable. McGland's only excuse is his verse; otherwise he is what Richard Boston calls the fool or clown, "someone who plays on the limits of acceptable behavior. We laugh at him because he goes over the limits, but as he does so he defines those limits for us, and all the time he is pushing them farther back."[6] His name was chosen as one "that would sound exactly like one of the old Scottish clans and yet represent the man." As is true of many comic writers, De Vries says he likes name that "have some thematic or connotative reference."[7]

Thus the name fits the man whose original wrote of "the force that through the green fuse drives the flower," whose fuse explores many a flower. McGland's real weakness, though, lies north of there, is his teeth: owing to childhood fights and natural chalkyness, he has only five uppers left; if he loses two more there won't be support enough for his bridge. It becomes a mania: "Toothlessness would be for McGland the moment of truth" (187). The sexual implications of teeth were well known to Freud, but their meaning has changed in recent literature, says Theodore Ziolkowski. In an article in *PMLA* he notes that "potency, beauty, or pain" are what teeth represent in cultural context, and that "as an image of sex and beauty" they "go back through Poe and the Bible to primitive myth and folklore."[8]

Ziolkowski notes that other diseases—TB, syphilis, cancer, and so on—have "been singled out from time to time to symbolize the state of society," but the incidence of tooth decay in particular "varies in a direct proportion of the level of civilization." Thus teeth, and troubles associated therewith, and dentists, have been used significantly by such modern authors as Grass, Bellow, Updike, Pynchon, Vonnegut, Sulzberger, Mann, and Koestler. There has been a change in the old meaning, however: ". . . by the end of the nineteenth century the conventional image of the tooth with its attributes of potency and beauty had been exhausted. . . . Writers like Koestler and Greene, who perceived society as an organism and were obsessed by their vision of its decay, found in teeth a familiar literary image that was now free to accept new and timely associations."[9]

Ziolkowski doesn't mention De Vries, although his work here could be used to prove either point: teeth as sexual potency or as social decay. Probably it's both, although the main thrust remains the pervasive absurdity with the dissolution that follows in De Vries's books whenever characters give in to the absurdity. To reinforce this absurdity, McGland is allowed to do something that often happens in De Vries's novels—gobbets of stories are recalled and used to prove a point without the stories themselves being integral to the work at large. These become, then, tales told within the novel; metaphorically they resemble a veteran telling war stories about people and places the hearer doesn't know. They lack force; they don't convince.

His mother's case is one of these. He remembers her as having had a double mastectomy, being afflicted with cataracts, and being unable to walk but still willing to crawl, singing pious hymns as she goes—sort of a Mother Theresa of Calcutta to her own case. His father blew his brains out. To McGland it's all a bad joke, although he thinks that perhaps to a possible deity it's a good one, if the deity is one "to whom the sight of a blind and mutilated old woman crawling on all fours through a mortgaged house thinking she is going to heaven is irresistibly funny" (188). Another war story involves a woman of ninety who is badly crippled, whose children and grandchildren have died, who grows vegetables and weeds her cemetery plots: "she represented human worth at its highest: virtue in a void. That final courage which consists in knowing courage to be useless" (247–48). She doesn't figure in the novel otherwise.

As for McGland's own afflictions (other than those visited on him by himself), he gets cluster migraines and has cervical arthritis. This last necessitates his "hanging" himself occasionally from a convenient lintel, using a contraption of straps and braces to do so. This subliminally sets one's mind for his demise.

His life wasn't bad, really. His poetry early made him a success; he married an attractive woman, Edith Chipps, who also worked at the BBC, and he became a literary lion; for a time, though, Edith's success eclipsed his when the role he read for radio was shifted to television. His appearance was not acceptable—apparently he *looks* like Dylan, too—and he was replaced by the handsome Alvin Mopworth. Mopworth at this stage is assumed by almost all to be homosexual since he likes women so much, everything being the opposite of what it appears. When Edith has an affair and thinks she has infected McGland it turns out he has infected her from his own liaison; probably *her* partner was Mopworth, whom she describes only as her "gay Lothario." She's so infuriated at having erroneously forgiven McGland that she says she wants never to see him again. Then to America, where his story merges with Spofford's.

Mrs. Punck, sure he's sleeping with Geneva, reads him moralistic verse and threatens to go on to Wordsworth unless he agrees to stop seeing her granddaughter. He agrees. Fortuitiously, Geneva soon happens on him when he's setting up his hanging contraption, mistakes it for something else, and begging that he stay his hand, offers herself; aware of her misunderstanding, he nonetheless accepts. Thus he inadvertently pays Mopworth back in advance, since Alvin will marry the girl in the third section of the novel. It justifies his epithet of the Welsh Rabbit. (Both of his parents were half Welsh, so it fits.)

Haxby, an excellent dentist and a strong personality, is not so tolerant—or unaware, anyway—of his wife's straying as is C.B.S. of his Bobsy's. When Gowan goes to him for a cure for the toothache, Haxby pulls the wrong one, meaning that one more, the fatal fourth, will have to go. That means a plate. Before that happens, McGland writes verse in which one is invited to join him and "Eat, drink, be merry with our backs to the abyss..." (242). He has deleted a line, "The world's too mad for anything but mirth," De Vries apparently feeling it wasn't good enough for the poem surrounding, but that it was important enough to be in the book. With his teeth gone McGland gets faced around to the abyss, and the madness overcomes the mirth; now comes home the alienation he "had for all the years of his sexual manhood carried ... mystically in his blood, the destination toward which he knew he moved" (245). He tries to kill himself with a mixture of ice cream and seconal, but fails.

Mrs. Punck rouses him to read him more penitential poetry, this time from Longfellow, and he vomits. To the soon-appearing Mopworth, now doing a book on him, he gives answers to the Ultimate Questions he's asked: the secret to life is locked, with the combination, in a safe; God is no Christian; man stinks, as the least bit of introspection ought to teach anyone (252). When Geneva presents herself and hints at her pregnancy he gives her a few hundred dollars he's received as an advance and on her departure hangs himself. On hearing of his demise, Geneva conveniently miscarries; in an also too-well-made stroke, Mrs. Punck marries Emil Rappaport. So it's over.

Thomas, whose work appeared in *Poetry* during De Vries's tenure and peak of influence there, was described by the novelist as "charming." And so is his stand-in, McGland, even when at his most despicable; described by others as being a man totally lacking in any concept of private property, McGland figures he can have, on the average, one out of every ten women he tries for. Yet he is here made at least somewhat sympathetic by De Vries, in part by making Bobsy Springer, her husband, Carl, her sister-in-law Lucille Haxby, and Haxby himself, all to be, in varying degree, toads. Not completely, of course: C.B.S. works hard at "communication" and Haxby, despite a too keen faith in speed reading, is a good dentist. As Peter Ustinov has said, the scales must be balanced to prevent boring the reader.

This De Vries does, so that the women and McGland just about deserve each other. But since McGland, although an approximation

of Dylan Thomas, is only that, it must be that De Vries is himself
unsympathetic to such people who increase rather than lighten the
load. Although McGland does lighten our load a little with his verse.

The third section, *Mopworth*, plays just a little on the old motif
of American Innocence (or Militant Ignorance) vs. European Experience, although his psyche suffers from gratuitous analysis in England
even as it does in the United States. He likes girls, and so is suspected
of inversion. A girl he tries to bed (if she doesn't, he says she'll hate
herself in the morning) says everyone admires how he's fighting
homosexuality. But it's worse in America, where he meets Geneva
as part of his research for a book on McGland; to divert attention
from her daughter's guilt, Mare claims *she* was herself the mistress.
This leads Mopworth to reflect on all the arty sorts—Rossetti, Dowson,
and Van Gogh come quickly to mind—who had mistresses from the
lower orders. (Some married them; he might have named Goethe
and Joyce, but doesn't.) Brahms and Moussorgsky messed around with
prostitutes, he recalls; luckily for them, all this was before psychoanalysis. Nonartists often enough have done the same sort of thing,
but that doesn't count.

Because of her mother's affair, Geneva is asked everywhere. Of
her George F. Will wrote that he thought it appropriate that she
" 'sometimes spelled the same word two different ways in the same
paragraph, thereby showing spontaneity.' Well, why not? According
to the new sensibility, spontaneous self-expression is an end in itself."
She is representative of what Will calls De Vries's main subject,
"the slightly Bohemian bourgeoisie, which is as national as McDon-
ald's."[10] She brings home with her for Christmas vacation a more
advanced specimen of her same species, Nectar Schmidt, whose parents
are divorced and gone; if Geneva is a creative speller, Nectar is an
imaginative elocutionist: *probably* she elides to "pry," and *actually*
becomes "ackshy." When Tad dates Geneva, Mopworth is paired with
Nectar; Nectar analyzes him as possessing a *basic* hostility toward
women, because he chases after so many of them. Alvin cannot stand
her, and much of the book concerns which of them—he or Nectar—
shall control what there is of Geneva's mind.

"Ackshy" he is hostile toward Nectar, fantasizing about stuffing
her body into a culvert and so on: "pry" it isn't Nectar's fault, though;
it's only that she is part of "the national crisis: what American women
were to do with their liberated minds and opened vistas occupied

half the magazines and a growing swarm of social anthropologists" (291). Her stops have been so played that she thinks there's music in her; there isn't. She strips and invites him to master her and prove wrong her estimation of him, then takes it amiss when he chooses not to. As she represents the incident to Geneva, it was an attempted rape (by him). After a scene at Indelicato's, where Alvin gets into (and wins) a fight because he is overheard calling a man a heterosexual, Geneva discovers he needs her, even as she had thought did McGland; a keener analyst than she, Mopworth discerns that she needs his need of her. So they marry.

Mopworth then recalls that McGland had wondered how anyone could "expect mankind to be happy in pairs when it is miserable separately" (313). The sophistry of the remark is not probed by De Vries, so he probably accepts it as truthful. Of all authors—since his books don't really begin till the principals are married—he ought to challenge McGland's observations, and perhaps he does so by centering his novels on the difficulties of marriage and not on the avoidance of it. As has been noted, very few serious American novelists write about marriage. Perhaps by doing so he is endorsing the Hebrew Midrash that has it that "an unmarried man is half a man"; that is, the natural state of mature humanity is married and in a group. McGland's statement, however, is more American.

Mopworth's difficulties with the biography have more to do with the poet's women, though: those who have slept with him clam up, and those who only claim to have shared his bed are chatterboxes. Also there is the undodgeable question: why did he kill himself? Edith, the widow, says she supposes everyone has it in him—she does; Mopworth, who doesn't, is silent. Through Tad Springer's father-in-law, the dentist who told McGland he was going to lose all his teeth, he finds out. Dr. Ormsby knows that "teeth are linked with virility in the masculine mind" (378), but he also knows that the "roots of suicide aren't clean cut like the roots of a tooth—" (379). He also knows it was the previous dentist who condemned McGland by pulling the wrong tooth, but he doesn't know who it was; he's certain that Haxby wouldn't make such a mistake. Of course it wasn't a mistake, as Mopworth soon finds; but if he printed the truth the publisher would be sued since Haxby could easily cover himself. So the book is ruined, because the tooth-pulling episode is the heart of it, and he can't leave it out. Geneva says he's only rationalizing a wish to drop it, and for once she's partly correct. Mopworth decides he's an actor, not a writer.

His marriage, meanwhile, is experiencing difficulties. He and Geneva have two boys and live in Woodsmoke. He does his share outside the home and does part of hers within it; still, she is not satisfied. All he wants is peace in the house, but it is Geneva who determines the weather in it, and often it is unsettled. Serial polygamy he thinks likely to take over. Into this comes, once again, Nectar, whom he hopes at least will be an ally against a neighbor who is a very popular and very bad writer, Jack Dumbrowski. In his books there would be "the innumerable 'You mean—?s,' the junky atmospheric 'somewhere,' that 'part of her' business, plus the host of descriptive stencils like 'a thickset man with beetling brows'..." (343). Mopworth picks a fight with him and largely wins it. Nectar and Jack—who is married—seem to like each other, though.

Visiting at the Mopworths', she continues to analyze but in a "nonjudgmental" way that infuriates Alvin; if he's that bad off then he ought to be not only judged but damned. After he takes as much of it as he can, he strikes back: "I think you're a man-hating, sexually frustrated, potential Lesbian," he tells Nectar, an "oral cannibal with a slightly sadistic streak—and I'm not criticizing you when I say that" (364). She accepts his judgment as clearing the air and gets on with her affair with Dumbrowski. That, too, infuriates Mopworth; not only was McGland a great success with women, so is his vulgar equivalent. It just isn't fair. Dumbrowski has many shabby affairs, and Minnie, his wife, knows about them. Alvin conducts only one, with Edith Chipps, McGland's widow. This adultery "made Mopworth if anything a better husband. Mellowed by pleasure, thankful for it (his ego of course soothed by the sense of romantic conquest), he went home a more kind and generous man, twice as willing to deserve the gratitude on deposit for him there by 'pitching in' after dinner and bathing the children. 'Another woman,' or man, is low on the list of causes for divorce. Infidelity has probably stabilized more marriages than it has shaken. It is from its discovery that the trouble arises" (412).

His theory here remarkably like that of *Playboy* philosopher-publisher Hugh Hefner, De Vries seems to be arguing that an acceptable way of discouraging overt serial polygamy is through the practice of the covert version. The thesis is suspect, on grounds logical; one presumes his preference is for monogamy since he prefers polygamy disguised as monogamy to open serial polygamy. The covert sexual excursions he endorses since they serve to preserve at least appearances if not the substance—hypocrisy is the tribute vice pays to virtue, that sort of thing. (It is only the shaky monogamous marriages that need preserving this way; adultery he does not recommend on principle, only as a sometime savior of monogamy.) He admits that discovery of these liaisons usually leads to divorce, but that is no more surprising than that apprehended criminals are more often sent to jail than those who aren't apprehended. The crime, however, remains and is just as destructive of the social fabric, whether the perpetrator is caught or no.

As to whether these adulteries are in any other way salubrious also is doubtful. If one assumes that coital sexual intercourse ought to be a moderately intimate relationship, then adulterous lovers will find themselves drifting into an involvement they can hardly live out; if, on the other hand, one is careful not to get emotionally entangled, but uses the other only as a punchboard, then that, too, is unfortunate. If both partners do this then the mutually masturbatory relationship in which each regards the other as a thing will result in their becoming rather like things—and this applies to the thinger as well as the thingee. Worse, if only one uses the other (while the other reacts in a more humane way, and gets "involved"), then, on discovery by the involved one that he or she is being used, there is hell to pay, especially if the involved one is female.

Also, De Vries's honest art proves his thinking wrong. One of the uses of art is to try out ideas. If the author can create a believable world in which his ideas work out then his ideas are acceptable, valid. But they never work out in De Vries's world. In Dumbrowski's case, Minnie divorces him; in Mopworth's own case, Geneva divorces him. The adultery, of course, is prompted by other things that are wrong in the marriage, but it hardly ever seems in De Vries's books to work out as an effective poultice. In this case it turns out rather well, though, since Jack and Nectar deserve each other, and Minnie finds another man, one who makes her blossom. What is being recommended, then, is divorce and remarriage, not adultery.

The case made through Mopworth's and Geneva's experiments also points to failure. On discovering that someone else is doing a better book on McGland than he can, and that Edith's book is more vibrant than his ever can be, he settles on acting. He does well enough there, but feels unappreciated at home: "He did his own work and a third of his wife's, dropped his moods to attend to hers, ministered to her humors and humored her wishes—and it was all taken for granted" (409). Geneva meanwhile is subjecting herself to the intellectual rigor of doing a degree in Elementary Education. When Mike is five and Amos three and a half, she decides to open with Nectar (newly divorced) a school for disturbed children. Children like her own, one presumes, although De Vries gives no personalities to them; perhaps that would take the book out of the realm of comedy altogether and leave it only with blackness.

Let Me Count the Ways

Although William Walsh says *Reuben, Reuben* is "one of those novels ... in which there are certain distortions of design, a deficiency in shaping the whole being De Vries's main technical weakness," he finds two exceptions in "the beautifully balanced ... *The Mackerel Plaza*" and the "splendidly finished ... *Let Me Count the Ways*."[11] This seems a just evaluation, especially of the last mentioned, more-or-less an academic novel, which is, as such, better than Bernard Malamud's, Mary McCarthy's, or Pamela Hansford Johnson's attempts at the same. At least Tom Waltz, son of a man who runs a moving-van line, is a junior-level academic; he tells the middle and major portion while Stan, the father, tells the endpieces.

Stan Waltz is that familiar De Vries creation, a self-educated blue-collar man particularly given to scoffing at belief in a deity; as an atheist he is the equivalent of the homosexual enemy of Winston Churchill who was said by the prime minister to be "the sort who gives sodomy a bad name." Few autodidacts have other than a fool for a teacher, and Stan is no exception; his salvation is that he comes to realize it. The reader's lesson learned is that we are all of us ultimately in his shoes.

Stan's wife, the former Elsie Wishnotski, gets saved—"plain low-down, cornball, meat-and-potatoes Jesus *Saves* saved ..." (5).[12] Thus they are equally paired, getting along fairly well in Slow Rapids, Indiana, in "the region," thirty miles from Chicago. They have a ten-year-old, Tom, a silent sort who seems not to know which parent to believe, and never does decide, even when he's older, although he conducts his later inquiries on a much more sophisticated level.

His mother wants to bring him up as a believer, his father as an atheist; his father suggests a compromise of agnostic. Elsie is ignorant but not stupid and knows no one can comfortably mugwump that one (sit the fence with his mug on one side and his wump on the other). An agnostic (except for those few who use it to mean anti-gnostic, the way Paul Tillich used atheist to mean antitheist) is a sophisticated atheist; pragmatically they are indistinguishable. Edith and Stan are equally paired on the issue, the only difference being that he thinks her "wonderful"—he appreciates the wisdom her super-ficial coarseness hides—but he doesn't realize how "wonderful" *he* is, how silly he is beneath the homemade education. He is rather like a failed Blake, if Eliot's evaluation of the poet is correct: the mystic's work seemed to him like an ingenious one-of-a-kind piece of cabinetry that, although interesting, one didn't care to see again. Blake's genius made it as clever as it is. Stan, however, lacks genius; his mind is a piece of gimcrackery.

Thus he and Edith amount to low-relief equivalents of the types De Vries more often writes about in Fairfield County, although he seldom puts both cultural levels in the same book. The multiple point-of-view technique in *Reuben, Reuben* is an exception, and there's something of that here when Stan takes over—except that he's an amalgam of his parents' view. He more nearly represents the father, though, since while De Vries often experiments with multiple points of view he seldom gives even one of them to a woman, until *Sauce for the Goose*, that is, when he did it well and added further balance and contrast to his work.

A section by Lena Salerno would be welcome; the wife of one of Stan's workers, she's "a horse, but at forty still firm in outline . . ." (12). Funny as a crutch and twice as perceptive, as Stan calls her, her near affair with her husband's boss is funny even by De Vries standards, the sort of thing that justifies the dust-jacket quotation from John P. Marquand that "one must go back to Laurence Sterne and *Tris-tram Shandy* and close to Cervantes to find the same quality of wis-dom combined with slapstick drollery. . . ." Tacky of taste in home furnishings, dress, and yard decor, she's keen on birth control, takes herself most seriously. She approaches intimacy with Stan, justifying it by Art's slovenly ways—he can belch the entire Pledge of Allegiance and the Ten Commandments—and Elsie is as arrogant in her humility as Christ was, so Stan is set. She gift-wraps herself in red silk lounging pajamas; she wants a little romance but when Stan lifts her she's too heavy and to avoid a hernia he ends up dragging her by her armpits into the bedroom over the threshold. That ends it.

A proto-affair with a condescending woman who liked him for being of the lower orders never quite made it, although she did manage to photograph him and his men throwing an old piano into a garbage dump. The three men stand among the droning flies and wonder, "Why? To what end? What for?" Ona Mervin works too hard to persuade him not to feel guilty afterwards—trying to convert the already-converted, Stan says—blaming the Puritans initially and then finally laying it in Adam's lap; Stan perceptively noticed that if the latter is so then it goes back a good deal farther than the *Mayflower*. She wants him to read Bertrand Russell and others in order to rid him of guilt he doesn't have. Stan sees no reason anyone should have to cram for the sack.

Then comes a spiritual crisis: Elsie accepts a pamphlet predicting the Second Coming, and soon. On 11 June, to be precise. That evening all hell breaks loose, and amid a lit-up sky and horrific noise Elsie gets the boy up and puts a shirt and tie on him, slicks his hair down so he'll look nice to meet the Lord, and Stan, panicked, baptizes himself under the cold-water tap. It's the local fireworks factory, exploding. Stan excuses himself by saying his was not a case of "a sinner reviving . . . but an atheist backsliding" (71). Then, aided by a beer, he attempts to show he can belch the books of the Bible in perfect order, but grows faint; as Elsie prays over him he gets the hiccups. They go away in time but they presage worse to come.

There is another attempt with Lena before she and Art are to leave the area for better business opportunities elsewhere, and she gives him a poem to remember her by; she neglects to tell him Elizabeth Barrett Browning wrote it. This soiree fails too when her pajamas split at the seams and there seems to her to be no glamour or loveliness in the world, not even in adultery: "What's the use! Everything is so awful! Everything is so absolutely and utterly hopeless!" (88). It was bad enough having to make do with Stan, but that ended it.

His next problem comes with his apprehension as a Peeping Tom, even though it was his own wife he was spying on. He gets off after arguing well with the desk sergeant, but tells too much since the young man he thought a plainclothesman really was a reporter. At least he didn't make page one. He escapes for a short while to Florida but returns in time to enter a poetry contest sponsored by the paper, to be judged personally by the editor himself. With Lena Salerno safely in Arizona he submits the Barrett sonnet and wins; when the publisher is apprised of his error, Stan is apprised of his. He goes on a classic bender and awakes with a chronic hangover. It lasts and lasts and lasts, with no need for refueling.

Elsie is able to run the business, and the years roll by—or spin by, considering Stan's condition. The son he thought would be saved from religion by his sense of humor grows up and goes to Polycarp College, from which came a professor who had offered an opinion on his father's psychology at the time of the peeper incident. That psychology has changed somewhat; Stan has found the meaning of life, and it is Love. Drunks usually are afforded the opportunity to speak baldly and in non sequitur fashion on great issues, and those with chronic hangovers apparently are allowed the same privilege. He wishes he'd died of terminal hiccups and merged with the dust, but since he didn't he has learned that "Simple human love that asks no quarter, seeks not itself, is not puffed up," that's what it's all about (114). We have to learn to give love or we are through. Of course he's on the receiving end of that (from Elsie and Tom) when he says it.

Tom's section is told by an educated intelligence and comes across as more honest, less cute. A senior at Polycarp College when his portion begins, he is

prey to fantasies. I imagine that there are people on this planet named Max Planck. I imagine that all matter is reducible to units of energy whirling in submicroscopic orbit, of which balls of roaring gas form the delirious counterpart in outer space. . . . I sometimes fancy that I am supported on a jointed improvisation of Tinker Toy called "bones," and that . . . this weird idea that sounds felicitous to the human ear could be produced by a man trained to draw tautened strands of horsetail across the dried entrails of cats, . . . that invisible organisms infested the palm of my hand, that people joined mouths in unlighted places preparatory to exchanging lavish tributes to one another's appearance. . . . (118–19)

Not only that, but he thinks he's seeing Aldebaran by light that left there at the time of Nebuchadnezzar; as for seeing itself, he fears that's done "by some kind of aspic embedded in two sockets in my head and transformed into comprehension by a scoop of albumin directly behind them..." (217). Thus there is this fundamental absurdity, that—at the least—matter can become so complex as to become aware of itself. Yet when his ignorant father rhapsodizes on much the same sort of thing it turns out banal; similarly, if his mother had intended her witticisms (she writes the president, and if he doesn't answer she'll try Uncle Sam) they would be ironic instead of only sad.

This last opinion is given by Marion Wellington, Tom's girl friend from Polycarp. She is from Evanston, as patrician as Americans get, and a believer, if only in the Episcopalian fashion. Tom threatens a rupture because of her belief, having earlier given up a girl because of her unbelief; he's rebelling against *both* his parents. Laodiceanism won't do, either. Yet within only a few years they both are back there on the staff, instructors with M.A.'s, hers in religion, his in English. He goes on dreaming, imagining that "clothed mammals alternately lose and recover their balance in a regulated error known as 'walking'" (118) and that the room is filled with a substance that includes oxygen, which he needs to inhale through two holes in his nose (132).

Otherwise he's normal, hates to see Marion sitting next to a poet-in-residence who signs himself Hodge!, and has an urge to ruin his teaching career because of the fraud he finds there: professors are promoted because of how well their colleagues like them and because of their reputations elsewhere, not because of skill at teaching; most literary research is ridiculous, harpies plucking pin feathers from some corpus or other and excreting their conclusion in six-point footnotes. When he breaks his leg (as did De Vries, although in a later portion of his life) he is restored by pity to the academic community. Also, his *faux pas* is so misunderstood that his status is improved rather than damaged; Tom reflects that he should have realized that such might happen—he wasn't the only jackass braying around in the world, after all.

Two familiar themes are worked the while: the growing number of people who divorce easily and early, and the surprising number of folk who need to be put away for a rest. No De Vries novel is without either. Nor the drollery; he rides home from the hospital in an ambulance, too, driven by the owner of Christ and Holy Trinity Garage, named for the next-door church (such is the name of a church in Westport), and he's ousted by his landlady when she discovers certain sentimental ballads of his composition, "Christmas at the Whorehouse" being typical. Meanwhile he does things like attend church on Sunday and participate fully, while reading in class the next day "A Free Man's Worship," by Bertrand Russell. The former is done in rebellion against his father; the latter, against his mother.

Tom is not himself a writer, not even would-be; rather he is one of those who drift into teaching literature because they spend their time reading good books. Then, finding they have to earn a living some way, they attempt to construct a virtue of their vice by entering a setting (a college) where they can formally invite others to join them in their pleasure. He does denigrate Shakespeare's efforts by writing parodies of his lines. It's embarrassing—although it's not meant to be—because, line by line, many can do as much; few, however, can write a series of plays in which the world is so well plumbed and scanned. More reasonable is Tom's entering an inane contest, the goal of which is to tell a movie starlet "what happiness is." His entry is hopelessly banal, as he knows, but he wins; and Angela Ravage wings out from the West Coast for a date that comes with his victory. Bagley, the president of Polycarp, surprisingly is intelligent enough to be embarrassed by what Tom Waltz has written. Waltz meant it, of course, as a burlesque of a travesty, something as hard to do as writing a satire of pornography. (Because pornography is already a satire of healthy sexuality, such an attempt would tie one too many tin cans on the dog's tail—it couldn't run with it.)

Angela isn't half bad—reads Sartre, knows she isn't much of an actress, finds mysticism unsatisfactory and calls philosophy the "enamel around the naked nerve": it's the mask reason gives to the fearful pulp beneath. Together they attend the funeral for the newly departed head of English, killed by too much insurance (he overworked to pay for it), where there oddly was a eulogy as part of an Episcopal service; then, on the way other than to the cemetery he notices all the other cars are following his. Trying to outrun them, he ends up leading a speeding funeral procession—grotesque enough, but even better when he leads them up a blind alley. So Waltz is put in charge of English—owing to death and resignations there is

no one else—and then, when Dr. Bagley has a heart attack, he's made
acting president. Bagley does this to get even with him, let him settle
all the paper work he has himself created.

Angela urges agnosticism on him, and against her he uses the arguments Marion Wellington has used on his agnosticism. Word of
this gets back to Marion and to Bagley and he's asked to see the
school psychologist, a woman who screens students and faculty by
means of their handwriting (Waltz's indicates latent sexual criminal-
ity). When she asks him varying probing questions he answers eruditely
on matters in no way related. Asked which parent he prefers, he
turns the talk to fascism; thus he parries her into noneffectiveness.
From that he proceeds to the most outrageous evangelical storefront
meeting, converts, goes to a bar, and sings blasphemous parodies of
the hymns he's just finished honestly belting out. The ensuing hangover lasts three days, and after it Marion agrees to marry him if only
he'll try affection rather than rebellion toward his parents.

Thus, with five-sixths of the book done, in effect a new novel (or
novella) begins. He and Marion live in the dorm in an apartment
provided for the housemaster; Angela disappears somewhere—her
presence was only to counterpoint Marion intellectually, so now she's
dropped (and whatever happened to Hodges, his rival?)—and Stan
Waltz sobers up, gingerly at first. This last has something, although
it's not clear what, to do with Tom's not having been affected after
all by a past indiscretion or two of his father's. Three new Harvard
men, the Three Little Prigs, are hired into the English department,
and their smug superiority brings Tom into action as a phantom BB
gun shooter (at their ankles) and ingenious harasser. One odious
fellow, Fangle, an "intellectual convert," finds JESUS SAVES stickers
securely fastened to his bumpers. Everything they get, they deserve,
theirs being "a species of aesthetic puritan, with principles as rigidly
intolerant and intellectual and artistic shortcomings as their New
England forebears were of moral" (262).

Then he wins another prize, his answer to "What Christmas Means
to Me" outdoing in banality even his "Happiness Is" effort; again the
president is not happy. It's a new president, the former having re-
covered sufficiently from his heart attack to be put away to rest in
the local private asylum. Marion also is embarrassed, weekends with
her parents, and Tom lucks on to an attractive girl in a bar just at
the moment the girl is telling her boyfriend that he's now her ex-

boyfriend. When Marion finds out about it she talks of divorce; one *"can't* separate sex from love" (284) except by hurting someone and he has hurt the girl. This hurting of the *other* woman is something Marion can't forgive. Tom notes this attitude as peculiarly Christian.

Since he has to get off campus anyway—because of the Prigs' having got evidence on him as their tormentor—he goes abroad on funds provided by Polycarp for needy associate professors. Smadbeck, who doesn't like the Harvardians either, arranges a promotion for Tom so that he might qualify for this benefice.

The book concludes with Stan's final narration. He has mellowed, finds his being narrow made Elsie so, and now he even goes to a liberal community church with her, meeting her halfway. The hymns there include "Spanish Cavalier," and they prefer to think of the crucifixion as occurring on "Pretty Good Friday." Tom meanwhile has gone out of curiosity to Lourdes, where he gets deathly sick. The trouble may have had something to do with a self-repair job he did on a tooth that lost a filling, but there's a moment when it looks to be a disease peculiar to sheep; this motif, which plays occasionally through De Vries's works, usually as a bleat from a sufferer, thus surfaces again here. Marion flies over to help him through his troubles, and it appears that the marriage will endure.

The illness remains a mystery, as does everything else: says Stan, the "universe is like a safe to which there is a combination. But the combination is locked up in the safe" (307). Thus by those familiar lines is the balance maintained, if reverent agnosticism can be seen as a fulcrum between belief and denial. Certainly the book is balanced, a well-cut jewel.

The Vale of Laughter

If *Let Me Count the Ways* is an exemplum of comic craftsmanship, then *The Vale of Laughter*, a mature fictional inquiry into the nature of comedy, shows how it got that way. The maturity shows in De Vries's resisting his tendency to too many swift one-liners ("Picked up a sliver.... I'm a great committeeman, you know. I sit on a lot of boards.") and to an overreliance on the *New Yorker* hors d'oeuvres ("Occasionally a jet went by, ripping the gray sky in two"). This tendency, unchecked, produces a novel that reads alternatingly like a joke book and excerpts of verse from the better literary quarterlies.

The inquiry into the theory of comedy involves a cursory summation of the opinions of some of the great philosophers who have addressed their minds to the question—Kant, Schopenhauer, Aristotle, Plato, Bergson, and a couple of others. To do this sort of probing and maintain the story line while doing it is no small feat, one that few American novelists are given to; since few of them have De Vries's intellect and erudition, it is a good thing that this is so.

This talk he manages to work in by having two principal characters who are interested in the subject—one of them a comic sort himself and the other a professor of psychology introspective enough to explore the subject. The first of these is Joe Sandwich, who, as is usual for De Vries's narrators, had one believing parent, his mother, and one disbelieving, a father who tolerated his spouse's seeing to it that their offspring had a traditional religious upbringing. Apparently it is from the father that the humorous vein springs, since Dad spent some years trying to think of an appetizing epigram to go out of this world with, something worthy of his benign disbelief. It ends as a joke, though, since—in one helluva thunderstorm—he hears an awesome clap, says "Jesus H. Christ," and expires. The line between profanity and prayer is thin, Sandwich notes, justifying a report to his mother that omitted the middle initial.

Raised Roman Catholic, Joe went as a child to confession and irritated the priest by confessing to good deeds. A clown in the house of God, he calls himself, something Roderick Jellema has also called his creator.[13] This tone is set from line one, in fact, when Melville's opening to *Moby-Dick* is parodied: "Call me, Ishmael," says Sandwich. "Feel absolutely free to." He's a stockbroker. Thus we are told this will be no diving-bell excursion to the bottom of a swimming pool by one failing to unravel the riddle of the cosmos; God is left out of it; man is silly enough by himself. The forte of Joe Sandwich is "the lower-case absurd that was [his] native and proper element and [not] the notorious upper-case" (135).[14] Although maybe not.

A man of a small and not too embarrassing South Side family, he had worked his way up by marrying Betty (Naughty) MacNaughton, daughter of a partner in a brokerage, a girl he first noticed doing a 1920s flaming youth parody, dancing the Charleston, even jumping rope with her pearl necklace: "... she would fling her arms into the air and push her hair upward in gestures of utter abandon. These writhing gyrations were all the more sensational because she was a plump girl—and more than merely plump. The implication of this takeoff was that she had herself acceded to a plane of wickedness, even profligacy, beside which that of another day was innocence itself" (58). She wets a finger, tests her hip for heat. Of course she's frigid, or next to it.

Joe is never convincing as a Roman Catholic; happily De Vries lets him lapse into being "a Christian at heart" and a pagan at everything else. When he marries Naughty he attends an Episcopal church to please her, as she attends it to please her mother (who looks pleasantly like a Rose Bowl float). That effectively puts an end to serious religious questions. It's as well: Sandwich's mother's sister had given him a copy of *Pilgrim's Progress* when he was eight; although it is undoubtedly the best book ever written by a Baptist, it has never had much readership among rank-and-file RCs. Further, insofar as Sandwich has any notion of sin whatsoever, his sensibility (or nonsensibility) is Calvinist; the Catholic God (except in the pitiable case of the Jansenist Irish) grades on the curve, and with this rather gentle anthropology sees man as being basically OK but needing to avoid specific sins. Joe, trying to assuage a guilt-ridden mistress (who might snitch on him to Naughty) by working off their dalliances with anonymous Good Works, doesn't believe it can be expiated that way. Of such is Reformation doctrine. Mrs. de Shambles, whose financial advisor he has become at the brokerage, eventually fades, only to come into focus again as one much admired by his rich Canadian uncle Hamilton (on his mother's side). To gain his money he proposes to Naughty that they name the child she's carrying for that heirless horse breeder.

Naughty eventually realizes that this means she has a Ham Sandwich in her stomach, but the idea of wealth prevails, even when the elder MacNaughton offers to restore his son-in-law to his will. Uncle Hamilton, given to speaking only in uncompleted introductory phrases, also has only one consuming but harmless interest, watching late-night movies. Since it happens that Mrs. de Shambles was once Laura Ribble, screen star, whose films are now seen only at that hour, she's a long while realizing that her popularity is owed to her being camp; but when she does grasp it she's only too happy to marry a man who worships her for different reasons. Thus the two of them are disposed of.

Naughty in the interim has grown tired of Sandwich's hilarity, to such clowning as using old rubber stamps to ink varying parts of his nude body: *overdue*, reads one appendage—the same one he likes to hang a tassel on, inviting her to "ring for service." A cousin, Benny Bonner, had analyzed Joe while on his way to a Clinical Psychology Ph.D., this affording many opportunities for musings on the nature of humor, religion, and abnormality. Religion is a refined form of superstition, says Benny, which at least leaves the faithful less afflicted than the unchurched; comics are hostile and anxiety-ridden. This amateurism will no longer do, however, and Joe is sent away—for a rest; he is dealt a gloomy shrink whom he manages to cheer up in a week or so, and with that he is released.

His worst problem has been at work anyway, where his diagnosed disease—possibly psychosomatic in origin—of Ménière's Syndrome is worsened by his having to look at the stock ticker. He gets positively seasick. To save him as much as possible for the job, his father-in-law sets him to writing (away from the Board) the weekly newsletter of advice to MacNaughton and Blair customers; this offers De Vries an opportunity to ridicule the pseudoscience of economics, especially as it is intensified by the use of computers. No sooner does he digest the data into the newsletter from the data—already semidigested— fed him from other sources than the market does just the opposite of what the band of experts had said it was to do. He clothes his opinions in the official jargon: the Inter-American Banana Corporation he says has "streamlined its entire executive structure" and in "July the marketing division will initiate an advanced booking program aimed at minimizing distress sales . . ." and so on (149). But it's all gibberish.

With the aid of computers, the gibberish is filtered into statistical columns that lend to it an odor of science, but they can do no more than that: he and Naughty do work for Sanity, Inc., a charitable sex-research organization, and take home for personal use a sexual graphing device so they can chart their own performance—ludicrously wired, they proceed—only to be interrupted by an important phone call from a client. Their scores—Joe's in particular—are not impressive, but their activity does lead to the engendering of little Ham. Otherwise, it's just plain silly; the bed is a "platter of noodles" (of wire) and he's so greased he feels he's ready to swim the channel. As is said of computers in general, Garbage In/Garbage Out.

Humor is the enemy of the puffed-up, or, as Boston says, "of the ideal."[15] Accordingly, when Sandwich reminisces about a date he had in his youth with a frump who enjoyed Marxist politics and "declamatory poetry of social protest," he discovers that the "girl had no humor, thus the laughs with which people can see themselves through under stress were out of the question here" (120–21). This is a situation noted by Professor J. A. Paulos, a mathematician at Temple University; in order to be able to see humor, one has to be able to hold two contrary possibilities at least momentarily in balance. This, says Paulos, is impossible for the dogmatic personality; for such a one, there is only One Truth (his or her dogma), and all that applies to it is susceptible to but one interpretation. Should there be any subject not related to the dogma, then that subject is trivial and not worth laughing about either.[16]

Then what is worth laughing about for those of us who are normally nondogmatic? Naughty accuses Joe of regarding "mankind as a joke and life as a farce" (143), which seems pretty close to De Vries's estimation of it. It is his way of maintaining a defense, but not—as many would suppose—against insanity, but against *sanity*. That is, if one assumes that Naughty's father is sane, that these serious folk who give their lives to managing stocks for people are sane, then significant numbers of us need some refuge from them, for they control the world. Saul Bellow remarks on such people in *Humboldt's Gift* when he observes that his family thinks it good to be concerned with the cure of foot problems, to be a podiatrist, but useless to yearn to study great ideas and literature. De Vries's defense against this bourgeois sensibility is humor: "One sees it through by frankly and freely embracing the total human farce of which he forms a modest part, a miniscule fragment in a hostile, or at any rate incomprehensible, Whole" (124).

Human life "goes on as it always has, and simply for what it is: a zoo in a jungle" (179). Just as zoos are clarifications of jungle life, they also lead to distortions of it; the animals have time to think, and thus to fall into needless confusion. The gloomy shrink Joe was sent to, who "sat sunk in a thick clump of chins, which gave him the downcast look of pigeons sitting on rooftops in cold weather" (111), is baffled by a logical riddle his patient has asked him. When Sandwich resolves it by saying one can't add and subtract at the same time, the impression given is that a little Logical Positivism will go a long way toward clearing up some of these confusions. About the Larger Questions of Life, unfortunately, the positivist solution is that of the legendary ostrich, a denial of their existence. De Vries seems unable to stick his head in the sand on those occasions where they arise, so he turns to mirth to see him through.

Thus will Sandwich's life toddle on, apparently with a dalliance here and there, even as there was one with Mrs. de Shambles; the next one up seems to be a promising Miss Wigglesworth, a secretary at MacNaughton and Blair, one who bends provocatively away from him and over coffee pots. This is where his portion of the narrative ends. About two-thirds of the way through, Wally Hines takes over, after having been only briefly mentioned by Sandwich as a Psych teacher of his in college. This shift is necessitated in part by Sandwich's death, it being very hard to deal with that subject in the first person. (Arthur Koestler manages it for Rubishov in *Darkness at Noon* by using limited third person, and Moses handles it in the Pentateuch. It's awkward, though.)

Still, the author could have a novel in which there were multiple intelligences—or at least *two* intelligences—working, and not in separate sections; De Vries is more than craftsman enough for that. He chooses not to, however, saying that he's more comfortable with first person (probably because, as John Gardner privately opined, "he's shy"). One may indeed learn what's going on inside De Vries's people (that is, inside De Vries: all writers are solipsists), but one will learn it from the outside. In this case, his wit is a defense against further intimacy, not only with deity, but with humankind. Thus another mind must take over.

Wally Hines is somewhat stand-offish himself, typed by his intended, Gloria Bunshaft, as being a Bleeding Madras type: in contact with other garments the once-fashionable fabric gets spoiled. So he stays away, except from Gloria, who, as a critic, he "liked parts of." She's one of his simple but damnably attractive sorts, one who has "just read the New Testament and loved it" (220). Also, like earlier characters, she mispronounces words: *pancakes* becomes "pangcakes," and *could we* elides into "kwee." In the De Vries canon, this quirk is damnable; and so, eventually, is Gloria. Nonetheless she is attractive as the Dumb Broad: "an archetype, almost a folk goddess, like the earth mother herself, perennially appealing to something in our deepest nature because she fulfills an irresistible need" (226). Conniving as they sometimes are, the one thing these women don't do is think

about; the men of De Vries's ilk do far too much of that, and the
Gloria Bunshafts are a pleasant respite from all that. They illustrate
that here is another, entirely acceptable, way of going at and through
life.

Hines the psychologist has a specialized interest in humor, knows
all the theories, but finds them each inadequate: "Nine-tenths of
what we laugh at answers to Bergson, another nine-tenths to Freud,
still another to Kant or Plato, and so on, leaving always that elusive
tenth that makes each definition like a woman trying to pack more
into a girdle than it will legitimately hold" (230). Because of this
interest he remembers Sandwich from student days; when the Sandwiches meet the Hineses at a Wisconsin resort where the latter pair
are honeymooning, a friendship begins.

Gloria he has married, despite his mother's protests; his mother
says no one respects marriage anymore, but is horrified when she
learns he wants to participate in it, even in his middle age. Were she
not Gentile, she'd be a good stage Jewish Mother, one whose clut-
tered yard reflects the souvenirs of where she has been. When a mistaken traveler stops and wants to buy a stork she sells it; she'll need
the money for her old age, when nobody comes to see her any more.
Wally marries anyway, Gloria having passed his test for compatibil-
ity: "If you can wake up in the morning and look over at somebody
who doesn't make you retch, you have got about all that can be
expected in this world. When we see what is embraced in a railway
station we know man wants but little here below" (234).

Early on, Wally begins to assume that Gloria needs more communion than monogamous marriage allows her, but no details are
offered and he doesn't seem distraught about it, only displeased.
Gloria finds Joe to be a riot, and Naughty and Wally grow in gentle
intimacy as a result; she wonders if he doesn't care about Gloria's
philandering—she's accustomed to Joe's—but he doesn't want to hear
of it. As for her, Wally tells her she knew Joe was a barrel of laughs
when she married him. Well, it has paled. Anyway, she has finally
figured him out: "What he does is *pretend to do what he's doing*"
(314). His victims forget that the shoe fits.

This analysis makes acceptable his demise. There is a square in
the town they are vacationing in, one that cyclists try to get around
in as brief a time as possible. Since one of the turns, if not negotiated,
leads to a hundred-foot drop onto a beach of Lake Superior, it is

imperative that one brake carefully. Joe Sandwich is determined to equal Wally Hines's effort and borrows his bike to try it; what he forgets is that Wally's European model has hand and not foot brakes. Joe disappears, pedaling madly backward, so that in "his green shirt, he was himself like a wreath flung handsomely into space, into a summer air through which it would sail forever as we watched" (324). Local boys fish for dimes as they race for in-place rental binoculars.

Gloria accuses Wally of murder, divorces him. His parting word as she leaves for Reno is, "Nymphomaniac!" Hers sent in reply asks how he would know. Of course Wally and Naughty get together, little Ham—a chip off the old block—making them already a family. Wally, calling death an old folk remedy, decides he's not quite ready for it yet. He'll stick around to see what next will amuse him. Thus ends what may as well be called, in De Vries's own terms, a tragifarce. This term he told Douglas Davis he prefers to tragi-comedy "Because of existentialist shooting for the upper case Absurd, you know, which regards the universe as meaningless and life as a joke, and hence no laughing matter."[17] In the novel he prefers the traditional word, however, when Joe tells a fellow broker that the "common denominator in tragedy and comedy [is] Desperation" (210).

And certainly the death of Joe Sandwich is Absurd, upper case. It is, surely, black humor, a subject not defined by its viciousness, since all humor is vicious. Viciousness is no particular distinction. The difference is that in the garden of black humor there are real toads. The toads are suffering, the people are real. But it's funny. De Vries's humor, says Walsh, has "the end effect [of being] neither negative nor cruel; in fact the comedy has a sad note and the mockery goes, strangely enough, with pity."[18] He has a touch of the black humorist; but he has *more* to him than that.

Mrs. Wallop

Part of his *more* is his sympathy for ordinary folk, well, almost ordinary folk like Emma Wallop. There are very few female clowns, although there are plenty of funny women. Of course they don't carry phallic cigars, floppy umbrellas, hooters, or wobbly canes: what they usually do in their malapropping way is offer false wisdom—that's what malaprops are—that works to ridicule the foolishness of the supposedly wise—Gracie Allen instead of George Burns. Emma Wallop is such a one. (Edith Chipps and Alvin Mopworth of *Reuben, Reuben* were to star in a soap called "The Wallops," but nothing is picked up on that here.) Her problem seems to come from having given "sucker" to a writer modeled approximately on Thomas Wolfe (or perhaps James Jones), one Randall Rivers from Tiverton, Indiana: large, hard-drinking, given to writing in Wolfean purple gushes, he has moved in with her as a roomer-boarder even though his own family lives in the same small city (had to get away from them); his fears are the usual ones for the romantic, he not loathing the "life to be faced because it was so great, but because it was so small" (6).[19] Emma, a widowed practical nurse, sees herself as the central and exposed figure in his book and of course resents it. Her own son is a writer fled to New York, who publishes occasionally, but she has to hear of it from Cora Frawley, mother of a set and costume designer (Emma assures Cora it could happen to anyone): Ralph Frawley knows Osgood Wallop, slightly. *Only* slightly, Emma hopes.

Ralph flies eveywhere, and is "beginning to look more and more as if he could do it without a plane" (11). It's on the increase, Emma thinks: one can't say whether a new baby is a boy or girl—instead we'll have to wait eighteen or twenty years to find out. Oriental wisdom also is in vogue, but she doesn't like Chinese aphorisms because "they don't stick to your ribs. An hour later and I'm hungry for another Chinese aphorism" (10). Astrology goes with it, and it's the bunk, "as any Capricorn with Mercury in his third house knows" (10). And on and on. Louis Hasley has written that while De Vries has been cutting down on the wit from book to book, the frenetic pace of the quips is a distraction so that even "when it comes from the mouth or mind of a character, it is likely to sound like the author cutting in. And, again in a total view of a given work, the reader must sometimes conclude that the events are manipulated to serve as a showcase for wit instead of the wit's being a natural part of the story."[20]

One way De Vries works at bringing it off is by having the narrator intelligent but ignorant, as was Spofford in *Reuben, Reuben*. This mitigates somewhat in Emma's excesses, and the book is helped further by the author finding excuses for her wit. Since she has been the landlady of a celebrity and since Randy Rivers has a Salingeresque hatred of interviewers, she gets to offer opinions on the artist (specifically on Rivers, but really on the *artist*), on society, on art (the

purpose of which "is to get man a cut above himself," says Emma
[19]).

As for "the origins of the artist presuming to look down his nose
at his fellow man" (29), Randall is characterized as descended from
parents who both married beneath themselves—his father by mating
with a hunky, Stella Slobkin, Stella by taking for husband Positive
Rivers, who, although very handsome and distinguished, doesn't have
the financial position he might have had he been less given to shady
dealings.

Emma also makes droll observations about the "Trick and Treat
style" of dress fashionable in the late 1960s among late adolescents,
some wearing bandmasters' jackets because their parents gave them
false values, girls trying to dewomanize themselves. One of this latter
group wears mattress-ticking pants but they fail to cover her forever
agitating rump; she's like a Renault, thinks Emma, with her engine
in the rear. All adolescents are a bit psychopathic, but this one, Virginia Quilty (why the oblique reference to Nabokov's *Lolita?*), a
senior at nearby Appleton (the college Osgood dropped out of), is
almost out of it. Besides that she's well connected, is from glamorous
Evanston, where her father is "a top commuter." But she's a little too
worshipful of writers. Emma tells her of a temperamental floor sander
and the technique of getting it right—something she knows about
because that's the work her husband did; artistic temperaments are
human temperaments, that's all.

De Vries, then, does not finally let the Artist get away with posit-
ing a great enmity between himself and the bourgeois: he merits no
special privileges and is in no way exempted from the ordinariness
of the human condition, a view similar to that of Kafka's in "Joseph-
ine," where a fieldmouse who sings very well wants to be let off
gleaning since she's an artist; when she puts on airs and refuses to
sing, her fellow mice simply cut off her ration—no work, no eat.
Eventually she sings around the campfire anyway, even if she has to
work by day, because that's the way artists are. Like Kafka, De Vries
gets fed up with artists who think they're special; unlike Kafka, his
own personal accommodation has been reasonably healthy. He seems
to be a good literary Matisse, then, a bourgeois artist.

Randy returns to Tiverton for a speech, and nervously tells the
overflow audience that writers of this day seek not moral meaning but
any meaning at all, even the *illusion* of meaning, the "last-ditch

existential consolation prize" (55). When he passes out from too much drink, Emma shepherds him to the hospital and then hides him in her house on his release, where he meets Miss Quilty and Will Gerstenslager, a lawyer friend of Emma's. Will is just the one to keep the press away, he looking so much like Mortimer Snerd that when he says he "doesn't know" something anyone would believe him. Virginia Quilty, less the type who wants to write than wants to be a writer, also wants to sleep with a writer and manages it. Emma gets rid of her by playing on Quilty's Evanston-bred tastes; when the girl is told of the Slobkin relatives of Randy's she's gone.

Emma reflects on her actions with Quilty and decides at Randy's hands they would be psychoanalyzed in the way that "Criminals are unmasked, dogooders understood" (115). Probably it was the sexual jealousy of an older woman for a younger. However Randy might handle it, De Vries has avoided making jealousy responsible by having Emma pass up an opportunity for a roll in bed with Randy, although it was there for the taking; she's not exploitative, and De Vries avoids prurience. And it's well that she did pass it up since her view of Randy changes when he—shocked by her mistake—says it's not *she* he wrote of but his *own* mother. Stella Slobkin Rivers was the punching bag (that's what mothers are these days, says Emma) and not his old landlady. It doesn't save her much, though, because from Cora Frawley she hears that Osgood Wallop has scored with a novella, and this one *is* about Emma. Obviously influenced by a distaste for *Portnoy's Complaint*, De Vries's Emma knows that what her boy has written about is "some sensitive youth unable to make a dime with the girls because of you-know-who" (125).

The middle section of the book is, in fact, Osgood's novella, *The Duchess of Obloquy*. In it Osgood names Tiverton, says it's a God-fearing area, tells of his mother speaking of sperm as a sort of pus, kind of a "number three" (131). Himself he calls Bunk St. Cloud, and, living in Greenwich Village, he has found there that boys dance with boys and girls with girls, just as the Dutch Reformed did back in Indiana. His difficulties, sexual and otherwise, with Mary Hackney don't seem monumental, although her agent, a black named (at the moment) Warshawski, does grate on him a bit; Warshawski does dialects—Irish, Italian, German—until one wonders who he really is. He surely doesn't know. Seemingly he has latent heterosexual tendencies since the baby that Mary abandons to Bunk—they've been living together—is quite dark. She has a six-month road tour, and Bunk is an unwed father. Nonetheless he and the black will collaborate on a play springing from their "joint sense of being pariahs (the one racial, the other cultural) in a community itself already really bad enough" (171).

Since the weekly checks from Mary aren't enough for baby and father, Bunk has to return to work as a waiter; but, finding that no day-care center will accept children from men, he must go in drag to drop off the kid. He's arrested, the baby goes to the mother, and the farce they are living will not be written.

Then it's back to Emma for the last third of the book. She's still mad about the muckraking of mothers: "This primordial life-slime I represent. Pardon *me*. I'm *sorry*. Excuse me for living" (195). Randy is back with her, perhaps from guilt about what he did to his mother (now dead, maybe as a result of his book); and he's suffering from a dearth of fan mail. With Randy and Will she entrains to New York, offering De Vries opportunity to complain about the government's letting the tracks and service go to hell (they dine on cowchips Aquitaine) while Congress flies free on nearly empty Air Force planes.

Confronting her son over the job of matricide he did in *Obloquy*, Emma considers why women become battleaxes, nags, bitches: the female was dealt child-bearing by nature while the male was able to use his free time to "organize the life the female produces," and then she loses even her role in production. Human females aren't distinguished only by being the sole animal of their sex to have orgasms: they also are the only ones to survive their reproductive years. Hence "Nature's supreme product: the widow" (209).

In this role she is free to criticize her son's blamed-on-her guilt: she doesn't think modern America feels much guilt at all, although the Puritans may have. If we did feel guilty we wouldn't let people rot and starve in ghettos or spend their lives in prison among beasts and perverts; the Puritans hanged them and got it over with (219–20). Maybe, but the commentary is gratuitous—unsupported by the story line since the novel isn't about ghettos and prisons. Since no particular course of social action is advanced by Mrs. Wallop, the gibe comes off as something the author probably little intended: a bitchy bit of point-scoring off her son Osgood, perhaps justifying his appraisal of her. It's true that he seems not to have a social conscience, but then neither has Emma till then had one worth noting. Most decent sorts agree, after all, that people are bad who "climb over each other's back for promotion, get rich dealing cancer in the form of cigarettes and death on the highways by manufacturing cars with horsepowers nobody on God's earth needs, to say nothing of concocting a lot of lying advertisements advertising these things with the profits from which we can subscribe our share to a country club costing a million dollars five blocks from where we successfully opposed a Synanon for the rehabilitation of drug addicts in a remodeled old livery stable" (220).

He could as well throw in advertising for alcohol. Something like 10 percent of the drinkers consume 70 percent of the booze; hence advertisements are directed mainly toward alcoholics, to get them to drink a particular brand. Then there's the ugliness of advertising in general, the hideousness of popular music. This latter he does complain of in several works (and usually in context), disgusted by the idiocy and vulgarity of it—even as vehemently as Solzhenitsyn has he complained. Like Solzhenitsyn, he seems not to realize that any one culture is of a piece, and that if a marketplace economy allows freedom in one area that it will allow it in others, too. But the book is not about that, and he ought to stay on subject. Osgood replies to her by saying he's moving in with Ralph Frawley.

Emma meets Pilsudski, the original for Warshawski, and notices he's light brown, something that someone might have noticed a little earlier; if physical descriptions of characters are to be given, they should be offered before the reader has a chance to form a picture to the contrary. She's surprised to find he's homosexual, too, since one thinks of blacks as so "natural"; but she knows by then that New York is full of *them*. From her natural-law point of view she argues with Osgood that it would be better to be nagged by Virginia Quilty— a relationship she's promoting—"than live in peace with a—" (241). She can't complete it, not when it involves her own son; she says only that "the one is with Nature and the other is against it" (241).

To help him she will back a film version of his novella with four-fifths of the $250,000 the stock her husband left her has grown to; she wants to spend it all, but Will won't let her. And a good thing, too: the film is absurd enough to be an arty classic (it opens with a lifeguard calling for help), but those don't pay. Still she has enough left to keep her from having to take in boarders again, although Pilsudski does spend some time with her (causing scandal) and she ends up having a warm feeling for his sort, especially after she maneuvers Virginia into a marriage with her son. Together they'll make a man out of Osgood, and she may marry Will. Marriage at their age seems as audacious as young people living together without it, though.

This silliness may be appropriate—instead of seeking Oedipal or other myths we ought to settle for less since "we are not gods or even heroes, but comic-strip characters" (295)—absurd, but with a little *a*. Pilsudski, doing a Jeremiad for a change, has preached as much; thus it seems in order when Emma suggests we may be becoming a nation of Lotus Eaters. She's even sentimental about the church steeples that are so increasingly outnumbered by the factory stacks and shopping centers: "The less you believe what it proclaims, the more you cherish what it recalls" (209).

Into Your Tent I'll Creep

Continuing to investigate the plight of modern women, De Vries makes the story of Al Banghart and Rose Piano in *Into Your Tent I'll Creep,* which begins in Chicago, a Pygmalion in reverse, she having been a high-school teacher of his, a woman in whose precise talk the semicolons can be heard; to her intellectual friends, who "disparage everything and approve of nothing," he's a find, and he—a factory worker—resents it just a little. So he looks up some old and less-cultured girl friends. These are of no special value to the book except to serve to introduce us to the brother, Artie, of one of them, Tut Carpenter; he's in his fourth or fifth nominal reincarnation as a rock singer, currently having renamed himself The Stopped Up Sink.

De Vries sings, as does Banghart, and has expert familiarity with poetry. Thus the modern musical desert is for him particularly dry. To make it worse, Artie was valedictorian of his high school, is college educated, but still speaks in the old blue-collar dialect. He's not so much the usual mental suicide one ordinarily thinks of rock singers as being as he is condescending to those still ignorant. Banghart complains that he was himself "an *honest* bum, just dirty, not anti-antiseptic. . . ."[21] Artie Carpenter seems to be one of the *nouveau pauvres* fashionable just then on college campuses (the early 1970s), sentimental romantics superficially identifying with the unfortunate.

He uses his guitar mainly as a percussion instrument and sings his words unintelligibly; why De Vries should complain about this latter situation isn't clear.

With Rose Piano, Al is overreaching himself a little; although she's only five years his senior, her cultural achievements are considerably in advance of his. When he misquotes Donne's "Batter Me, Three Personed God" so that it sounds as if it were written in favor of sexual license she corrects him; but then she enjoys "constantly correcting [your] grammar, your opinions about life and letters, challenging you at every turn, it was all part of a pattern" (35). She's a Feminist, but not unbearably so, and they make jokes about sexual hostility.

He's for sexual liberty, even for marriage—just because it's no longer regarded as permanent doesn't make it valueless. She agrees and turns the affirmation to one that includes domesticity, saying that it, too, is as natural as sex (a favorite De Vries attitude); since they are compatible in bed and she likes condescending and he's a climber it's agreed they'll marry. He'll tend the house while she works. Thus De Vries tries out for comic size the role reversal that many women militate for.

They are wed in a double ceremony read by a friend of Rose's, Shorty Hopwell, minister of a liberal church, the other couple being two who are divorcing, for again "Modern Community had made divorce a sacrament" (67). Shorty's obscene sermon knocks marriage; and then, recommending a merger of Christianity with the new paganism if the former is to survive, he offers communion with a Beaujolais with a good bouquet and "a crusty brown loaf flown in from France, but remarkably inexpensive. 'Break and eat, I doubt whether you've ever tasted better'" (71). The Stopped Up Sink, looking like Yeats's beast slouching toward Bethlehem to be born, provides the prothalamion: "She ya gonna gotcha frucks / Alla wella muncha grucks..." (73).

Settled in with Rose teaching at private Classic High, Al talks like a detergent commercial over the back fence to a neighbor whose husband travels a lot. It's easy, his work is done by noon, and it's no more suffocating than the career in the hat factory he gave up for Rose. Women who think running a punch press or meeting one's quota in sales is more fulfilling than housework are fools. Maybe, but what De Vries doesn't mention is that the punch-press operator isn't dependent on the housewife for income—for maintaining the home, yes, and all that appertains thereto, but for income, no. That's a very large distinction since the one with the money also most often has more control of major decisions. De Vries just doesn't face that.

Rose eventually is embarrassed anyway because people are smiling behind her back; besides, Al has become entirely too friendly with the neighbor, Rochelle Landgrabber. George, her husband, has confronted Banghart, but has been confused by the swish act the latter has put on, lisping but asking the while if he too has gotten one of those crank calls accusing him, Al, of being initimate with Rochelle. Every other husband, he twitters, has had one—hasn't he, too? George is only too glad to escape, but as he leaves Rose enters: she has heard it, but is pleased: instead of divorcing her parasite she'll keep him since he's a man, after all. Al gets a job selling door to door.

Affecting a harelip and limp to enlist sympathy, he does pretty well. Their income up, they move to a better neighborhood, one in which he sees Hjnorty (he hasn't shed his daily accent yet) Hopwood. It leads through Shorty and the Sink to a job with a record company where there are two coworkers of Al's, one dewy and rather above-it-all and one fortyish; the latter he can "rap with," Miss Tompkins being "a woman with whom all bets are off, sexually" (115). Damnably, nothing happens with either of them—why introduce them to the reader?—but Al begins to take clients to better and better restaurants as he sells more and more records, and he becomes well educated by the menus handed him like parchment diplomas. After four years of marriage, Al and Rose are on the Gold Coast and far from South Side origins. He resents going back to Feeley's, a steak and chop place he's known of old, but he has to go there with customers who have "discovered" it. Feeley doesn't know about camp and is dismayed, except profits are way up. Rose assures him it's all right, that he's *not* slumming in his own past. She quotes Proust: "Don't you realize that it's neither the same place you went to, nor the same you that went? Can't you grasp that? Have you read the end of *Swann's Way* yet, where it is necessary for Mme. Swann not to appear in the Bois de Boulogne for it not to exist..." (138)—a favorite passage of De Vries's, a favorite mind-teasing concept.

Other troubles are on the horizon; Shorty is beginning to quote with approval certain of Eliot's pious opinions, and they fear he'll be converted. If so, "he would be washed up as a minister" (141). Still, the old caroling group, much mellowed, belts out "Buffalo Gals" on Christmas Eve before unfriendly bungalows; so it hasn't happened yet. Then Al wants to write, shells out for a correspondence course that costs $800, but doesn't know anything about the rich he writes about at first, or whores. Rose could have told him as much, and does. So he goes to find out.

From the rich he gardens for he learns only terms like penis envy, antiheroes, and environmental degradation; but on Division Street it's different. None of the girls seems to have a heart of gold, and in no time he fears he's "picked up a nail." Because MDs have to report such cases to the authorities, he tries a vet. Since it's malpractice if he looks at him officially in his office—Dr. Beansod is doing it only because an overheard conversation allows Banghart to lead him to think he can get him in (or keep him out of) a certain country club—because of this Al exhibits the offending member to the doc on a park bench, just in time for Murphy of the vice squad to catch them. A quick plea of guilty and a fifty-dollar fine and he's home in time for dinner with their guest, the Reverend Shorty.

Shorty, alas, is gone—converted, and fired, of course, since the gabardine crowd doesn't care over much about the Jesus Saves routine. Rose is also about to fire her rhinestone-in-the-rough; indeed, she wants to help Shorty, and takes him East with her when she gets a college teaching job in Connecticut. He has become one of those who have slipped "out beyond human connection—except with others like himself" (178). She knows that otherwise sensible people take leave of them "on the subject of religion. Sometimes a little madness in the realm of faith stabilizes the rest of the psyche" (179). She tells Al that it's Karl Barth who hooked Shorty; because the Scriptures don't quite mesh doesn't mean they aren't true, just as two sane witnesses will differently report an event—but the event happened. After a few half-hearted attempts at suicide—Al still wants to be a writer—he follows her to Connecticut, where the madness continues.

Seeing Rose platonically allied with Shorty, now grown fat, is too much for Al, and again he contemplates suicide, this time by seeking out Long Island Sound, just in time to get mistaken for a member of an Audubon group going out to look at waterfowl among the islands. So he goes... what the hell? But that's eighteen instead of the figured seventeen, and when the catamaran loses one and then the other engine and it looks like they'll sink, that extra one is too much.

Someone tunes in Shorty on a transistor—he preaches in Bridgeport, of course, not Westport—and another sings "Nearer, My God, to Thee," but most significant is the reaction of Fred Laycock, Jr., of Darien: "You live your life doing the right thing, never step out of line, oh, maybe pad the entertainment on your income tax a little or renew a magazine on a special offer intended for new subscribers only . . ." (210). De Vries is very fair, and gives secular jackasses equal time.

Then it's over-the-side time for Al, whose departing line (cf. Barth, above) is sworn by witnesses to be three different and conflicting sets of words. It's shallow, though, and they save him *and* the cat, and it's not long after he comes to in the hospital that Rose Piano is there, too, willing to take him back. Or be taken back. She has discarded a no-account and wants to collect a hero. For once the ball is in his court, and he plays it well. They buy a colonial. He sets up as an answering service and agent for repair and service men; he locates and schedules them, and from their munificent rewards he extracts 10 percent. There's still philandering here and there, but generally he's winding down.

What De Vries has done here is the literary equivalent of the scientific examination of a hypothesis: let's try out this notion in fictional form and if it works out, then it may do so as well in the real life that so often looks to art for its norms, in this case men and women in reversed roles. He seems to think it won't really do, not for long. But it's good for some laughs.

Chapter Seven

The Decline and Fall
of Nearly Everything

Forever Panting

If in *Into Your Tent I'll Creep* De Vries tried out role-reversal, in *Forever Panting* he gets around to that favorite universal taboo of all Romantics, incest. Romanticism is egoistic, and incest is the closest one can come to having sexual intercourse with oneself. The incest in question is only legal, though, not the biological kind; thus De Vries hedges his bets just a little. He's not yet ready for total decadence. (But it's coming.)

Stewart Smackenfeldt, another Chicago Dutch Reformed parvenu, is an actor who does well enough to live in Connecticut, although he needs occasional help from his mother-in-law, Ginger Truepenny, mother of his wife, Dolly, a playwright. Ginger is forty-five, ten years his senior, even as he is ten years Dolly's, and has some money she inherited from her deceased first husband. (She had a second, whom she divorced, the "dreadful Art Buckett, who was said to throw peanuts into the air and catch them in his mouth" [60].)[1] Attractive, lithe—she exercises and even gets Stew to join her in them—and well turned out, she's another malapropper ("He's a pseudo-masochist") who seems unaware of her lure casting. Anyway, she's Dolly's aunt, not her mother—she just raised Dolly and is called "mother"— another hedge: De Vries said he originally had them mother and daughter, but decided against it.

The problem seems to be the moral one between spirit and flesh that St. Paul wrote so much about, although in this case Stew's Blodgett looks likely to be strong enough to force an ontological split as well. For Blodgett is what he calls what would be "the 'old Adam' of Christianity, or 'old man' as the Apostle Paul kept terming it ..." (267). This heavy bear who goes with him eats too much, causing dieting problems for a man who must keep up appearances for professional reasons; he's lost 600 pounds since his marriage, although not all at once. Blodgett has other longings that cause even more trouble, making Stew, when married to Dolly, long for Ginger; married to Ginger he has the hots for Dolly, or for Birdie Truepenny, Dolly's few-years-younger cousin, despite Ginger's saying Whoy for Why, and despite her doing an MA thesis in psychology with him as the subject.

Anyway, Smackenfeldt knows the spirit "is guilty of evils often worse than the bestial variants it presumably bridles..." (4); and he prefers to think of them as two men handcuffed each to each, although he finds it impossible to tell which is escorting which to the state prison. Although the Id has never heard of psychoanalysis, the Superego has—and uses it against itself; the depravity is complete, not just physical. Thus this theme based on 1 Corinthians 5 ("One of you is even sleeping with his mother-in-law") is informed by Calvinism, which was informed by Augustinianism; in *The Institutes* Calvin quotes Augustine more than anyone else except St. Paul. And of course Augustine was a Paulinist (with some Platonist influence, but that may be going too far). It's not a Freudian tune, then, although De Vries admires the man well enough; said he, "I think you have to judge Freud in the light of the validity of his two discoveries— the importance of the unconscious and of sex in our lives. Both of these are corroborated by human experience. The collateral absurdities of psychoanalysis result from its determination to interpret absolutely everything in light of them."[2]

This limited commitment is all to the good since although the basics of The Master are likely to survive yet awhile, the discoveries revealed by Frank Sulloway in *Freud, Biologist of the Mind* show that the underlying assumption of that psychiatrist's work derives from a belief in the "recapitulation" theory of Ernst Haeckel. That "ontogeny recapitulates phylogeny" has not been wholly acceptable in scientific circles since 1930 or so matters little here since the real basis for *Panting* is not Freudianism but Paulinism, and that (along with Platonism) is a perennial favorite. He simply has to mask it for those who don't know Paul. De Vries, whose college education ended about the time Haeckel went out of vogue and who still believes the theory, thus suffers nothing artistically. (His favorite litterateurs—including Stevens and especially Eliot, who is quoted or alluded to in every novel—are also those a bright English major would have studied in the late 1920s and early 1930s.)

Anyway, Ginger is a type that the De Vries narrator finds attractive; trim and stylish (De Vries men notice fabrics, colors, textures), she is "one of those women who manage to be both dizzy and intelligent" (10). People like that also conveniently function as joke-makers; at a Pinter play she wonders where in hell the prompter is. Also she can guess pretty well who the people are Stew happens to be imitating at the moment, while Dolly can't: Smackenfeldt is another of the De Vries men who isn't too sure who he is, which is to say he's very aware that we are all of us actors playing roles—but he's also aware that those who pass for sane *aren't* aware they're playing roles. His superiority lies in his realizing how tenuous is his hold on health. Thus "Smackenfeldt's sanity hung by a single thread: the belief that he was Edwin Booth" (24).

As an actor of Booth's stature, he can then proceed to play any number of other roles, including the one he's in at the moment, that of a priest, Father Plight, in a weakish piece that hasn't long to go. In several of his roles he debates about matrimony, adapting to the institution of marriage Churchill's notion that democracy is the worst system in the world except for all the others that have been tried. Not since Charles Darwin decided to wed has the subject been so thoroughly worked, although with more color than the biologist could mix. (Darwin made two lists—one pro and one con—and toted them up; finding the former ahead, he married.)

His own problems, aside from those resulting from his attraction to Ginger, come from Zap Spontini, an ad man whose work in Additives was so good that he's been made "Vice President in Charge of Subtractives. You know—products containing-no" (53). Zap likes Dolly, who returns the interest, although it's hard to see why: Zap won't join Stew in singing a parody of "America the Beautiful" in which polluters' role in defacing the country is satirized because a number of his accounts include those polluters; and, banality personified, he offers Stew a role in a commercial as an ear of corn. Not only that, he uses *hopefully* without its modifying anything. Occasionally they ask each other to step outside.

Zap sees possibilities in Dolly as a model, and they spend time— too much of it—in the city together. This offers mitigration for what is brewing between husband and mother-in-law; they stay comfortably at home, where " 'Zoals het klokje thuis tikt, tikt het nergens.' As the clock ticks at home, ticks it nowhere" (125). As Dolly rejects him nightly it increasingly seems justified that he allow Blodgett to go along with his Peter O'Toole—his term for his coolly civilized super-ego—and have a go at Ginger. The problem has been to decide which of his desires was to win out; as he has had to explain to Birdie, these conflict. Augustine, discoverer of the Will, could not have put it better. Ginger almost spoils it by saying, "We're mad, do you hear" (141). But he goes on anyway.

Since there are no children involved and since Dolly is herself adulterous, the philandering has no victims other than the immediate participants. Thus they step over the line, which Stew points out to Dolly as being as natural a step—once it's taken—as hers with Zap: "Because we're doing what comes naturally. People rarely do what they don't want to do" (145). While Augustine holds that people *never* do what they don't want to do, there being not two wills but one, De Vries's Smackenfeldt is close enough. The interesting part is that what we want to do, "what comes naturally," suggests that human nature is depraved. And so one marriage ends and another begins. Stew disagrees that he's making a statement thereby—that even a mother-in-law is better than a wife—and he insists it's not a male-female conflict of the kind that moderns seem to feel most acutely, it's only a people-people conflict. Stew marries Ginger.

Certainly there is novelty in the arrangement since in our culture there is between son-in-law and mother-in-law what Radcliffe-Brown calls a "joking relationship." This he says is "a relationship between two persons in which one is by custom permitted, and in some instances required, to tease or make fun of the other, who is required to take no offense." He calls it a peculiar combination of friendliness and antagonism.[3] The instances given suggest that the situation is designed to prevent sexual congress, as with sons-in-law and mothers-in-law where she has almost wifely complaining privileges but he does not have commensurate sexual privileges. Probably mothers-in-law cause more trouble for daughters-in-law than for sons-in-law (it's fathers-in-law who trouble *them*) but there is no son-in-law joking relationship with fathers-in-law; there is no need for it, there being no possibility of coitus between them, no danger of breaking the incest taboo.

Of Ginger and Stew's marrying, their old acquaintances take little notice: "Perhaps too many people were going to the moon and converting soybeans into clothing fabrics and construction materials" (164). Dolly's latest play looks promising, but Smackenfeldt's roles are declining so he gets a job in a corporation. Finding it unendurable, he goes about firing people he has no authority over, but who believe he does; he figures it's a rescue for them. When he tries it on the president, he himself loses his place. There's still Ginger's money, though, so they survive.

Since mother and daughter still get along, they can meet to talk, including talking about Stew. These confabs provide occasions for a number of one-liners, the elder asking the younger if he had told her about his former times—once in particular when "It was Christmas eve, and he was penniless and hungry." This was the time when, in Pennsylvania, he was hitchhiking, "slouching toward Bethlehem" (175). Such digressions illustrate what Hasley calls the problem of our wittiest writer—the problem of undisciplined wit, which here could be defined as unsubstantiated intelligence, disembodied intelligence, a joke with legs. The story, what there is of it, is devised for the sake of a laugh; thus contextual motivation is lacking. With De Vries this is a compulsion (which he recognizes) that no doubt delights his readers, but keeps his art from being all that it could.

Anyway, marriage has decaffeinated sex with Ginger, and now he has the hots for his stepdaughter. Dolly's losing it for Zap, too, as she works again on her play, now faltering; and it begins to look as if it might make it to New York about the time they get back together. Meanwhile Stew has involved himself in a local Citizens Rezoning Committee, the goal of which is to allow apartments in the town, which habitations might have Negroes in them. To conceal the radical nature of his sentiments he speaks in a stage black dialect; he has been tormented as a Dutch kid by other immigrant children, so he is sympathetic. Only the blacks on the committee are amused, and Stew is removed by his elbows from the room. Such rough treatment serves to pop more one-liners and shows he's on the verge of collapse; Ginger calls in a psychiatrist, Doc Pathfinder, who guesses that it's battle fatigue from the sex war, and if the play flops he'll snap out of his current delusion that he's Sir Walter Raleigh. The play, although improved, "just misses" and closes in a week. Thus Ginger has found in Doc a replacement for Stew; her fourth husband will be ten years her senior, even as her third was ten years her junior. Birdie will marry, too, she and her fellow graduate student-husband having found that wedding-gift booty is useful if one would have the wherewithal to resist the materialistic life.

Thus the work is well made, and no one gets much hurt. As for the sex war, Stew (subbing for De Vries) thinks it caused by journalists trying to fill up space: "We've been sold this bill of goods that there's a war going on between us, and, accepting it, we expect hostilities, and so partly produce them. Those self-fulfilling prophecies" (272–73). The sex war is a myth, there being nothing one can "pin on the sexual relations [that] isn't true of human relations in general" (273). Dolly accepts that, although she notes that he does tend to dramatize himself. It's tough being Stewart Smackenfeldt, and he sometimes wonders whether he's right for the part. But he'll play it.

The Glory of the Hummingbird

The waters darken a bit in the next work, one concerned more with public than personal transgressions. The title of *The Glory of the Hummingbird* comes from T. S. Eliot's "Marina," a line that reads entire: "Those who glitter with the glory of the hummingbird, meaning / Death." Jim Tickler, his name derived from the Dutch for bricklayer, has grown up in Wabash, Indiana, and has dreams of the Chicago lakefront. Jim is youngest of eight, his father a pharmaceutical salesman with thoroughly banal tastes—Bliss Carman, the Sousaphone—who in different circumstances might have been more polished. The same could be said for the mother, the believing half of the pair, who drags Oompah (because he plays his tuba in the local marching band) to the nearby Presbyterian church. Jim is embarrassed by them and—the usual thing—is embarrassed by his embarrassment.

Mrs. Tickler is saving trading stamps in order to pay for a divorce; an all-expense-paid trip to Reno is just under 200 books. Her husband meanwhile submits competent verse (probably De Vries's own left-handed stuff) to a writer's colony where his son is on the staff; Jim got his position because the authorities liked his uncompleted (and soon discarded) novel, *Munching on Mrs. Dalrymple*. Once there, Oompah dons beret and polo sweater, pedals a bicycle, and enjoys his leave of absence from McKesson and Robbins, until some fellow writers notice the poems he offered all have been in print already, by other authors, in *Harper's*, the *New Yorker*, the *Atlantic*. Like father, like son—Oompah wants to glitter and bends if not breaks the law to do so; even so will it be with Jim.

While Jim is living with a former college roommate near the old Evanston campus he meets Amy Wintermoots, a Northwestern graduate, and her dad, prominent in something called marketing counseling; Jim offers a name for a new brand of frozen wiener, Hot Diggity Dogs: "Nothing was ever to be the same again" (67).[4] Parties at Amy's house he enjoys, especially since her parents dine rather than eat, and there he meets interesting people, including the well-heeled and round-heeled Mrs. Flamsteed, widowed Limousine Liberal editor of *Consumer Review*.

Tickler begins to write speeches for Jake Wintermoots, the latter being asked because of his prominence to give many of them to the Kiwanis, for business seminars, and the like. Then Jim has to write one for his boss to give at his alma mater, Yuppa Prairie College. The school, somewhere in North Dakota, needs money, and will give Jake an honorary degree; in exchange he is asked to lecture on "Moral Values in a Changing World." The speech he reads well enough, but, alas, few successful businessmen are prepared for question-and-answer sessions with students who ask whether man is instinctively monogamous. It's all over when another asks about his having spoken to the need for "evolving an Existential morality in the post-Christian world" and wants to know what existentialism is.

Jake needs work, although with time he, too, just might glitter with the glory of the hummingbird, which would suit his son-in-law to be, Jim and Amy having decided on marriage after a successful weekend at a local hotel. She opts for a large North Shore wedding even though he has warned her of his uncle who drinks cold coffee right from the spout, of his mother who says irregardless: does she want *them* at a gala affair? She does. Mrs. Flamsteed, among the guests, invites Jim to tour her operation—she says such a visit will be the devil sightseeing a cathedral. *Consumer Review* is an important journal, the humorless Ralph Nader having been their guest the week before. Jim, panting at his own wedding over a guest twice his age, agrees.

Jake (Hopefully) Wintermoots, having decided to seek the Republican senatorial nomination, replaces Jim with a safer and duller

writer. While Amy, now an M.A. in sociology, works late at a settlement house for boys, Jim catches one of Jake's speeches, and sleep-
walks out of it, to the delight of the press. He has to hide out till it
blows over. In the hiatus he thinks of the cracking-up priest in Scott
Fitzgerald's story, "Absolution," a cleric "racked by dreams of the
worldly pleasures he has given up for sanctity." The priest tells a
young boy whose confession he is hearing that "When a lot of people
get together in the best places thing go glimmering." Thus Father
Schwartz is like Tickler, having made, or having wanted to make,
a "sort of Pilgrim's Progress in reverse; as though our young Christian,
his back turned on the City of God, set his face like flint for the
beckoning glamors of Vanity Fair" (137).

And so he does. Jim, typically for the Elect young men De Vries
writes about, lands on his feet and gets to appear on a show called
"Little Red Poolroom." In this show, modeled on "The $64,000
Question" of a decade earlier, Tommy Trotter, bumped by Tickler,
strongly suggests Charles Van Doren, even as the Angela Burwash
brings to mind Alfrieda Von Nardoff. Since the show is sponsored by
a cosmetics company, the producers like to keep on it people the
audience responds to favorably; thus they help them a bit with the
questions they'll be likely to get. Not that Tickler needs much help
with his biblical category, and he wins on his first time out with no
coaching. He knows that butter is mentioned in one of the Psalms,
that *shibboleth* is a word pronounceable to Gileadites but not to
Ephraimites, and so on.

The people on the show *are* learned, but things are relative—like
Pirandello, like Vaihinger: "The illusion is the reality, and vice versa"
(156). To the irony of Tickler's topic being Scripture is added the
irony that the sponsors on opening night push a rejuvenating face
cream, something called New Lease on Life. Tickler's take, over the
weeks, is something in excess of $100,000, but that goes to the
settlement house that Amy works for; his real award is that he has
arrived in Vanity Fair at last; a new suburban street in Wabash is
to be named for him, an honorary degree is offered, he's interviewed,
his autograph is sought. And he and Amy take in a lad, Chip Griswold,
from the settlement.

Thus comes back a sort of character not seen since the earliest of
De Vries's novels, where similar types appeared in one of the out-of-
print works and in a couple of those still in circulation. These are

fellows whose moral deficiencies are matched by elocutionary sins: Chip steals, listens to humanoid recording groups like the Viable Alternatives and the Veiled Threats, and cannot distinguish verbally between such words as *saw* and *soar*. His father deserted his mother, who, unbeknownst to the former, later died of a drug overdose. What Tickler and Amy can't figure out initially, having read no earlier De Vries works, is that it is precisely Jim's rectitude that provokes Chip's hostile acts. This problem shortly will be solved.

In the interim the Ticklers are invited to a White House dinner. Although he and Amy are hardly the featured guests, Jim does get to speak to the Nixons and to the Vice President, whose gimlet eyes skewer him, divining, perhaps, his perfidy. Agnew being one who then presented himself as morally circumspect in the midst of a corrupt civilization, it bothers Jim to be so confronted.

De Vries's digs at holier-than-thou conservatives, people who seem largely the same from generation to generation, are balanced—lest one be led to think that sanctity consists of voting right (that is, left)— by our meeting once again Mrs. Flamsteed. Her sorts are those "who over the years scolded you for taking vacations in Spain and Greece, chided you for buying lettuce and grapes when striking labor unions asked you to boycott them..." (195). Or, in Tickler's parents' day, told you not to listen to "Amos 'n' Andy."

Crisis: Angela Burwash has found Christ and has to make a clean breast of it (this was *before* Colson, wasn't it?); ironically it was her listening to Tickler identify snippets from Scripture that got her to reading the Book and that was what grabbed her. So Jim resigns from Wintersmoots's firm and takes employment with Mrs. F. Her address is at a large house with spacious lawns, but it seems slightly insane inside as she herself does; in the presence of others she tells him that while working for the CIA she found that the Russians were spraying our sidewalks with poisons that would decay us from the feet up. Indeed, it *is* an asylum—she's there incognito checking it out for her *Review*.

This behavior is appropriate, since she is a little wacky, professing belief in metempsychosis, arguing that the "phenomenon of *déjà-vu* is one for which there is no explanation except that we are reliving memories of other existences" (213–14). She errs. Whatever the experience does point to, weird as it is, it is *not* reincarnation since the "already seen" experiences are so strange precisely because they seem to be prerecordings of *this* life, not intimations of some other that has already been lived (unless it is this life that is being repeated, but that's not the general drift of reincarnation). It does hauntingly suggest Calvinism in that it is just when we seem most sure we are freely making choices that one of these damned flashes comes along and says, oh, no, it's already settled: see, here's an insight for you. Then the veil drops again. Calvin gave little space to predestination in *The Institutes*, but it is a feature later generations seized on as typical.

As is true of most of those who believe they've lived before, Rosé (Rosay) thinks she was rather prominent last time around: John the Baptist to be precise, then as now "a voice crying in the wilderness of shoddy merchandise and reprehensible practices" (216). She, too, has been to the White House, with the Kennedys (as were the De Vrieses), although she appears not to have gone to bed with her host—too big a gathering. Like most Liberals, she does not count sex as reprehensible, since it is a personal weakness; Liberals tend to strength on public morality, while being personally predatory; Conservatives are just the reverse. Thus she argues not for promiscuity but for "any legitimate pleasure not destructive to another" (227). She agrees with Russell that "marriage should be permanent if at all possible, but that it should not exclude other relationships" (227). Thus readers of De Vries have an immediate instance of *déjà-vu*, these very opinions having occurred before and before and before.

It doesn't matter. Most novelists write pretty much the same thing over and over. Witty ones will tell the same jokes more than once, reuse an image (breasts like paired door buzzers, say) they find good. The Song of Solomon does it, too. It doesn't mean that here is a mystical glimpse into the noumenal, one that intimates immortality or much of anything at all. It is simply something that comics do, comic writers or the stand-up variety; they do it because their audiences enjoy it, can participate as they anticipate. It is the reason one goes to see a particular comic a *second* time, and every time thereafter. It is why one reads more than one novel by a serious comic writer one finds to be to one's tastes. So we hear once more of Lord Russell.

Usually these sentiments come from someone less asinine than Rosé, generally from the protagonist, or maybe it only seems that it's normal for men to have to rationalize adultery (while intending to keep their marriages intact) but odd for a woman to do so. Certainly it is a clear instance of Puritanism, the esssence of that attitude being Justification; one can do anything so long as it is moral, however perverse one's understanding of "what is moral" might be. This attitude is true equally of secular Puritans, it being a feature more of a personality type than of a religious sentiment (although from time to time the two do merge). Often these scrupulous consciences overwork it so that by the time they finish justifying whatever they want to do, it isn't fun doing it any more. But then no one ever accused the Puritan personality of trying to enjoy life.

Rosé even calls herself a Puritan of the marketplace, although she seems to think that her Puritaism totally transcends the sexual sphere—"where of course we've all been quite liberared" (235). She is of the ilk that, were she an Episcopal bishop, would campaign for abortion and against bingo. Thus with everything squared away she can go to bed with Jim. Says Tickler, she "had every virtue but virtue" (236).

He works hard on evaluating products, condemning even Hot Diggity Dogs for adulterating the product. He comes down hard on wrongdoers, says his secretary. Then Angela Burwash does it, comes clean, confesses, arrayed in a silver gown and seated on a dais; in spilling her guts she thus recaptures the glory of her quiz-queen days, indeed surpasses it. She's enormously proud to be humble, even with every platinum hair in place, while Tickler's situation is a disaster in all areas except for that of life with Chip. Says Jim, Chip's "home life was so traumatic that he seethed with rage at the sight of any house with the composure and integrity of this one..." (251). Now that Tickler doesn't make Chip's own father look like such a bum he's a much more cooperative kid.

Jim hides, waiting the subpoena he knows will come from a congressional committee chaired by a Sam Irvin-like character who quotes and misquotes Scripture and Shakespeare. Even as Irvin secured re-election by a pattern of racist voting so does this one; Jim dreams of telling him this is simply his, Tickler's version of the justifyitng Irvin did—Irvin's racism allowed his return to the Senate and otherwise liberal voting. Of course De Vries is just a little sore that the liberals who lionized Irvin for his work on Nixonian corruption (he wasn't nearly as effective with Korean pay-offs that seem to have gone mainly to Democrats) ignored the distasteful parts of his earlier record.

Even as Irvin gave to Shakespeare a gobbet from Byron's "Don Juan," this chairman gives to Goethe a line that belongs in Marlowe's

Dr. Faustus; wisely, Tickler lets it pass. Then he admits to a deep
and scalding remorse which he does feel, however temporarily, and
he's let off. As for the Van Dorens and Von Nardoffs, nothing happened to them, either, since what they did was not illegal.

Unfortunately Chip—before he reformed—sent an anonymous letter
to Amy in which he told her about Jim and Rosé, he having overheard too much on the phone. Confronted with his liaison with Saint
Jezebel, as Amy calls her, Jim protests that it had nothing to do with
her, anyway: the argument seems to run to the effect that what two
people do with each other in no way affects anyone else. In fact it
would seem not to affect the individuals even in relation to each
other—it just makes the individual feel better or worse insofar as
his own self is concerned. This must be so if the already-seen (*dejà
vu*) argument of De Vries is to be followed out; if there is no personal relationship developed in an adulterous affair, then likely there
isn't much more of one in a marital affair. This may be, but if it's
so then Beckett's depiction of people trapped each in his own garbage
can is realism of a very basic sort. Nonetheless, De Vries has Tickler
say that he has "a sneaking suspicion that adultery has kept more
marriages afloat than it has sunk" (270).

In an interview with Douglas Davis eight years before *The Glory
of the Hummingbird* saw print De Vries was asked about his fascination with adultery and whether he considered it immoral. He replied
that he was being asked how long a piece of string is. It mattered
as to whether there is "a victim, real or potential? And even that
can't be answered in the abstract, only with the closest reference to
the parties concerned. There are good husbands and wives who are
not physically loyal, and there are mates faithful unto death who kill
each other daily. Give us the former any time." He thought adultery
seldom the actual cause of divorce (But is it sometimes the cause or
at least savior of successful marriages?) and he thinks Russell's recom-
mendations are winning out: "marriage should be regarded as permanent if at all possible even though it ought not to exclude other
relations. But that is an ideal that may ask an awful lot of an innocent
person." That is, the nonadulterous partner may not be generous
enough. Anyway, "Marriage remains still the most satisfactory frame-
work for the sexual emotions."[5] One could wish he had never heard
of *Marriage and Morals*.

This tale ends tidily, though, with Amy returning after a brief walk-out and Chip shaping up. Jim gets his job back with his father-in-law, so he doesn't finally find the marketplace economy so bad after all. That is, the marketplace morality follows from the economy, and it is that economy that gives us The Stopped Up Sink, The Veiled Threats, and so on. If something can be sold, sell it. Now that is just what Jake Wintermoots and Jim Tickler do. As a *New Yorker* man De Vries is one of those aristocrats of the soul trapped in a bourgeois world. The people he writes of and ultimately endorses are just those who have turned a neat profit in that very marketplace. So he's one of them himself, their funny apologist. All he seems to be saying here is that the status quo can be maintained yet awhile even without requiring strict marital fidelity. The Decline and Fall, then, is really only a shaking up and sifting out, the same thing that has always gone on.

I Hear America Swinging

But in Iowa? That's where *I Hear America Swinging* happens, the book prefaced by a delicious parody of Whitman—De Vries is in all areas an excellent mimic—that begins with the book's title, and sings of all the swinging: ". . . The butcher singing as he wraps the meat diagonally on the / wrapping paper, never straight, always diagonally / Thinking as he wraps how he will swing with the fair cus- / tomer come nightfall, / The school teacher, also now free and swinging, never / lonely now, none thirsting for love, none a parched vir- / gin ever, / Herself swinging in turn also with the choirmaster . . ." (v).[6] The tentative but rejected cover design had another parody, this one of Grant Wood's familiar *American Gothic* with the dour man and woman ogling each other. The jacket decided on shows a satyr tootling his pipes on the porch of a general store and does as well.

The point seems to be that while the East has gone to sophisticated hell, so long as the heartland remaineth then yet there is hope. Just why sophistication should equate with hell (and plainness not) is a notion derived no doubt from the author's pietistic origins and suave goals, although a moment's observation and reflection should reveal that it need not be so. Although Christian Scripture was written only in *koine* Greek, still it was put together by educated men; and no one can deny that the Nicene Creed is subtle. One presumes these people were pious, too. On the other hand, most of the political monsters of this century have been men of intelligence who lacked education: Mussolini, Hitler, Mao, Amin, Stalin; these are typical of the "worst" who seem always to be "full of passionate intensity."

Yet decadence and sophistication here are seen to go together. Bill Bumpers is from Muscatine but has gone East for an education, then returned to Demeter University in his native state to do a dissertation in some pseudoscience or other on "Causes of Divorce in Southeastern Rural Iowa." (Kathinka Loeser, sometime associate editor of *Poetry* and since 1943 the wife of Peter De Vries, is from the area; through his association with her he knows the place.) But it's not a statistical study and not an anthology of case histories, so his committee says it won't do. The reason it won't do for him to rewrite it, thinks Bumpers, is that it's "a mare's nest, the stuff we call human nature being finally as incalculable as it is . . ." (7).

He can put together some meaningless statistics for them, but no one knows what's going on in someone else's interior. He does want to be a marriage counselor, though, so he can investigate this dying institution of marriage as one who studies the automobile in "neither the showroom nor the junkyard but the repair garage" (9). Since no one cares what the qualifying Ph.D. is actually *in*, he shifts to English, where, Demeter being a progressive school, a novel in the form of a graduate thesis serves as a dissertation. He just renames it *The Apple of Discord*—after the golden one a goddess pitched to Aphrodite, Hera, and Athena—and sets it in Troy, Iowa. Then it's on to Middle City to set up shop and wait for trade.

For a while he does no more than pimp for psychiatrists, sending on to them patients to bed in the interest of therapy. Then comes Hattie Brown, in early midlife, wearing a checkered coat and a straw bonnet hatpinned down and a Scott Fitzgerald sweatshirt. Her husband, Herkimer (Heck) Brown, has fallen in with a fast set that has coffee after and not with their meals, leading him to read the Bible here and there for its literary merits and sending him off to Buster Keaton film festivals. As for dusting the crops, the maid can do it. Things have indeed come to a pretty pass, which is just what Heck names his farm—Pretty Pass.

Next appears Hattie's mother, called Ma, purveyor of Mother Sigafoos's Bloody Mary Mix; she wears granny glasses and a poke bonnet, but only for advertising purposes. A business rival, Ma Godolphin, is mistress of the salon her son-in-law frequents. From her circle he has learned his "inner-city laugh" but it seems to the mother-in-law not to be only a change in styles of humor from olden days: "They *did* their work, is the thing. They didn't knock the work ethic they call it now days. They didn't gallivant; lollygag; fornicate; blaspheme; snooze. They didn't tell you 'Have a nice weekend,' being as how it was Wednesday" (33).

She is aware that in Jeremiah there is a passage that talks about wife-swapping, although she reads it as prophecy instead of as a general deploring of a situation already at hand in the prophet's own day. Bumpers knows better, but this theme, that decadence is perennial, is not developed further; nor is much given to the notion that what Jeremiah called sin moderns call therapy, although it seems certain the people he was railing about thought of it as something like therapy or free expression, too. Ma Sigafoos is a native Iowan, from Dubuque, and knows what's what; for one thing, Ma Godolphin not only covets her Land's Sakes Brands—or the name, at least—but she also wants the Browns' Pretty Pass. She buys them up for agribusiness instead of encouraging the family farm to continue. That's just how wicked things are. Ma says it's bad: "When farmers say look instead of listen, let alone tell you they haven't the vaguest idea, we're through. I mean it's Decline-and-Fall time, kiddies. . . . Fade out to Nero fiddling on the roof" (49).

This all begins to sound as if the author thinks sophistication has gone too far: while it was all right in an earlier day and so long as only certain members of Vanity Fair did it, well, now it has gone too far, like a politician whose values remain constant during his life while the world changes, so that one who starts out seeming decidedly liberal ends up modestly so, if at all. Is De Vries a literary Hubert Humphrey? Possibly, but probably not. What is more likely is that the "national slightly bohemian suburban bourgeoisie" that is De Vries's subject for analysis now and then needs a new sort of needling—even in Iowa.

Bumpers suggests that Hattie allow the fallow-lying of Heck for a few months, but with the proviso that he read the Bible all the way through. Ma Sigafoos hopes maybe he'll turn a Malcolm Muggeridge. It doesn't happen, of course; De Vries can't manage Christians like that, that famous British journalist being neither himself a fool nor one who thinks Christ was. What does happen is that Heck discovers

concubinage was common in the days of the patriarchs and beyond;
so he moves a local sculptor, Opal Kitchener, in with them. She
works out fairly well, doesn't mind or mock the souvenir pillows.
Certainly she's against the puritan sex ethic; when she says it has
to go, Heck agrees and says the same is true for the work ethic. The
arrangement wears thin after a bit, but Hattie takes to the hired
man who's doing Heck's work; she wants him to do Heck's night
work, too, and moves him in. Clem Clammidge moves in as Opal
leaves: "I know it isn't exactly what you had in mind," Hattie says,
"but it *is a ménage à trois*" (64).

Unfortunately the new decadence is far-reaching, and Clem leaves
his chores for work evaluating local art galleries. He functions as "a
counter-irritant" to primitive art; he's a primitive art critic. A chap
named Kublensky "aimed at a progressively more drastic refinement of
the principle of minimal form" (70) and achieved it by putting up
labeled pedestals with nothing on them; two of them, *Mrs. Rumple-
meyer's Flesh* and *Feigned Orgasm*, soon had red stars pasted on the
labels—sold. Called "the Grandma Moses of exegesis," (70) he's an
instant success. How a hired hand is so quickly transmogrified is not
made clear but it does allow the author to lower the teeming level of
his wit basket.

Clem being no further use on the farm, they next try Charlie
Achorn, one of the half-dozen local shirtsleeve philosophers who sit
around "on tilted chairs encircling the Today's Special bin at the
supermarket" (78) kicking Kierkegaard around, as well as Jaspers,
Heidegger, Husserl, Camus, Sartre, and, whenever Ham Abernathy
gets his lick in, Vaihinger. Abner Teasdale fancies Eliot, as someone
always does. From among them Hattie takes Charlie to work on her
modern Brook Farm, a place similar to the original in that no one
there wants to work; but the sexuality is a little more frank at Pretty
Pass, and no one drowns. Otherwise it is still the same as Hawthorne
found it to be; literature and manure don't mix. Heck, worn thin by
life in a utopia, can hardly wait for a break at St. Tropez. With Charlie,
there are now four in the family bed.

That number quickly recedes when Clem moves out, he being in
danger of losing his job because of creeping sophistication; the sow's
ear has become a silk purse, and, caught between his two personae,
he knows not which mask to wear. Fortunately Bumpers meets an old
friend, Artie Pringle, who's into the occult, to include orgies, and

Bumpers is invited. Typically, the episode is not erotic. As Hasley observes of De Vries's work, "Of sex there is a great deal. It inspires numerous witticisms, a few of them bawdy, besides having generally disruptive effects on the lives of the characters. Sexual impulses drive the characters to marital infidelity, deception, quarrels, and alcoholic truth sessions, as well as occasional divorce. Of prurience or eroticism there is never a line."[7] In this instance it's mainly disgusting, leaving Bumpers with the "suspicion that this was probably the last moist heap" to which he would be asked (121).

He does get Clem set up on the touring circle with Archie, though, and he meets Archie's rather pure secretary, Claire de Lune; she won't even join the Baredevils, mainly because she already has a boyfriend. With Ma Sigafoos he tries to reclaim values by going with her to her father's old church, but, alas, the cleric is a clown who reads the Twenty-third Psalm the way Charles Laughton would, and so on. In the basement brunch, called Aprés Church mothers talk of their daughters' no-fault pregnancies, of their work as whores during their Non-Resident Terms at college. Nothing much left there.

Bumpers is torn between an erudite waitress and Miss de Lune (her first name was her parents' joke), but the former ruins it when she calls herself a counterperson, talks of chairpeople and even of personkind: Bumpers has the same respect for English as has De Vries, and turns to Claire. He attends a black mass, invited by Pringle, and has misgivings about receiving the vaginally intincted host, but accepts on the Calvinist ground that he doesn't believe in transubstantiation anyway. Then, in a scene reminiscent of the passage in Hawthorne's "Young Goodman Brown" where the man sees his bride also in attendance at the Satan worship, Bumpers spies Claire. She's going to strip on the diving board and join the Baredevils, having broken off with her boyfriend. He can't watch, but when she has toweled off and suited up for a while—before the orgy begins—he persuades her not to take her final vows, and to go off with him instead. As Lord Russell points out in *Marriage and Morals*, if you add sex and jealousy you get marriage.

On their honeymoon he watches the leaves patterning on the motel ceiling as the streetlight plays their shadows so, and, his bride asleep beside him, reflects on his first love, a Greta Vermeer. When they were newly out of separate colleges, he spent some time under such a tree with her. Earlier, cycling her at age twelve to a catechism class at her Dutch Reformed congregation, they had an accident. His snazzy bike was hurt somewhat, but not they. She had been rehearsing her dreadful theology without internalizing a drop of it while he sweetly and chastely adored her. Now he knows that "Intellects who make a profession of explaining to us what we are about tell us that romantic love, classically so-called, is an idealization of the desired sexual object generated by a delay in its possession." But he thinks it's more than that, that "at some stage of the game at least idealization is instinctive, waiting on nothing" (207).

How is this to be read? That De Vries is one more American writer who isn't comfortable with adult sexuality? No great writer in our canon seems to be: not Hawthorne, Melville, James, Twain, Crane, Dreiser, Hemingway, Faulkner. They're all like Salinger's Holden Caulfield, trying to keep their little sisters pure and on the merry-go-round and when they can't do it going mad. They resent not being allowed to stay in what they imagine to be the Garden. Since these authors are American, and the critics and readers who hallow them are American, it must be that this is an American sentiment. How to get back into the Garden?

Some (like Archie Pringle and his Baredevils) take off their fig leaves and hope to reenter thereby. All that results, of course, is that they are naked; humanity cannot copulate innocently like animals—humanity can't do anything innocently. It is a strength of De Vries's that he realizes this even as he sentimentalizes about Greta Vermeer; he sees no Christian solution to the problem but rather sees it only as the human condition. It's not a problem, for in the word *problem* is implied the word *solution*. It is simply a situation.

And thus as Claire dreams beside him he dreams too while he looks at the shifting shadows, recalling that Greta Vermeer had married early and divorced early, that she lives in Muscatine, or so he has heard. On their way back from their honeymoon near Fond du Lac they just might route themselves that way.

Madder Music

Robert Swirling is a typical De Vries character, with a Dutch Reformed background (né Zwirling) that blights with guilt his sexploits. He varies only in that at forty he's a little older. The usual terminal satyriasis is there. And this makes for his distress, that and the Calvinist theology that may prompt it. He longs for a Catholic background and the gentler anthropology that goes with it, theirs being a deity that maybe sees the Fall as less disastrous and man not a total wipe-out; or maybe the Catholic God just grades on the curve— with any kind of luck you might make Purgatory with a D or even a D— and thence eventually on to Heaven. Not so with Calvinism, whose God grades Pass-Fail, but not the easy P-F of current academe and liberal religion, but a sort where everyone deserves an F, and God gives a P to those whom He chooses, to His Elect. Swirling senses the vote has gone against him. As a Catholic it would be

Twenty Hail Marys and the thing is done. But as a Calvinist, that Puritan doubled in spades, that unexorcisable Pauline bluenose scourge of the flesh, as a Calvinist with your catechism not only in your brains and your guts but in your very balls, the guilt is unresolvable. The check is never paid. Nothing on account will stop the dun on your conscience. Somebody else must foot the bill. Of course somebody else had—that was the atonement in which the Catholics also believed, but somehow they could see it as all marked paid and forget about it and enjoy them- selves. Or so it seemed to Swirling. (153)[8]

The novel's title is one that Alvin Mopworth had for his unfinished book on Gowan McGland but there is no tie-in to that here; it's part of the most famous poem of Ernest Dowson (d. 1900) in which the speaker remembers an old love even while embracing others. Swirl- ing's guilt, not fully perceived at the opening, has evinced itself in his Marxist conversion: his wife complains that her husband thinks he's Groucho. And indeed he has the maddening patter of Eliot's favorite comic (the two, Eliot and Marx, met and enjoyed each other only shortly before the former's death). The psychiatrist asks the wife what "does Freud find the two basic human drives most released in humor? Sex and aggression. And what is Groucho's chief stock-in- trade? Lechery and insult" (9).

Swirling cracks up at an NAACP benefit at which he was to play Marx; his wife for a time went along with the scheme, was even his foil—she was an actress manqué—but no more. It all began when Swirling had found and read a hidden letter of condolence his wife, Enid (who smokes cigars), was preparing to send a friend. He thinks it's for his own funeral; she wrote their wedding ceremony, after all.

Enid, arriving, interrupts his reverie to tell him Becky Tingle has come with her, that he should come downstairs—this may be the day she finishes a sentence. Becky is short and militant, a realtor and one who goes to "improvement" classes; at the moment she's in on one that includes a discussion of Eliot's "Prufrock," and the De Vriesian Swirling can't resist dropping in. This allows the author his chance to get his lick in, giving credence to the notion that just as literary critics often are frustrated poets and novelists, so are poets and novelists often frustrated literary critics. Swirling's own life meanwhile is being measured out with coffee spoons, with little left in the cannister.

He and Becky leave the class together, and the inevitable happens. His and Enid's is an open marriage, the unlatched gate to which he thinks his wife has swung open a time or two—so there's precedent. His collaborator almost spoils things when she whispers in his ear that he's "making Becky Tingle," but he pretends he hasn't heard: "He was no Prufrock, nor was he meant to be" (56). He reflects that perhaps all this has been agreed upon by Enid and Becky anyway, but he's glad to get it under any conditions; thus "they rushed together into that First Garden to which kind nature lets us intermittently return, the primordial Eden to whose gates Sin—so far from being the cause of our exile—is often as not the very key. What rubbish! And how deliriously true!" (57).

Hers is a garage apartment and Swirling has to avoid being seen by the landlady, Mrs. Pesky, and there is much *Angst* involved, although it is only by Becky's (or someone else's) delectable privates that sense is made in his world—"that slashed plum, that halved strawberry, that succulent bivalve about to swallow him whole . . ." (63). Even if it's exurban existential nonporn, it's exciting, anyway, and convenient once her brother, Pomfret, leaves for a while, except she calls him Bobolink and says *Sheesh!* He does wonder why he feels guilty if he has Enid's tacit approval. When Pomfret returns they tryst at a house listed only with Becky's agency.

But they are undressed when a woman from another agency comes to show the house to Enid. She finds them in the closet, and thus he learns he isn't dying; no, it wasn't arranged between Becky and her, and no she wasn't keeping a secret the doctor told her. He complains that he forgave her her affairs, and that pops Enid's cork; such forgiveness implies something needed forgiving. She begins to see Leo Ludlow, whose marriage also is breaking up, although not because of Enid any more than Swirling's is ending because of Becky. When Becky blackmails him by saying *she* might not have long to live, he marries her. They rent from Enid the house Swirling formerly has lived in with her.

Even as Becky is a syntactical cubist, breaking up and rearranging sentences, Pomfret is a stylist, a mannerist of the decadent sort, given to noting such things as that the quality of murals in restaurants parallels that of food in museums. Given to English affectations and never to work, Becky's double stepbrother is no blood relation at all; but he is terribly precious, a Prufrock who *just doesn't care*, and Swirling would like to suck his guts out with a vacuum-cleaner hose. Instead he gets the village wit a job as an extemporaneous poet at a newly opened sophisticates' cabaret where Pomfret does very well. Bob and Becky share a table on opening night with another newly-wed couple, Leo and Enid. While Becky and Pomfret dance a bit, Swirling hits it off with another entertainer, a folksinger called the Miller's Daughter, putting her on to sublet Becky's old garage apartment.

Naturally it isn't long before Swirling is sitting listening to Julia (Miller's Daughter) Griswold play her zither, both he and she naked. He decides he's unsuited for either monogamy or adultery—bored by the one, made guilty by the other—but he gets on well with Julia, who compliments him for finding the combination of her safe, allowing "deep orgasms." Should he change? No, "Life has no destination, except the old glue factory, so enjoy the ride" (126). He will continue in his morality, to enjoy such pleasure that causes no one else pain. His guilt pales, anyway, when he catches Becky and Pomfret enjoying each other incestuously. (Does that cause anyone else pain?) The fault is his, anyway, Becky indignantly asserts, for having such bad grace as to catch them at it.

Swirling, feeling guilty, does what he usually does in such circumstances: he visits his father at Maple Lodge, a church-run home. His father longs for the three-generation household, but how can his son "explain to his poor old church-elder father what they all were there, now, in the notorious suburbs: the Bohemian bourgeoisie" (140). Becky has never even met him, nor he her mother.

The return opens up the possibility of religious debates, something Swirling ought not to have to go through—nor should De Vries think his readers need it—especially since the debates are the ones current in the early years of this century. Fortunately, Mrs. (Honk if you love

Jesus) Pesky has a mind formed about that time, too, and she hits it off with Swirling *père*, especially as the son has caused the father to lose his faith; this gives Mrs. Pesky a mission. At a delightfully vulgar service even the son is converted, *pro tempore*, and his father soon sells for $50,000 a pot-cleaning device he's patented. Everything thus is tidy there.

But with fifty or so pages to go, something has to happen. It does. Swirling gets involved with a black girl, Pauline Winchester, who works at the Museum of Modern Art to which Swirling might be able to sell his Jawlensky (the till then unsuccessful blue Russian painter). Once she begins visiting his garage apartment it's only a matter of time till his "mother" (stepmother, that is: Mrs. Pesky has married Dad) catches them. Pauline gets out of it by pretending in an audacious drawl to be the maid. She does think Swirling a little old to be hiding, and she gets in a De Vriesian lick against liberal hypocrisy, how they think it's fine "when it's a Cause. Out there. When it's majority rule for Rhodesia, way out chonder, and civil rights in Mississippi here. But when it strikes any closer to home than that, it's no go" (177). Her scathing is Pauline indeed.

Swirling's coming out for meaningful open housing does lead to an NAACP benefit at which he is to be Groucho. He gets into it a little too deeply, loving the license granted, but he gashes his shin on a step while fleeing an outraged husband and has to be taken to the hospital. Although he's not in serious condition, his heart is fibrillating and, asked by a nurse whether he believes in God, he says, "I'm dying to meet Him" (201).

And when he is reborn, he *is* Groucho. Dr. Josko suggests they traumatize him back to his senses, and Pauline cooperates; she'll seduce him anew (as Groucho he doesn't recall Swirling) and then claim pregnancy, reinforcing her dismay with a six-and-a-half-foot-tall "brother." Fleeing from Jumbo leads Swirling to make such jumps and leaps (on to roofs, down drainpipes) as brings him home to his senses. But on resuming a normal relationship with Pauline he finds she *is* pregnant. He'll marry her, even if it is Groucho's child.

When they get a house that Becky sells them, Pauline invites Becky to share digs till she gets a decent place of her own to stay. Swirling subsequently finds them unabashedly enjoying each other sexually. So blacks are no better than whites, he reasons. Then Pomfret returns and with him a buddy named Buddy; that makes four who romp together. This time Swirling escapes into W. C. Fields. Humor is indeed a way of handling heartbreak.

This seems to be the way not only for Swirling, but for his creator as well. Assuming the psychologists right when they say that we are all of us two-faced, one can see the fruit of this by looking at a picture of De Vries. The right half of the face is the part of us we present to the world, the left shows how we really feel about things—assuming right-handedness, that is. Since most of us notice only the right half of anyone's face, one who looked at De Vries would see the right half of a comic mask; doubling it over would give us a complete comic. The left side of his face, however, is half of a tragic mask. De Vries is right-handed, and laughs.

Richard Boston has written that the first use of humor is "for the relief of pain. When one thinks of the funniest people and the greatest laughers, what is most conspicuous about them is their melancholia, and it is from this that their laughter springs. Dr. Johnson is a classic case, Byron another. Mark Twain, who must have been one of the most consistently funny people who ever lived, was a desperately unhappy and guilt-ridden man (he himself said that the source of humor is not joy but sorrow). Even the apparently sunny Sydney Smith was melancholic."[9] Smith is once mentioned favorably by De Vries in a frontispiece, where he quotes the Englishman's request that a certain cleric not assume Smith isn't serious just because he's funny, even as the cleric isn't serious just because he's grave. What, then, is the drift of De Vries's seriousness? Look to what he said about James Thurber.

Thurber, admired by De Vries and helper of De Vries, was said by De Vries to write mainly of the Comic Prufrock, indeed to *be* the Comic Prufrock. This was in one of the two essays he thought enough of to include in *Without a Stitch in Time.* Apparently De Vries thought the master had covered that field well enough for him to plow elsewhere, or maybe it was only that Thurber's tendencies were toward paranoia while De Vries's incline much more in the direction of schizophrenia. That's why Swirling and all the others shift so easily from one personality to another. And they are not Comic Prufrocks; they dare to eat the peach. The result is sheer disaster, although one way or another his folk manage to live with it. They are Prufrocks who express themselves.

The pleasure that hurts no one else seems hard to come by, all of life being a web. Anyway, whenever was there a pleasure without a pain (food is best when one is hungry, etc.)? De Vries produces, deplores, meditates, celebrates a garden-variety decadence. Although the modern situation needn't be so read, and any number of social anthropologists, etc., see in modern turns of events much that is salubrious, and predict a general upturn, De Vries has difficulties with it that, no doubt about it, come from his religious upbringing. Roderick Jellema says he "is a masterful religious clown whose comedy of escape is always a failure. He always ends up where he started. What he gives us is the comedy of Original Sin."[10]

Because his life began somewhat like Bob Swirling's he, like Swirling, has a sort of binocular vision that enables him to compare cultures much more acutely than can the ordinary social anthropologist. Wesley A. Kort, writing in *Shriven Selves*, sees this as coming from the immigrant isolation in Chicago and the "slick, nonreligious, enlightened mentality" of Connecticut. "What De Vries has not been able to do in his fiction is to suggest that the Chicago origins, with their incestuous cultural and religious inversion, are all bad and that Eastern exurbia, with its forms of rebellion and relativity, is all good." He "sees the uncertainty of moderns less pathetic than the Fundamentalist mentality he deplores." Something in each holds him: in the old life, it was their belief; in the new it is their "tolerance and honesty." He can't put them together, though, says Kort, since "Religious convictions and contemporary uncertainty cannot be easily joined" and he spits out of his mouth as distasteful the religious humanism of Laodiceanism.[11]

To be truthful, he has put them together pretty well—in his fiction. He has had time, and has taken time, to prepare a face: a tragicomic face. A lot of people like it. They are used to seeing something like it in the mirror.

Chapter Eight
Remarks from a Slanting Deck
Consenting Adults

Consenting Adults or The Duchess Will Be Furious (1980) was originally to be called *Venus on the Half Shell* until De Vries learned a Vonnegut character had already used the title. Since there was another book called *Consenting Adult* (singular), he decided to append the part about the duchess's fury to the new title. Actually the duchess isn't all that important to the book, although as the local artist/aesthete who is married to a doctor (only a chiropractor, really) she does help set the tone of Pocock, Illinois. Teddy, or Puck, or Punk Peacham does not, he having a father given to a close facsimile of yearly winter hibernation; but Punk is a familiar enough De Vriesian narrator, embarrassed by his origins and hoping to do better. The duchess does ride his consciousness, though, and is the sort of mother he would adopt. She serves as an intelligent older female, needed now and then to set things straight.

One oddity in this one is that while the topic throughout is marriage, it is not till the end that Punk weds Columbine, one of the duchess's many children. It is familiar enough in other respects, to include mention of favored literary figures—Santayana, Stevens, Eliot, Pound, Housman, Hardy, Forster, Beckett, Sartre, Descartes, Schopenhauer, and Magritte to name a few. Their mention is relevant to Punk's tendency to teeter on the edge of the existential abyss, a vantage which he invites Columbine, some years his junior, to share. Mrs. d'Amboise points out a familiar De Vries code, that women generally do not care for such a pose: "That's another difference between the sexes. Men flog their brains about these questions, but has there ever been a woman philosopher? We're the custodians of life who dislike its being questioned. We don't like to bring it into the world only to have it doubted" (25).[1]

Colly does not like Entropy. It's bad enough that there are "galaxies of galaxies whirling in a mad void..." without there being any Mind of God from which they sprang (22). Still he goes occasionally to their weekend place, By a Dam Site, just below the Michigan border; in Pocock that's as much sophistication as is to be had. During much of the book, though, Punk gets on with the consequences of his "illusionectomy," settling into a sort of Protestant Atheism: "There was no God and Jesus Christ was his Son..."(29). (Catholic Atheism holds that "There is no God and Mary is His Mother.) Part of the consequence of it being an Einsteinean rather than Newtonian (or Aristotelian) cosmos is a sexual frenzy; says one of the duchess's sons, Ambrose (to Punk's Augustine? No.), "This was all predicted by Pascal. Pascal said that the loss of God would lead to two things. Megalomania or erotomania, or both" (195).

It begins with Snooky von Sickle, built like a Clydesdale—which attracts him, and he's attracted still more when he learns she's an heiress. But she and Ambrose eventually ally, although later, in New York, the old "pre-existing nonconformity" of Punk is invited back in, and they enjoy her *en sandwich*, during which passage the writing turns as close to lascivious as De Vries has ever come. For a time the relationship looks difficult, but they are moderns and resolve that their "triangle was going to work because we were going to *make* it work" (177). Then Punk falls madly for the Peppermint Sisters, a set of identical triplets. At first they think they will talk it all over "like six intelligent people," but instead give it up: Snookly will stay married to Ambrose, they will never know whose son it is she bears, and Punk returns to Columbine.

Before that occurrence he had a fling at Officer Kathy Arpeggio, a New Woman who was briefly a daughter-in-law to the duchess, whom Punk wants to take *in uniform,* gunbelt and all. He daydreams an orgy with several New Women, something like a female set of "The Village People" (except for being more masculine), but it doesn't happen.

Other currents play through, among them the specter of a fellow named Skimpole and called the Prophet. His business mainly is to issue Jeremiads, something prophets alone are allowed to do *non sequitur*, or, more precisely, in a fashion that otherwise would be decried as *deus ex machina*. Besides predicting a flash flood, a burst gas main, and the Mayor's ruptured appendix (90), he holds forth on the general decadence of the affluent: "...the Lord will say,

'Screw your portfolios, what are these things to me in which ye have put your trust, yea the fly-by-night growth stocks someone let you in on the ground floor on, the electronic shares that skyrocketed from 8½ to 2¼ ...'" (46). Further he warns that "... if the works which are done in thee had been done in Evanston and Westport and Sausalito, they would long ago have repented in sackcloth and ashes" (45). And "'Up yours,' saith the Lord God of Hosts..." (119). It is these, of course, that are the truly revelational notes in the book: the reasoning is atheistical, and the Word provides as nice a counterpoint as any Evangelical might desire. That sort has ever seen Reason and Faith as contrarities, and so does it occur here. By couching the proclamations in obscenities De Vries at once manages to amuse and to get away with warnings.

And what of those who are neither Evangelical nor much bothered by Entropy? At the highest levels (those found, one presumes, in Evanston, Westport, and Sausalito) it amounts to eating cherries jubilee, and trying to ignore other difficulties. At a lower level, it amounts to attending Rotary. It is people who give "financial reports at the Tuesday luncheons at the Holiday Inn," it is being "fully cognizant" and filled with "increasing awareness" (210). These are the people who go about furtively searching the crevasses of couches, publicly urging their allies to make their sales achievements such that this will be "a banner year." Thus De Vries writes that "There is something to be said for insanity, always granting that being a secretary-treasurer is the norm" (215).

In other words, humor is a defense against sanity. America he thinks of "as polarized between two sets of James brothers... Frank and Jesse at one end and Henry and William at the other ..." (210). Say that to a secretary-treasurer and see what you get.

At the end there occurs marriage to Columbine, virginal and suffering from anorexia nervosa; presently she gains weight and becomes pregnant, so the way of the feminine, of the yea-sayer, does triumph, at least in the cosmos that is the creation of De Vries.

Sauce for the Goose

This is especially true in *Sauce for the Goose*, although without the masculine agonizing; since it is written from the point of view of a female that much is spared us. Daisy Dobbin does have her identity crises, but they deal more with her than the universe. In particular she assumes, because of a playmate's catty remark, that she is adopted; nay, she prays it. Her mother is one who goes frequently from Terre Haute, her home, to Grand Rapids, because "that's where it's at," and her father is no better. Even Daisy spent three weeks there once for the famous Meatloaf Writers Conference, almost developing a relationship with a homosexual young author named Scudder, but he is dropped and never reappears.

At Kidderminster College she is friendly with Bobsy Diesel, known for her ineptitude in bed as *Lay Misérable*, and it is this Bo who gets Daisy a job working undercover for *Femme* to ferret out matters of sexual harassment at various journals. She does find it, but not always in the way she had expected. After working on a Long Island weekly for some years after college she is on the fringes of thirty, and on the fringes of publishing. Disconcertingly the born-again atheist Daisy frequently finds middle-aged Christian men pressing tracts upon her. (Technically she's Episcopalian, "that most tepid of denominations," which church she dreams one night has "been bought by Minnesota Mining in a much-touted takeover" (48–49).[2]

At the opposite extreme is Dog Bokum, "who thinks *Playboy* glorifies women, and who glorifies them himself by taking them out for what he calls lunch-hour quickies, or nooners" (65–66). There is also the owner of *Metropole*, Dirk Dolfin, a Dutchman who owns ventures from Amsterdam to Curaçao, who is well dressed, suave, and competent. Both of the men seem to be De Vries, perhaps De Vries in light and dark varieties, like Heineken's. Daisy's old enemy, the one who as a child said Daisy was adopted, has set her cap for Dirk and plans to marry him as soon as her divorce is final. This makes a problem, for Daisy is soon sleeping with Dirk, even before she finds out if there is a promotion in it for her. Bo Diesel is not happy about that and makes her own play for Daisy. Does this mean those most pressing for Women's Liberation are like Bo, a militant feminist "beating off men who weren't trying to get to her . . .?" (36).

It does seem so, since although De Vries argues forcibly for equality of fornicatory opportunity, he also says, "Men are rivals; women, enemies" (99). This is in reference to the old childhood enemy-friend, Effie Sniffen, now Daisy's rival for Dirk; when Daisy sees her at a hotel with him, she feels as though she's been kicked in the stomach. This scene follows one in which Effie assures Daisy that she does indeed know the difference between infralapsarianism and supralapsarianism, these being topics Dirk likes to bring up as pillow talk. His grandfather was a dominie. If Effie knows that the latter means God predestined (instead of only *allowed*, as in the former) the Fall of man from grace and before the Fall chose the Elect (instead of afterward, as in infralapsarianism), if Effie knows this then she has learned it on Dirk's pillow. A kick in the stomach indeed, "sexual harassment at its worst" (100).

Ultimately Daisy settles down, learns she's not adopted, marries this forty-year-old Dutchman who "has twenty-two suits and always stands as though he's being measured for a twenty-third" (197). Harassment and exploitation are eradicated at *Metropole*, "without dethroning Eros" (217). There is even an authorial statement that although "Right wing politicians raise their snouts from the public troughs long enough to call for a return to God" they could be correct for once, for "high time it may well be" (217). She has had an encounter with Dog, "the moral mongrel," and Dirk has had to see it's no different from his liaison with Effie. Thus declared equal, they marry.

Marriage is the one constant in De Vries—that is, it's the one *approved* constant; it, too, is questioned, as is the basis for everything else, but marriage is the one unity he sees as fundamental and constant. It is not a matter of people's finding in it a small refuge or a cosmos out of the great chaos, but rather it is the basis for everything else that stands. Such is the ultimate analysis of the thrust of De Vries's writing. The penultimate point to be made is that he is a serious comedian of manners, one who fled the Celestial City for Vanity Fair and that he is very good at remarking what he has found there and that this in itself is quite an achievement, but the ultimate is that what is working here is something like a metaphor found in The Song of Solomon.

The book of Canaanite love poetry was allowed in scripture because it was attributed (wrongly) to Solomon and because it was susceptible (for Hebrews) to interpretation as a parable of God's love for His Israel, or (for Greeks) as Christ's love for His Church. De Vries is susceptible to the same sort of thing; love leads to marriage, and marriage survives. Nothing else in the world makes any sense, except that we are only a random collision of atoms—and the atoms themselves don't seem too substantial these days. Ordinarily this absurdity matters little, paralleling the life one lives from coffee spoon to coffee spoon. Then, if one finds love, all is transmogrified into something worthwhile. If that love be lost, then the world is no longer the old humdrum place but is an insane asylum kept by a madman; marriage is the stay against that. No one can live very long at the keen pitch of romantic love, although many try to do so by going through a succession of such loves, an exercise that is bound to lead to something like one's becoming a Dog Bokum, obsessed finally more with sex than with love. Marriage stays that.

Man's love for woman and his marriage with her means God loves people and is not divorced from them.

The reason it seems likely that De Vries sees marriage as a paradigm of the divine-human union and not only as a reasonable and convenient method of organizing one's life is the relentlessness with which he asserts the fundamental absurdity of life. He is like certain evangelical divines who use their considerable reasoning ability to argue that there is no reason for believing in what they profess to believe; this they do because, seeing faith and reason as contraries (man being so fallen as to have lost his reason), they rely totally on revelation, on faith. And they find that faith corrupted which is supported by reason. Thus does De Vries argue against there being reason for anything much. And then there breaks in the revelation— the same one, time after time: the metaphor is marriage, and it speaks of a greater covenant.

Otherwise, why would he not let that—marriage—go too, in an absurd world? Why hold on to it alone? Because if that goes then it all goes.

Chapter Nine
What the Others Have to Say

In order to work effectively as the critic of another's writings one should be smarter or better educated or at least have the advantage of time. Clearly, no one who has written on De Vries—this present writer obviously included—has the first two qualities, and no one can have the last, not for some decades to come. When these decades have gone, after De Vries has written his last, then we will be able to see whether he got his wish, that later generations would say *Yes*, that he was indeed six months ahead of his time.

This last clause is the sort of thing that throws people off, as Roderick Jellema says: "His real trouble—ours, rather—is not that he is too serious, but that he is too funny." As a result, "...the big literary quarterlies are silent. This has meant that De Vries's reputation has been left to the hazards of single-shot book-reviewing. And that in turn means that almost no one has explored the wholeness of his work and the inter-relationships among the various novels. His reputation is still adrift in a shifting stream of literary chit-chat."[1] His reputation in England already was secure then, and since those words were written (1966) some of the best American quarterlies have broken their silence, and segments of books written on the current literary scene have been given to him and his works.

Louis Hasley, writing in the *South Atlantic Quarterly*, has complained of De Vries's handling of point-of-view, the first technical problem authors address themselves to; critics are right behind them. He says that "De Vries fails to maintain sufficient distance from his story, tending to identify with his leading male character, who may be either the first-person narrator or a third-person point-of-view character. The portrait of such a protagonist, with a makeup given to arbitrariness in his actions, is often weakened by what must strike the reader as insufficient motivation and an incapacity to sustain a truly human relationship."[2]

Robertson Davies, in *A Voice from the Attic*, finds just the opposite to be the case:

It is no accident that the best novels of one of the most inventive and successful among American humorists, Peter De Vries, are related in the first person. A writer may choose this method of narration for many reasons, and nobody believes that the "I" of the story is the "I" of the writer; nevertheless, a man who is writing in the first person even of a creature of his own invention has a potent force at work upon him which prevents his work from escaping into the realm of the inhumanly clever. Mr. De Vries produces excellent comic effects by his revelation of his central character, his narrator, in several aspects—as he sees himself, as he hopes the world sees him, as he discovers, to his dismay, that the world actually *does* see him. His narrator . . . is a man of lively intelligence, scornful of his achievement, doubtful of his effectuality with women, and given to fantasy; the complexity of this invention serves the author well, for he is able to present both his principle character and his story on several levels.[3]

Further, he says the novels "do not suffer from the sags which are the characteristic faults of comic novels," and they work together as unities rather than "incidents and phrases" (242).

He commends De Vries as belonging among company such as Sinclair Lewis, Joyce Cary, Pamela Hansford Johnson, and Angus Wilson; all of these he says resemble Robert Smith Surtees, who he says possesses "that faculty of impersonation which is one of the best gifts a novelist can claim. When he writes about a man, he becomes that man, while retaining his watchful, chronicler's identity as well."[4] Jellema agrees with Davies that the use of first-person narrators "prevents his work from escaping into the realm of the inhumanly clever," and adds that it "spares us from the low spots which are characteristic of comic novels written in third person."[5] Thus the report on De Vries's use of point of view is generally favorable, if mixed.

So far as subject matter goes, human sexuality is a topic surfacing in every De Vries novel. His debt to Freud he has acknowledged—for the man's calling attention to the importance of sexuality and of the subconscious—although he playfully told Israel Shenker that "dreams have become dullsville," since the sexual revolution is recognized by everyone except the "Victorian censor."[6] Hasley observed that while "sex is always involved, other things are important—in fact, the whole complex of urban mores and morals: marriage, sex, family, divorce, money, status, even the vestiges of religion."[7] In short, it seems to be the metaphor used for everything else.

So much does this appear to be the case that one suspects De Vries of being a Freudian coded backwards: instead of sexual horrors being expressed (in dream code) as social horrors, we have social horrors—or, maybe, malaise—coded as sexual debacles. Everything is going to hell in a handbasket, and nowhere is it clearer than in the relationship of the sexes. While he still believed at the time of the interview with Richard Sale that a woman would merge her life more in a man's than vice versa, still he hedged his bets by saying that if the social anthropologists had their way with them then it may be disaster. At least he thinks it will happen "if it reaches a stage where there's more 'Me' to her thinking than there is 'Us,' it may be that'll be bye-bye ballgame as far as the institution of marriage is concerned."[8] He did expect something similar to take its place, though, if that eventuality comes to be: domestication he says is an instinct, although one notes that desperate men often defend their opinions that way—even St. Paul did, against the Greeks, when he said they knew "in their hearts" that homosexuality was wrong.

Desperation also drives some people into a form of bitterness that is called black humor. Is he one of them? To Sale he denied it, saying, "One ticket doesn't make you a speeder." He did agree with Sale's suggestion "that art depicting the seamy side can go so far that its prevalence can become part of the seamy side itself."[9] Like *Candy*, which supposedly was a satire on pornography but failed because pornography is already a satire (on decent sexuality) and one can't satirize satire—a tin can tied on a dog's tail will be dragged along, but a tin can tied on a tin can just sits there.

De Vries told both Newquist and Davis that he did not care to be called a satirist. Those folks, he averred, shoot to kill; but the "humorist brings his prey back alive." To them both he also said that his point was "something perfectly plain: that we're all absurd variations of one another."[10] To Hasley, because Don Wanderhope in *The Blood of the Lamb* says man has only his trinity to "Reason, Courage, and Grace," De Vries is a secular humanist. He puts him "on the side of spirit and intelligence,"[11] as does the poet D. J. Enright in an essay mainly consisting of a review of one book by and one book about Vladimir Nabokov. After lamenting that no one had done

a book on De Vries—like Nabokov a wit and a "word-boy"—he says
De Vries "despairs of his fellow beings without ceasing to love them
altogether and finds the human condition pretty rough but still the
only one we have. ..." Nabokov, per contra, loved memories, and,
of course, is "much more amenable to high-level discussion."[12]

Wit is a defense weapon, as is all wordplay, as well as a weapon
of aggression. In a most perceptive book review in *Life* in 1969,
Leonore Fleischer examined De Vries's blackest effort, *The Cat's
Pajamas & Witch's Milk.* She said his people were like those cartoon
characters who overran precipices and continued to do all right even
though running on air—until they looked down. Then they fell
screaming to temporary deaths. "What black humor does is to reveal
the comic aspects of the tragic and horrifying. Peter De Vries gives
black humor an extra half-twist. He invents a comic situation, as
comfy as a TV family comedy, fills it with gags and, when you're
laughing your head off, he pulls away the grinning clown's mask and
shows you the grinning skull beneath it."[13]

He tells a Dionysiac tale in Apollonian terms, she goes on to say,
functioning as "God's little wiseacre; his essentially pessimistic view
of the human condition, his understanding that most of us are not
the lords and owners of our fates, that we are in need of God's personal
reassurances and comfort and will reject the inferior human Brand X,
is expressed in terms of the gag and the pun. ..."[14] Hasley says that
"his need is not only to amuse readers but also to divert himself.
And from what?"[15] From Dutch Reformed Calvinism, he thinks. So
is he a secular humanist or isn't he?

Jellema says De Vries will not take the middle ground between
"belief in a radical Christian faith which turns the world inside out
and acquiescence in a pathetic, meaningless world." He sees him as
Hawthorne saw Melville, comfortable neither in belief nor in unbelief,
and, similarly, "too honest and courageous not to try to do one or
the other." No Door-keeper in the house of the Lord he, says Jellema.[16]
William Walsh points out that the fundamentalism De Vries "was
born to, primitive, Dutch, Calvinist, is decidedly tougher than its
American version. ..." Thus he calls him a "Calvinist clown and
metaphysical comedian," except that the jokes are not the nail-
puncture types Americans are used to: "It connects with an attitude,
is continuous and organic. ..."[17] He compares it to an Hegelian dialec-
tic being run through a projector backwards till it ends in a thesis

which is more or less a footnote. Or, as De Vries has written, all our stories, our fates, are palindromes.

To conclude, he has taken a most bourgeois form of Christianity—the one that shaped him—and made it into art, despite Calvinism's being deadly toward art. But so is being bourgeois deadly, so that's a redundancy. And yet the bourgeoisie prospers, says Herman Hesse, because certain tormented souls—Steppenwolves—join with and support the bourgeoisie: there "is always a large number of strong and wild natures who share the life of the fold." They are kept there by lingering sentiment, although they hold that the bourgeoisie's motto of "He who is not against me is for me" is exactly backwards. A few Steppenwolves escape and live the unconditioned life and go down in flames, but most don't. Those who conform do have one resource left, though, says Hesse: humor: "Humor has always something bourgeois in it, although the true bourgeois is incapable of understanding it."

"Humor alone, that magnificent discovery of those who are cut short in their calling to highest endeavor, those who falling short of tragedy are yet as rich in gifts as in affliction, humor alone (perhaps the most inborn and brilliant achievement of the spirit) attains to the impossible and brings every aspect of human existence within the rays of its prism." This humor allows one to be in the world and yet not of it. De Vries himself, concerned that his mask not be misunderstood, suggested that passage of Hesse as relevant to his work. It's a long way from the *New Yorker* attitude of the aristocrat caught in a bourgeois world. Or maybe not: Harry Haller, the Steppenwolf, is condemned by Mozart to "apprehend the humor of life, its gallows-humor." He is "to live and to learn to laugh."[18]

Notes and References

Chapter One

1. Interview with author, Westport, Connecticut, January 1976.
2. Roy Newquist, "Peter De Vries," in *Counterpoint* (Chicago, 1964), pp. 146–47.
3. Letter to the author, 25 May 1976.
4. Newquist, "Peter De Vries," p. 147.
5. The younger sister, Ann, attended Wheaton College and Calvin College, and then taught in Christian Reformed grade schools while she was caring for her father. After his death she married a widower, also a member of the Chicago Dutch Reformed community. Her brother wrote that "After nearly a decade of richly deserved happy years with him, she died on March 1, 1970.... She had no children, but through Evert acquired fourteen grandchildren, in addition to three or four stepchildren." Personal letter to the author, 25 May 1976.
6. William Walsh, "The Combination Is in the Safe," *Encounter* 40 (1973):80.
7. *Dialogue*, The Calvin College Alumni Journal, April 1975, p. 21. Other quotations identified in text.
8. Interview with the author, 2 May 1976.
9. Newquist, "Peter De Vries," p. 147.
10. Ibid., p. 146.
11. Burton Bernstein, *Thurber: A Biography* (New York: Dodd, Mead & Co., 1975), p. 360.
12. Ibid., p. 361.
13. *Poetry* 52 (January 1938), p. 323.
14. Israel Shenker, "Peter De Vries," in *Words and Their Masters* (New York, 1974), p. 96.

Chapter Two

1. *But Who Wakes the Bugler?* (Boston, 1940). All page references are to this edition.
2. Newquist, "Peter De Vries," p. 153.
3. *Wilson Library Bulletin* 33, (March 1959):460.
4. *The Handsome Heart* (New York, 1943). All page references are to this edition.

5. *Angels Can't Do Better* (New York, 1944). All page references are to this edition.

Chapter Three

1. *The Tunnel of Love* (Boston, 1954). All page references are to this edition.
2. Saul Bellow, *Humboldt's Gift* (New York: Viking, 1975), p. 92.
3. Louis Hasley, "The Hamlet of Peter De Vries: To Wit or Not to Wit," *South Atlantic Quarterly* 70 (1971):470.
4. *Comfort Me With Apples* (Boston, 1956), p. 3. All page references are to this edition.
5. Richard B. Sale, "An Interview in New York with Peter De Vries," *Studies in the Novel* 1 (1969):36.
6. Douglas M. Davis, "An Interview with Peter De Vries," *College English* 28 (1967):526.
7. Shenker, "Peter De Vries," p. 100.
8. *The Mackerel Plaza* (Boston, 1958). All page references are to this edition.
9. Phyllis McGinley, *Times Three* (New York, 1960), p. 134.
10. Richard Boston, *An Anatomy of Laughter* (London, 1974), p. 152.
11. Newquist, "Peter De Vries," p. 154.
12. *Time*, 17 January 1977, p. 85.
13. Walsh, "Combination," pp. 79–80.
14. Roderick Jellema, *Peter De Vries* (Grand Rapids, Mich., 1966), p. 18.
15. Richard Boston, *An Anatomy of Laughter* (London, 1974), p. 231.
16. David W. Noble, *The Eternal Adam and the New World Garden* (New York: George Braziller, 1968), p. 5.
17. Jay B. Hubbell, *Who Are the Major American Authors?* (Durham: Duke University Press, 1972), pp. 301–2.
18. *The Tents of Wickedness* (Boston, 1959). All page references are to this edition.
19. Hasley, "Hamlet," p. 471.
20. Jellema, *Peter De Vries*, p. 19.
21. For a fuller discussion of this point see James H. Bowden, "Exlit," *College English* 38 (November 1976):287–91.

Chapter Four

1. *Through the Fields of Clover* (Boston, 1961). All page references are to this edition.
2. Jellema, *Peter De Vries*, p. 24.

3. Boston, *Anatomy*, pp. 221, 229.
4. Hasley, "Hamlet," p. 468.
5. Newquist, "Peter De Vries," pp. 149–50.
6. Jellema, *Peter De Vries*, p. 24.

Chapter Five

1. *The Blood of the Lamb* (Boston, 1962). All page references are to this edition.
2. *Angels Can't Do Better*, pp. 17, 19.
3. *The Cat's Pajamas & Witch's Milk* (Boston, 1968). All page references are to this edition.

Chapter Six

1. Newquist, "Peter De Vries," p. 152.
2. Sale, "Interview," p. 369.
3. Boston, *Anatomy*, p. 135.
4. Ibid., p. 37.
5. *Reuben, Reuben* (Boston, 1964). All page references are to this edition.
6. Boston, *Anatomy*, p. 160.
7. Davis, "Interview," p. 526.
8. Theodore Ziolkowski, "The Telltale Teeth: Psychodontia to Sociodontia," *PMLA* (91) (January 1976):11, 14.
9. Ibid., pp. 19–21.
10. George Will, *Newsweek*, 9 February 1976, p. 84.
11. Walsh, "Combination," pp. 78–79.
12. *Let Me Count the Ways* (Boston, 1965). All page references are to this edition.
13. Jellema, *Peter De Vries*, p. 31.
14. *The Vale of Laughter* (Boston, 1967). All page references are to this edition.
15. Boston, *Anatomy*, p. 76.
16. John Allen Paulos, *Mathematics and Humor* (Chicago: University of Chicago Press, 1980), p. 27.
17. Davis, "Interview," p. 525.
18. Walsh, "Combination," p. 78.
19. *Mrs. Wallop* (Boston, 1970). All page references are to this edition.
20. Hasley, "Hamlet," pp. 467–68.
21. *Into Your Tent I'll Creep* (Boston, 1971). All page references are to this edition.

Chapter Seven

1. *Forever Panting* (Boston, 1973). All page references are to this edition.
2. Davis, "Interview," p. 528.
3. Boston, *Anatomy*, p. 58.
4. *The Glory of the Hummingbird* (Boston, 1974). All page references are to this edition.
5. Davis, "Interview," pp. 526–27.
6. *I Hear America Swinging* (Boston, 1976). All page references are to this edition.
7. Hasley, "Hamlet," p. 474.
8. *Madder Music* (Boston, 1977). All page references are to this edition.
9. Boston, *Anatomy*, p. 237.
10. Jellema, *Peter De Vries*, p. 43.
11. Wesley A. Kort, *Shriven Selves* (Philadelphia, 1972), pp. 62–63.

Chapter Eight

1. *Consenting Adults or The Duchess Will Be Furious.* (Boston, 1980). All page references are to this edition.
2. *Sauce for the Goose* (Boston, 1981). All page references are to this edition.

Chapter Nine

1. Jellema, *Peter De Vries*, p. 7.
2. Hasley, "Hamlet," p. 467.
3. Robertson Davies, *A Voice from the Attic* (New York, 1972), p. 241.
4. Ibid., p. 150.
5. Jellema, *Peter De Vries*, p. 19.
6. Shenker, "Peter De Vries," p. 98.
7. Hasley, "Hamlet," p. 470.
8. Sale, "Interview," p. 366.
9. Ibid., p. 368.
10. Newquist, *Peter De Vries*, p. 148; Davis, "Interview," p. 525.
11. Hasley, "Hamlet," p. 474.
12. D. J. Enright, "Nabokov's Way," *New York Review of Books*, 3 November 1966, p. 3.
13. Leonore Fleischer, *Life*, 13 December 1968, pp. 16–17.
14. Ibid., pp. 16–17.

15. Hasley, "Hamlet," p. 473.

16. Jellema, *Peter De Vries*, pp. 23, 40, 44.

17. Walsh, "Combination," pp. 74, 79.

18. All quotations from Hermann Hesse, *Steppenwolf* (New York: Bantam Books, 1963), pp. 61–63, 246.

Selected Bibliography

PRIMARY SOURCES

1. Novels

Angels Can't Do Better. New York: Coward-McCann, 1944.
The Blood of the Lamb. New York: Little, Brown and Co., 1962.
But Who Wakes the Bugler? Boston: Houghton Mifflin Co., 1940.
The Cat's Pajamas & Witch's Milk. Boston: Little, Brown and Co., 1968.
Comfort Me with Apples. Boston: Little, Brown and Co., 1956.
Consenting Adults or The Duchess Will Be Furious. Boston: Little, Brown and Co., 1980.
Forever Panting. Boston: Little, Brown and Co., 1973.
The Glory of the Hummingbird. Boston: Little, Brown and Co., 1974.
The Handsome Heart. New York: Coward-McCann, 1943.
I Hear America Swinging. Boston: Little, Brown and Co., 1976.
Into Your Tent I'll Creep. Boston: Little, Brown and Co., 1971.
Let Me Count the Ways. Boston: Little, Brown and Co., 1965.
The Mackerel Plaza. Boston: Little, Brown and Co., 1958.
Madder Music. Boston: Little, Brown and Co., 1977.
Mrs. Wallop. Boston: Little, Brown and Co., 1970.
No, But I Saw the Movie. Boston: Little, Brown and Co., 1952.
Reuben, Reuben. Boston: Little, Brown and Co., 1964.
Sauce for the Goose. Boston: Little, Brown and Co., 1981.
The Tents of Wickedness. Boston: Little, Brown and Co., 1959.
Through the Fields of Clover. Boston: Little, Brown and Co., 1961.
The Tunnel of Love. Boston: Little, Brown and Co., 1954.
The Vale of Laughter. Boston: Little, Brown and Co., 1967.
Without a Stitch in Time. Boston: Little, Brown and Co., 1972.

2. Play

With Joseph Fields. *The Tunnel of Love.* Boston: Little, Brown and Co., 1956.

SECONDARY SOURCES

1. Bibliography

Bowden, Edwin T. *Peter De Vries, a Bibliography, 1934–1977.* Austin:

The University of Texas Humanities Research Center, 1978. The definitive bibliography of De Vries's original books and contributions to books.

2. Books

Boston, Richard. *An Anatomy of Laughter*. London: Collins, 1974. Boston puts De Vries with the black humorists, adding that he is better at producing comedy than analyzing it.

Davies, Robertson. *A Voice from the Attic*. New York: Viking Press, 1972. Among other things, De Vries is commended for his gift of impersonation.

Jellema, Roderick. *Peter De Vries*. Grand Rapids, Mich.: William B. Ecrdmans Publishers, 1966. One of the "Contemporary Writers in Christian Perspective" series, this early monograph covers the first eight novels: Jellema is very good at placing his author just where the series title promises.

Kort, Wesley A. *Shriven Selves*. Philadelphia: Fortress Press, 1972. Along with Styron, Malamud, Updike, and Powers, Kort considers De Vries as one more of "Abraham's third sons," those who are comfortable neither in the faithful community of Isaac nor in the make-it-as-best-you can world of Ishmael.

3. Articles

Davis, Douglas M. "An Interview with Peter De Vries." *College English* 28 (1967):524–28. Much of the same material also appears in Newquist's interview, cited below.

Hasley, Louis. "The Hamlet of Peter De Vries: To Wit or Not to Wit." *South Atlantic Quarterly* 70 (1971):467–76. A look mainly at De Vries's use and maybe overuse of wit.

Newquist, Roy. "Peter De Vries." In: *Counterpoint*. Chicago: Rand McNally & Co., 1964, pp. 149–54. This book is a collection of sixty-three interviews with authors, columnists, and publishers. The standard questions are asked and the standard answers given.

Sale, Richard B. "An Interview in New York with Peter De Vries." *Studies in the Novel* 1 (1969):364–69. Is De Vries a black humorist? What of the war between the sexes? And so on.

Shenker, Israel. "Peter De Vries." In: *Words and Their Masters*. Garden City, N.Y.: Doubleday, 1974, pp. 96–100. Here De Vries gives way mainly to showing his mastery of words, and he is funny.

Walsh, William. "The Combination Is in the Safe." *Encounter* 40 (1973):74–80. Walsh's focus is on De Vries as a "Calvinist clown and metaphysical comedian."

Index